ARSENAL:

UNDERSTANDING

IN THE

KOSTA TSIPIS

WEAPONS

NUCLEAR AGE

SIMON AND SCHUSTER | NEW YORK

10   9   8   7   6   5   4   3   2   1

Library of Congress Cataloging in Publication Data

Tsipis, Kosta, date.

Arsenal: Understanding weapons in the nuclear age.

Includes index.
1. Atomic weapons.   2. Atomic warfare.   I. Title.
U264.T78   1983   355.8'25119   83-13530
ISBN 0-671-44073-X

To Mikael, Andreas, Yanni
and the rest of this earth's children
for whom we must preserve
a livable world

ACKNOWLEDGMENTS

My gratitude naturally belongs to Alice Mayhew, Ann Godoff, and Deborah Posner for the careful and caring editing of the manuscript, and to Gail Morchower and Susan Belinky go my thanks for their labors as the text evolved from a set of seminar notes to a readable typed manuscript. I would also like to thank Professor L. Sartori and Messrs. M. Bunn and J. Romm for their careful reading of the manuscript and their useful suggestions for changes.

My wife Judith's cheerful enthusiasm for the book lightened the disruptions and dislocations of the family's lifestyle occasioned by its writing.

Ultimately the roots of this book start with Bernie Feld, who inspired my commitment to the study of nuclear weapons and their effects, and with Max Stanley, whose early and constant confidence in my work in this field made it all possible.

Over the years the following foundations supported my research, from which much of the material in this book derives: Bydale Foundation; CS Fund; Field Foundation; Ford Foundation; HKH Foundation; Kendall Foundation; Levinson Foundation; Ruth Mott Fund; Needmor Fund; Ottinger Foundation; Rockefeller Family Fund; Rockefeller Foundation; Stern Fund. I am grateful for their support.

CONTENTS

FOREWORD

INCREASINGLY, decisions on public policy issues affecting all of us are made on the relatively narrow basis of scientific and technical considerations. As a result, the general public has had a diminishing role in arriving at such decisions; more and more, they are left to the experts to make. In a democratic society like the United States, this trend poses several problems. It alienates the public from the polity of the nation. It subverts the democratic principles of governance by de facto disenfranchisement of a very large segment of the public. Furthermore, it leaves public policy prey to the parochial interests of unelected experts whose notion of the national interest is at best narrowly defined and at worst confused with their own interest.

In the case of nuclear weapons, the American public has been totally and deliberately excluded from policy decisions which are vital for its very survival. The experts who develop weapons systems, be they military, technological, or scientific, not only claim the exclusive right to make decisions on matters of weapons policy—on the grounds that they are the only ones who possess both the necessary information and the technical means to evaluate it—but also actively try to prevent the general public from gaining enough knowledge about nuclear weapons and their effects to enter the debate. This self-created elite presents the physics and technology of these weapons systems as too complex for the average person ever to understand.

This book attempts to disprove this claim. There are indeed a myriad of technical and scientific details about nuclear weapons and their delivery systems and performance,

9

but most of them are not included in this book. There are two reasons for that. Some of these details are justly considered to be national military secrets which cannot and should not be divulged. Some of them may bear on policy decisions—or may not. We obviously cannot know. But of the information that is publicly available, the fact is that much of it simply is not necessary in order to make responsible, judicious decisions on matters of national defense and weapons policy. The minutia of technology do not count much when it comes to deciding whether or not a given weapon system should be deployed. What does count are general questions such as: Will the weapon do what it is supposed to do? Do we need it, and if so, for what mission, serving what national purpose? How much will the weapon cost? Does it make this country more secure? Does it make peace more assured? Would it lead to unpleasant surprises? Is there another weapon system that we already have, or that is cheaper, better, or more rugged, that can perform the same mission? These are the questions citizens should be asking our military, our technologists, and the Congress, which authorizes the spending of public funds for these weapons. But the irony is that the public is not always aware what the relevant information is, nor that the information is in fact readily available, and so delegates its decision-making powers to the experts.

No one is going to become an instant expert by reading this book. But the information presented here will permit you to comprehend the nature of nuclear weapons, and to decide, on your own, their utility for our national security. By presenting it, we take the first steps in exposing the issues of nuclear weapons and nuclear war to informed public debate. If citizens are sufficiently informed, it becomes appropriate for them to question the actions of their elected representatives and to challenge the opinions of the military and scientific technocracy. Let us hope that we will have time for such informed debate.

ARSENAL:

UNDERSTANDING WEAPONS

IN THE NUCLEAR AGE

1

THE DISCOVERY
OF THE NUCLEAR FORCE

PHYSICISTS do not like mysteries. Expose a physicist to a new phenomenon and he wants to explain it, reduce it to facts and phenomena that he already understands. It was, of course, this desire to eliminate the unexplained that led to the discovery of the nuclear force. But the earliest researchers in radioactivity and nuclear structure never envisioned the complex chain of historical events which would transform their quiet, detached experiments into the basis of a devastating military technology. The story of the discovery, gradual understanding, and eventual military application of the nuclear force is a classic model for the relationship between pure research and national policy; it is also a good introduction to the basic physics of today's nuclear weapons.

In 1896, Henri Becquerel, whose father and grandfather were also physicists, was professor of physics at both the Ecole Polytechnique and the Musée d'Histoire Naturelle. He was interested in luminescence, the fact that some crystals glow in the dark after they have been exposed to light. When he heard of Roentgen's discovery of x-rays, he set out to determine if luminescent crystals were also a source of x-rays. Roentgen had exposed photographic plates wrapped in black paper to a burst of x-rays from his apparatus, so Becquerel tried to repeat the experiment by exposing wrapped photographic plates to luminescent crystals which had been exposed to light (causing them to luminesce). His attempts did not yield any positive results until he tried a crystal of potassium uranyl sulfate; when he developed this plate there was a black spot where the crystal had lain on the opaque wrapping. Why was this crystal different from all the others? Was something other than luminescence responsible for exposing the plate?

To test this idea, Becquerel put a crystal of uranyl sulfate that had not been exposed to light on a wrapped photographic plate and shut it in a dark cupboard. Sure enough, even though the crystal did not luminesce, the photographic plate was exposed. This confirmed his guess that it was not luminescence but some other emission from the crystal that darkened the plate.

As he tried more and more crystals he found that only those containing uranium had this property of darkening his photographic plates. Becquerel suspected that the uranium in the crystals must be emitting something that acted like x-rays, ionizing the silver iodide of the plate. His suspicions were confirmed when he borrowed some pure metallic uranium from a chemist and found that it too could expose a wrapped photographic plate. But Becquerel was interested in luminescence and not in the properties of uranium, however novel and strange they might be. He made his discoveries public, but after about a year he dropped his investigation of uranium, unaware that he had been the first scientist to observe the nuclear force at work.

The mysterious phenomenon Becquerel had observed was more intriguing to a young Polish woman, Marie Sklodowska, married to Pierre Curie, who was a professor at the Ecole Municipale de Physique. In 1897, for her Ph.D. thesis, Marie Curie systematically went about finding other substances and elements that had the same odd property as uranium. Eventually she discovered a series of elements that are naturally radioactive. However, she did not attempt to find out what it was that those substances were emitting. It was another young physicist, from New Zealand, who became interested in the nature of radioactivity itself. He was Ernest Rutherford, who is unquestionably the father of the nuclear age.

In 1898, Rutherford found that uranium actually produced two different emissions. He called them alpha rays (α-rays) and beta rays (β-rays). But he soon discovered that the β-ray was actually an electron and the α-ray a much heavier particle—and for this reason replaced the term "ray" with "particle." Five years later he made the momentous observation that the unknown reaction that caused the α-particle to be emitted from uranium released about a million times more energy than the ordinary chemical reactions scientists were familiar with. Rutherford postulated that the force that made the α-particle pop out of uranium was not the same force that caused chemical reactions such as oxidation or other familiar ionizations, but a new, much more powerful one, which he dubbed the strong force.

This led him to two more momentous discoveries. In 1911 he discovered that the α-particle was not really a single particle, but a helium nucleus which we now know consists of four nucleons (as we call the constituent particles of a nucleus): two positively charged particles called protons and two neutral particles, as heavy as the protons. In addition, by bombarding thin metallic foils with alpha particles and observing the way the particles scattered as they passed through the foil, he discovered that matter consisted of atoms having a nucleus (his word) made up of protons and neutrons, and electrons revolving around the nucleus.

When, in 1920, the Danish physicist Niels Bohr postulated that despite their electromagnetic properties, the electrons remain revolving around the nucleus rather than falling into it by radiating away their energy, the concept of the atom as we now know it was virtually complete. But not many people paid attention to the atomic theory; no one in 1920 thought that the nucleus and this mysterious strong, or nuclear, force had any practical applications.

Ten years later, as additional details of the structure of the nucleus and the nature of the strong force were discovered, the picture started changing rapidly. First, two German physicists, W. Bothe and H. Becker, discovered in 1930 that when they bombarded beryllium with α-particles the beryllium emitted a very penetrating neutral particle. Soon afterward, Irene Curie, Marie Curie's eldest daughter, and her husband, Frederic Joliot, found that this neutral particle could knock protons out of paraffin or cellophane, but they didn't identify it with the neutron. This connection had to wait until 1932, when James Chadwick, a British physicist, measured the recoiling of protons hit by this object and showed that it was as heavy as a proton and was therefore a neutron. Thus, by 1933, all the pieces of the puzzle were known. All that was needed was a leap of imagination to see the potential practical applications.

Late in 1933, Leo Szilard, an enormously bright and self-confident Hungarian physicist who had gotten his Ph.D. and made his reputation as a genius in Berlin, read in *Nature*, the British scientific journal, that no less a physicist than Ernest Rutherford—now Lord Rutherford—had called any ideas of deriving energy from the nucleus "the merest moonshine." Szilard had never settled down to do systematic work in physics, but had a number of attributes that would set him apart again and again in the next ten years from even his most brilliant colleagues: He was constantly preoccupied with ways to apply physical discoveries to everyday life, and his astounding foresight allowed him to see clearly the broader implications of a physical discovery. And he had read H. G. Wells' fiction book, *The World Set Free*, written in 1913, that predicted the extraction of vast quantities of energy from the atom.

Undaunted by Rutherford's assertions, Szilard continued to speculate. If an element could be found with nuclei that could be split by neutrons and would emit two neutrons when they absorb one, then such an element, if assembled in sufficiently large mass, could sustain a nuclear chain reaction releasing great amounts of energy. Szilard realized that the magnitude of this energy was such that an explosive device based on the nuclear force would profoundly alter the nature of war, affecting even the course of history. In 1934, while living in London, he applied for a patent which described the production of energy by means of a nuclear chain reaction. Szilard assigned the patent to the British Admiralty, because, unlike other physicists, he realized the enormous military and industrial applications of the chain reaction and, he explained, "did not want this patent to become public." This is the first hint of his subsequent efforts to keep knowledge of nuclear phenomena secret, for fear the Nazis would build a nuclear weapon first.

It did not take physicists long to prove Szilard's physics

right. In 1938, Otto Hahn and Fritz Strassman, two German physicists working independently of Szilard, bombarded uranium 238 with neutrons and, by chemical analysis of the results, found that the uranium had not merely changed to another heavy nucleus, but had fissioned into barium and krypton, two elements with much smaller nuclei. By Christmas of 1938, Lise Meitner and her nephew, Otto Frisch, had calculated that the sum of the masses of the fission products was much smaller than the mass of the uranium and therefore some mass must have been turned into energy (according to Einstein's prediction that $E = mc^2$) as part of the uranium fission process. The practical potential of these discoveries was further enhanced when it was discovered that the number of neutrons in the barium and krypton nuclei of Hahn's and Strassman's fission products was smaller than the number of neutrons in the original uranium nucleus. The fission process liberated not only energy but also additional neutrons.

In the first week of January 1939, when the news of all this reached Szilard, who by this time was in the United States, it galvanized him into a frenzy of activity aimed at two purposes: first, to test whether the extra neutrons emitted from fissioning uranium had the right amount of energy to split additional uranium nuclei; and second, to keep the details and the importance of the discovery secret from the Germans. Szilard went to see Enrico Fermi at Columbia University. Because of his long experience with neutron experiments, Fermi had also thought of the possibility of a chain reaction. Unlike Szilard, Fermi was not concerned with the prospects of constructing a nuclear bomb. Fermi was a conscientious, pure physicist who thought the conservative thing to do was not to make alarmist predictions. Szilard was the clairvoyant pragmatist who thought that the responsible thing to do was imagine the worst—that such a bomb would be possible—and act accordingly.

Szilard borrowed $2,000 from a friend, with which he rented a gram of radium from the Radium Chemical Company in Chicago, and with a block of beryllium from England, produced neutrons by bombarding the beryllium with the alpha particles spontaneously emitted from the radium. Then, on March 3, 1939, he exposed a piece of

uranium to these neutrons and, with the help of some
equipment built by Walter Zinn, another physicist at Columbia, saw neutrons being emitted from the fissioned uranium. Fermi, using different apparatus and techniques,
confirmed Szilard's work. This was the first indication of
the feasibility of the bomb. Szilard thought that the U.S.
government should be immediately informed, and indeed
Fermi went to Washington and spoke privately to a committee consisting mainly of physicists working for the
Navy. However, apparently the Navy committee did not
grasp the significance of the discoveries, because nothing
came of the meeting.

Meanwhile, the Joliots in Paris observed the same phenomenon, but they acted quite differently. The Joliots
rather nonchalantly proceeded to publish the result. Szilard mounted a frantic campaign, enlisting practically every
major physicist in the United States and England, and tried
to convince Frederic Joliot not to publish their discovery
for fear that the Germans would grasp its importance and
start building a bomb. But it seems that the Joliots must
have been informally competing with their colleagues in
Berlin and, in typical French spirit, wanted to show them
how much better the French were. So they ignored Szilard
and the others and proceeded to publish their findings.
After all, they *wanted* the Germans to know! The truth is,
physicists of that time did not know how to handle discoveries that had importance beyond pure science. Except for
Szilard and a few other émigré physicists in the United
States who had tasted Nazism and were aware of the implications of Germany's growing militarism, the vast majority
of physicists were unprepared to play a role in shaping
national policy.

After the Joliots refused to keep their results secret, the
Columbia experiments were also published and the basic
physics for assembling a nuclear bomb became virtually
public knowledge. Szilard believed it was now only a matter of time before the Nazis constructed a nuclear bomb;
after all, they had a large group of brilliant physicists, even
after the Jewish exodus from the German universities and
laboratories. Szilard was convinced that a race to build the
first weapon now existed between Germany and the United

States, but he was practically alone in this belief. Fermi went off on vacation for the summer; the Navy continued to ignore increasingly encouraging data that a chain reaction could be produced in a pile of uranium and graphite.

After several futile attempts to interest the U.S. government, Szilard decided President Roosevelt must be approached directly. With Edward Teller, he drove out to the Hamptons on Long Island where Einstein was spending the summer, and on August 2, Einstein wrote to Roosevelt, explaining to him the discoveries of the nuclear physicists and their momentous implications. Einstein suggested a method by which the government could keep in close touch with the physicists working on chain reactions in America, and he urged that government funds be provided to expedite experimentation.

The letter, finally delivered to Roosevelt on October 11, 1939, resulted in the appointment of a "uranium committee" to meet with the physicists. For a year and a half, with splendid bureaucratic indifference, the committee did little to promote the necessary experiments. After all, it was not the custom at that time for the government to fund experiments, especially at universities, and the committee saw little reason to break precedent for a group of largely foreign scientists (Szilard, Fermi, Wigner, and Teller were all émigrés).

Even after the Committee on Uranium was reorganized by Vannevar Bush early in the summer of 1940, it didn't perform much better. But by spring 1941 the committee learned of two important new discoveries: In England, Rudolf Peierls had shown conclusively that if one used U^{235}, an isotope of the naturally more abundant form of uranium, U^{238}, in a chain reaction, a bomb small enough to be carried by an airplane could be made. At the same time, Glenn Seaborg, an American physicist at Berkeley, created plutonium (Pu^{239}), a new element that also fissioned when bombarded by neutrons and emitted more than one neutron in the process, even more readily than U^{235}. The committee, faced with multiple choices on which way the research on chain reactions should go, bogged down. Impatient scientists around the country began to criticize Bush, who in early 1942 finally transferred the chain-reaction effort into the so-called S-1 section of the newly created Office of Scientific Research and Development, whose purpose was to coordinate and promote all war-related scientific research. In May the S-1 scientists recommended that efforts be concentrated simultaneously on separating U^{235} from U^{238} and on building a uranium reactor to produce plutonium via a chain reaction.

Both the separation of uranium and the creation of plutonium involved the construction of massive installations and the coordination of thousands of skilled scientists, engineers, and technical workers to operate them. Bush realized that no civilian agency could muster the resources necessary for such a massive effort, especially during the first months of the U.S. involvement in World War II. So at his urging, the Army set up the Manhattan Project, and on September 25, 1942, General Leslie Groves was appointed to head it. The race to make the bomb before the Germans had truly begun. Groves appointed Robert Oppenheimer scientific director of the project, and in turn Oppenheimer assembled a team of physicists, chemists, and metallurgists and other engineers, whose task was to transform the physicists' experimental discoveries into an atomic bomb. To ensure secrecy, the scientists were isolated at Los Alamos, New Mexico.

The task was enormous. There is a vast difference between an experimental setup to observe or measure a physical phenomenon and a functional piece of apparatus, like a bomb, that utilizes the phenomenon as its essential working principle. Bridging that gap requires many new technologies, which leads to a considerable time lag between discovery and application.* Any bomb, for example, must be made small enough to be carried by a plane. It must blow up when you want it to, but never at any other time. It must be safe and rugged for transporting and immune to human clumsiness and error. As is often the case, for the scientists at Los Alamos there was a myriad of technical details that had to be dealt with, a legion of problems that

---

* Major weapons systems that derive from what we now call "a technological breakthrough" take about ten years to develop from the day that the physical phenomenon on which it is based is recognized as a useful working principle for a weapon.

had to be solved so that the solution of one did not interfere with the solution of another. Many problems that can be ignored in the laboratory must be faced and solved in the design of a working system.

The physicists at Los Alamos knew that a neutron emitted by a fissioned uranium nucleus travels on the average a few centimeters in uranium before it hits another nucleus and splits it. To produce a chain reaction, the majority of neutrons created during nuclear fission need to travel in at least several centimeters of uranium in order to have more than a 50% probability of splitting another nucleus. This distance is in part what determines the *size* of the uranium mass that will sustain a chain reaction and explode if injected with neutrons. The minimum size needed is called the critical mass. It depends not only on the average distance (or mean free path, as physicists call it) a neutron would travel between its generation and its collision with another nucleus, but also on the purity and density of the uranium and whether or not it is surrounded by a material that reflects exiting neutrons back into the uranium mass.

The problem was to control the chain reaction in order to keep the bomb from going off unpredictably while making sure that it did explode when it was time to do so. They came upon a simple but ingenious solution: to separate the uranium in the bomb into several pieces, each smaller than the critical mass, so that a chain reaction cannot ensue. These separate pieces can then be brought together rapidly so that their sum exceeds the critical mass. If at the same time some initiating neutrons are injected into the center of the assembled pieces, the chain reaction will start and enough nuclei will fission to release a very large amount of energy.

So the physicists at Los Alamos assembled the first uranium 235 bomb as follows: They devised a cannonlike tube, put one subcritical piece of uranium in one end and another subcritical piece at the other, and then topped off the tube with high explosives. When the explosives detonated they pushed the two pieces of uranium together; since their combined mass would then be critical, the entire weapon would explode. The scheme appeared so foolproof that the U^{235} bomb was never tested before it was actually used in war—on August 6, 1945, over the Japanese city of Hiroshima.

While the design of a uranium bomb proceeded, Glenn Seaborg discovered that plutonium was even easier to fission, and that it took less plutonium than U^{235} to form a critical mass. In addition, separating U^{235} from the much more abundant U^{238} was an expensive and difficult procedure. So in the early days of the Manhattan Project it was realized that plutonium would be a better bomb material. But there was a hitch that the physicists had not encountered until they came to assemble a plutonium bomb, and that was Pu^{240}, an isotope of the fissionable plutonium, Pu^{239}, which is used in nuclear weapons. Pu^{240} is formed when Pu^{239} absorbs a neutron without fissioning, and it will prevent a chain reaction from proceeding if significant quantities accumulate in a weapon. In addition, Pu^{240} fissions spontaneously, emitting several neutrons that could start a premature chain reaction. Since at any given time there will always be some nuclei in a mass of Pu^{240} undergoing spontaneous fission, one cannot put a critical mass of plutonium together in the fashion of the U^{235} bomb. In the thousandth of a second or so that it takes the two subcritical masses of fissionable material to get together in the "gun assembly," spontaneously fissioning plutonium nuclei would cause enough additional fissioning to release sufficient energy to blow the weapon apart, thereby terminating the chain reaction before significant amounts of energy were released.

As with uranium, whether a mass of plutonium is subcritical or not depends upon the length of the mean free path of a neutron traveling within it. For example, if the radius of a sphere of plutonium is larger than the mean free path, then chances are that a neutron will hit the nucleus of an atom before escaping. Such a sphere is said to have a supercritical mass.* If the radius is smaller than a neutron's mean free path in it, then the sphere has a subcritical mass.

---

* In a "critical" mass, exactly one new neutron is generated for every neutron that is lost—either by leaving the mass or by being absorbed. In a supercritical mass, more neutrons are created than are lost. In the fast chain reaction that causes a nuclear explosion, on the average two neutrons are generated for each one lost.

Since, as we have seen, the spontaneous fissioning of Pu^{240} prevents us from assembling a critical mass fast enough, the only alternative left is to reduce the mean free path of the neutron from larger to smaller than the sphere's radius. The physicists at Los Alamos hit upon the idea of assembling the plutonium into a sphere with a low enough density so that the sphere did not constitute a critical mass, and then increasing its density by sudden compression. The average distance neutrons travel in a material is inversely proportional to its density; the higher the density the shorter the mean free path. Thus squeezing the sphere quickly would decrease the mean free path before enough plutonium nuclei could fission, causing a fizzle; instead, the entire mass would fission explosively.

But how could the plutonium be squeezed and how fast must it be done? A Cal Tech physicist, Seth Nedermeyer, suggested surrounding the plutonium sphere with high explosives and detonating them all within a millionth of a second, thus squeezing the plutonium mass suddenly and drastically. Suppose the sphere starts out with a radius equal to one mean free path, a distance we will call 1.0. Halving the volume of the sphere doubles its density and therefore halves the mean free path of a neutron in it, yielding a mean free path of 0.5. But the radius of the compressed sphere is 0.8. So the radius of the compressed sphere is equivalent to 1.6 (0.8/0.5) mean free paths, and therefore the sphere is highly supercritical. Predictably, though, the concept of drastic compression is far simpler to invent than to make work.

The success of the plutonium bomb depended on the flawless performance of the implosion scheme to squeeze the sphere. The implementation of the scheme was entrusted to George Kistiakowsky, an explosives expert from the Department of Chemistry at Harvard. Kistiakowsky developed special explosive "lenses" which fit perfectly around the plutonium sphere and which, when fired properly, squeezed the plutonium rapidly and uniformly and caused it to explode. To successfully design these lenses, however, he had to overcome an unusual geometric problem. Figure 1a shows how it is geometrically possible to completely surround a sphere of plutonium with pieces of

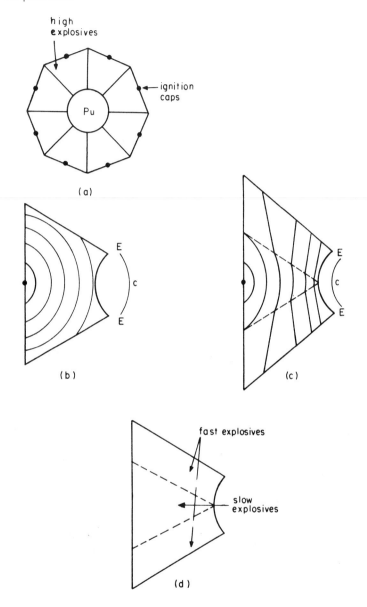

FIGURE 1. The working details of the implosion process.

high explosives that can be ignited simultaneously. This arrangement, however, would not squeeze the plutonium, but rather would shatter and scatter it because of the shock wave created by the explosion. As Figure 1b illustrates, the shock wave is an ever-expanding series of concentric spheres. Since when it hit the plutonium, its center (C) would be ahead of its edges (E), it would shatter the sphere rather than squeeze it. What Kistiakowsky needed was a shock wave that reached the plutonium in the shape shown in Figure 1c: The edges (E) would be ahead of the center (C) in such a fashion that the shock wave would hug the surface of the plutonium sphere and squeeze it uniformly. To achieve that, Kistiakowsky designed pieces of explosives that consisted of two parts: the center, made of slow explosives, in which the shock wave would travel more slowly, and the edges, made of fast explosives, in which the shock wave would travel faster (Figure 1d). Upon detonation, the shock wave starts out as a convex spherical surface, but very quickly the center slows down and the edges catch up and pass it, so that by the time the shock wave reaches the plutonium sphere, it has assumed the concave form shown in Figure 1c.

Kistiakowsky's explosive lenses not only had to generate a shock wave that would match the exact curvature of the surface of the plutonium sphere, but also had to produce compression waves all arriving at the surface of the sphere at exactly the same instant. Even though Kistiakowsky, with characteristic self-confidence, assured everyone that the implosion scheme would work, it was necessary to test the principle, not only to find out whether it would work at all, but also, since the energy released by the nuclear explosion depended on how well this very delicate scheme worked, to find out how much energy the plutonium bomb would yield, and what the military could expect from its detonation. Before the first test, estimates ranged from the equivalent of an explosion of 100 metric tons of TNT to 10,000 metric tons.

On July 16, 1945, the first nuclear weapon detonation on earth took place at Alamogordo, New Mexico, as a test of the implosion principle's feasibility. It was a spectacular success. For the first time in history, the strong force had released an appreciable amount of energy, equivalent to almost 20,000 metric tons of TNT, by fissioning nuclei of plutonium into smaller nuclei and thereby releasing the excess energy exactly as predicted by Meitner and Frisch six and a half years earlier.

The scientists and engineers who had produced the bomb were elated with their success. For the physicists, the detonation was a major scientific milestone—proof of the predicted existence and extraordinary properties of the nuclear force. But many were also appalled by the destructive might of the weapon, and embarrassed as well by the fact that, as it turned out, there was no race between the forces of good and evil: Germany had surrendered in May and it had become clear that the Nazis had not made a serious attempt to develop nuclear weapons. They did contribute, however, ballistic and cruise missiles to the arsenals of mankind; today, the combination of the American bomb and the German missile has created the technological conditions that animate the present arms race.

Szilard, the champion of secrecy and the prime force behind the rush into the development of a nuclear bomb, did not seem to be upset by his miscalculation of German intentions and activities. Thinking, as usual, of future implications, he now felt that the secrecy he had once so strongly advocated would cause an unavoidable nuclear arms race between the United States and the Soviet Union, a race that would come to threaten the very existence of mankind. He tried to see Roosevelt, but before he had a chance to do so, Roosevelt died. Niels Bohr, who had similar concerns, did manage to see Roosevelt and voice his fears of a nuclear race, unless the United States shared its mastery of the nuclear chain reaction with other nations, specifically the Soviet Union. Roosevelt, it appears, took Bohr's fears seriously and mentioned them to Winston Churchill. The English Prime Minister not only disagreed but recommended that Bohr be put under surveillance.

At the same time, another debate was raging in the United States among those associated with the Manhattan Project. Many scientists believed that nuclear weapons should not be used against the Allies' one remaining foe, Japan; that country was already defeated and was trying to sue for peace. Many proposed a demonstration; the Japanese could be invited to witness the awesome fury of the strong force in action on a remote deserted island. But the military and political leadership in the United States rejected the idea. Astonishingly enough, the U.S. military did not seem to be impressed by its new weapon. At Alamogordo the steel tower on which the bomb had rested had been totally vaporized and the desert sand had been turned to glass by the intense heat for several hundred feet in all directions, but the impassive General Groves felt that if he was not impressed, the Japanese generals would not be either. It was decided to stage a show of might over a Japanese city, and Hiroshima was chosen. Another tug-of-war developed between the nuclear scientists and the military and political authorities: The scientists wanted to warn the Japanese to evacuate the city. The military refused, saying that an evacuation would humiliate the United States if the bomb didn't work.

The decision to drop nuclear weapons on Japan and the reasoning behind it are still open to question. Some believe that it was necessary in order to end the war quickly and spare additional American and Japanese lives that would have been lost in an American invasion of Japan. Some reformist historians claim that the bomb was dropped on Hiroshima in order to impress Stalin with U.S. might and thereby achieve more favorable results during the Potsdam negotiations on postwar zones of influence. In any case, no one has a good explanation for the second bomb, dropped on Nagasaki. There is general agreement on one point, however: It was a matter of momentum. Once the decision had been made and scientists and Air Force crews were gathered on Tinian Island for the assembly and delivery of what would be the second plutonium bomb ever made,* it would have taken active intervention to stop it. No one in a position to do so intervened.

Nuclear weapons must have appeared particularly attractive to the United States at the end of World War II. They

---

* The Hiroshima bomb, as noted earlier, was a uranium bomb, and the scientists at Los Alamos were so sure that it would work that it was never tested; the Nagasaki bomb was a plutonium bomb, like the one tested three weeks before at Alamogordo.

promised an inexpensive way of wreaking destruction upon enemy territory without having to defeat enemy land armies. Equally important, American leadership felt certain that the secrecy employed during development of the bomb would ensure that control of it remained firmly with the United States. The U.S. military hoped that where conventional strategic bombing had failed—and by August 1945 they knew that in Germany, at least, it had failed to disrupt the German war effort the way the military had expected—nuclear bombing would promise such an overwhelming threat of destruction that the United States would assume undisputed world dominance. This undisputed dominance lasted merely four years: On August 29, 1949, the Soviet Union exploded its first atom bomb. Subsequently, other nations would also test nuclear weapons. The race that Szilard had feared was on. From the quiet, disinterested research of Becquerel, the Curies, Rutherford, and others had emerged the most powerful physical force ever to threaten civilization.

2

THE PHYSICS
OF A NUCLEAR EXPLOSION

NUCLEAR WEAPONS are rather small. Some of them fit in cannon shells; others, such as those that are carried and dropped by planes, may be about the size of a refrigerator. The tremendous amount of energy that is released when a nuclear weapon detonates seems inconceivably out of proportion to the size of the weapon. Where does this energy come from, how much is it exactly, how is it released and how fast, and in what form does it get into the surrounding space? To answer these questions, we must first review some elementary physics.

An atom consists of a heavy nucleus, which has a net positive charge, and a group of electrons that revolve around it. The electrons carry negative electric charge and so are attracted to the positive nucleus. The force between electric charges that keeps the electrons revolving around the nucleus is the electromagnetic force.

The nucleus of an atom consists of neutrons and protons. Neutrons and protons are roughly equivalent in weight and are each about 2,000 times heavier than an electron. The number of protons determines what the element is, and the sum of neutrons and protons determines the element's atomic weight. For example, the element uranium has atoms with nuclei that contain 92 protons—that is the definition of uranium—and 146 neutrons, for a total atomic weight of 238.*

* There are also atoms of uranium with only 143 neutrons in their nuclei for a total atomic weight of 235. This kind of uranium is known as an isotope; it has the same number of protons but a different number of neutrons. Scientific notation distinguishes between various isotopes in the

It is an experimental fact that a nucleus weighs less than the sum of the weights of the protons and neutrons that constitute it. That is, the mass of a nucleus is less than the sum of the individual masses of its protons and neutrons. According to the law of conservation of matter, no mass can ever disappear. So this "missing mass" must have gone somewhere. Actually, it has transformed itself into energy according to Einstein's famous formula $E = m \cdot c^2$, where E is energy, m is mass, and c^2 is the speed of light squared. So if the missing mass is m, the amount of energy it has transformed itself into is $m \cdot c^2$. This is the energy released to the world outside the nucleus as the neutrons and protons bind themselves together to form the nucleus. Accordingly it is called the "binding energy" of the nucleus. If one calculates the binding energy of the nuclei of an element and then divides it by its atomic weight, one finds that the binding energy per nucleon (neutron or proton) varies from element to element. Plotting the binding energy per nucleon against the atomic weight of the various elements and their isotopes gives the curve in Figure 2.

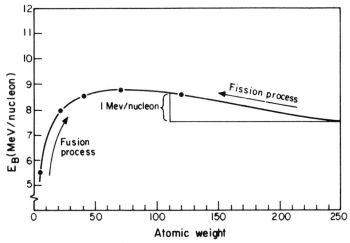

FIGURE 2. The curve of binding energy.

following manner: We write U^{238}_{92} for ordinary uranium, and U^{235}_{92} for the lighter isotope that was so important to the first uranium nuclear bomb.

The curve of binding energy shows that the protons and neutrons inside nuclei with atomic weights between, approximately, 40 and 120 are more tightly bound than the nucleons inside very light nuclei like deuterium, tritium, and helium and the very heavy nuclei like uranium and plutonium. And in fact, the very large, but still stable, nuclei like those of uranium and plutonium are not very hard to fission.

The individual nucleons inside tightly bound nuclei have, on the average, less motion or kinetic energy than the nucleons inside the nuclei of such elements as uranium or plutonium, which are not tightly bound. So when a uranium nucleus splits into two smaller nuclei, the same nucleons have less kinetic energy in the new nuclei than they had inside the big, fat uranium nucleus that could barely hold itself together.

How much energy is lost by each nucleon as the uranium nucleus splits, and what happens to it? As you look at the curve of binding energy, you see that each nucleon of the uranium nucleus that has ended up in the two smaller nuclei is, on the average, bound to the new nucleus by 8 Mev* (million electron volts) of energy, while in the original uranium nucleus it was bound by only 7 Mev. In other words, a nucleon inside a uranium nucleus would need 7 extra Mev of kinetic energy in order to leap out of the nucleus, but inside the smaller nucleus the same nucleon would need 8 Mev extra kinetic energy to free itself from the nucleus. So each nucleon has lost on the average about 1 Mev of energy as the uranium fissions into two fragments. Since the uranium nucleus has 238 nucleons, *the total energy released during its fission into the two lighter elements will be about 238 Mev per atom.* This energy, which escapes into the environment when a nucleus splits, gives a nuclear weapon its destructive power.

How much energy is 238 Mev? Even though the energy released by a nuclear interaction is, atom for atom, about a million times more than that released by a chemical (electromagnetic) reaction, the amount released by one atom is pretty puny: 238 Mev is about nine millionths of a millionth

* 1 Mev = $1.6 \cdot 10^{-13}$ joules = $1.6 \cdot 10^{-6}$ ergs.

$(9 \cdot 10^{-12})$ of a calorie. But just 1 gram of uranium contains $2.5 \cdot 10^{21}$ nuclei, so if all of them were split at once, the energy released would be $22.5 \cdot 10^9$ calories.* The 238 Mev per atom released by a nuclear reaction is such an enormous amount of energy because this process involves rearranging the nucleons of tightly bound nuclei. Electromagnetic processes, on the other hand, like the explosion of TNT, involve the rearrangement of electrons *around* the nucleus, and yield only a few electron volts per atom, because the binding energy of electrons is far smaller than that of the nucleons within a nucleus.

But, as Szilard realized, in order to release all the energy from a large number of nuclei by nuclear fission, one must find a self-sustaining way to split lots of heavy nuclei within a very short time. Since the nucleus is held together by the binding energy, a mechanism is needed to provide for each nucleus enough extra energy to break it up. And since (as Hahn and Strassman discovered) the impact of a modestly energetic neutron provides enough energy to fracture a uranium or plutonium nucleus, the problem is to cause enough neutrons to interact with a large number of nuclei (nearly 10^{23} of them) in a very small period of time (about a millionth of a second) and break them up. Now, it just so happens that every time a uranium 235 nucleus fissions into two fragments, it releases, on the average, two neutrons, each of which has enough energy to break up another uranium nucleus (if it hits one), which in turn releases two more neutrons, and so on, thus producing a chain reaction (Figure 3.)

For all we know, this is a completely fortuitous circumstance. The neutrons released need not have the right energy to split uranium nuclei. (In fact, for both uranium 235 and plutonium 239, the neutrons produced during fission can in turn fission additional such nuclei.) But it could very well have been that only one neutron was released for each fissioned uranium nucleus. That wouldn't have been enough for a chain reaction, firstly, because a newly gen-

* For comparison, the explosion of 1 gram of chemical high explosives such as TNT releases 25 million billion Mev, which is the same as 10^3 calories (a mere 1,000 calories).

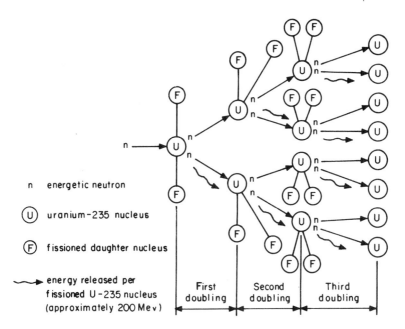

FIGURE 3. The chain reaction principle.

n energetic neutron

(U) uranium-235 nucleus

(F) fissioned daughter nucleus

➤ energy released per fissioned U-235 nucleus (approximately 200 Mev)

First doubling | Second doubling | Third doubling

erated neutron is sometimes harmlessly absorbed by a neighboring nucleus, and secondly, because a neutron sometimes misses all the other nuclei and flies out of the uranium sphere. But even if these things never happened and every new neutron generated split another nucleus, in order to fission 10^{23} nuclei one step at a time it would take about 10^{13} seconds, or about a million years.

The fact that, on the average, *two* neutrons are emitted from each split uranium nucleus makes a nuclear explosion possible. Since the number of emitted neutrons doubles with each step, starting with one neutron, it will take on the average only about eighty doubling steps to produce enough neutrons to fission completely 10^{23} uranium nuclei (see Appendix A). How long does it take to complete eighty doubling steps? First, we must know how long it takes for one doubling step to happen. Since the nuclear interaction that splits the nucleus is practically instantaneous (10^{-22}

sec), the duration of one step is as long as it takes the neutron to go from the uranium nucleus that generated it to the one it splits. On the average, the neutron travels 3 centimeters before it hits a nucleus, and since it travels at about a tenth the speed of light (speed of light is $3 \cdot 10^{10}$ cm/sec), it takes about a nanosecond (a nanosecond is one billionth of a second), that is, 10^{-9} second, to complete one step. So the entire process of fissioning a gram mole* of uranium takes about 80 nanoseconds. It is interesting to note that after seventy doubling steps there are still only 10^{21} neutrons, which is 1% of the number needed to completely fission a gram mole. Therefore, only about 1% of all the available nuclei have been fissioned during the first seventy nanoseconds, which means that 99% of the energy in a nuclear explosion is released within the last 10 nanoseconds.

Let us now see how much energy is released when a small amount of uranium or plutonium is fissioned (in fission process, the properties of plutonium and uranium are almost identical). Consider a sphere of 5 kilograms (5,000 grams) of plutonium, which is about the size of the "trigger" used in a modern fusion nuclear weapon. Such a sphere would be 330 cm³ in volume and 8.5 cm in diameter. Now, since this sphere contains $1.2 \cdot 10^{25}$ nuclei and each one, when it fissions, releases about 200 Mev of energy, the energy released by the complete fission of every nucleus inside that sphere would be

$$1.2 \cdot 10^{25} \cdot 200 = 2.4 \cdot 10^{27} \text{ Mev}$$

which is equivalent to 10^{14} calories.† Actually, only about 30% of the nuclei fission in a real weapon, so realistically the energy released by a bomb that contained 5 kilograms of plutonium would be nearer $3 \cdot 10^{13}$ calories. So the energy per unit volume of the sphere will be $3 \cdot 10^{13}/330$ or $9 \cdot 10^{10}$

---

* A gram mole (from gram molecule) is the quantity of an element that has a weight in grams numerically equal to its atomic weight. Thus, 1 gram mole of U^{235} = 235 grams, and 1 gram mole of Pu^{239} = 239 grams. The gram mole of *any* element contains $6 \cdot 10^{23}$ atoms.

† 1 Mev = $3.8 \cdot 10^{-14}$ calories. (It is common practice in physics to round to the nearest order of magnitude, so while $[3.8 \cdot 10^{-14}] \cdot [2.4 \cdot 10^{27}] = 9 \cdot 10^{13}$, the answer is given as 10^{14}.)

calories/cm^3, which translates into a temperature for the sphere of about 130 million degrees centigrade (see Appendix A). Since the sphere has not had enough time to expand in those first 80 nanoseconds, the pressure inside will rise in direct proportion to the temperature, from an initial pressure of 1 atmosphere to about 100 million atmospheres. Thus, 80 nanoseconds after the initiation of the nuclear reaction, the 5-kilogram plutonium sphere has become a 5-kilogram mass of smaller nuclei having a temperature of 100 million degrees and a pressure of 100 million atmospheres. These are the conditions in the center of the sun. Indeed, a nuclear detonation is a miniature sun shining momentarily on earth.

The energy of $3 \cdot 10^{13}$ calories is equal to that released by the detonation of 30 million kilograms, or 30,000 metric tons, of high explosives. That much dynamite would constitute a cube almost 30 meters on a side, with a volume almost 100 million times that of the 8.5-centimeter plutonium sphere.

So far we have considered only the splitting or fissioning of large nuclei into smaller ones. But modern weapons also depend upon the energy released in the process of *fusing* small nuclei into larger ones, that is, moving from the leftmost edge of the curve of binding energy (Figure 2) toward its peak. In the fusion process, nuclei of two lighter elements are literally fused together to form a heavier element. Fusion nuclear weapons generally use the elements deuterium and tritium for this process. Deuterium is an element with a nucleus consisting of one proton and one neutron. Tritium is an element with a nucleus consisting of one proton and two neutrons. Their atoms are like a hydrogen atom—they are, in fact, isotopes of hydrogen. Specifically, fusing together two deuterium nuclei to get a helium nucleus and a neutron yields about 3 Mev of energy:

$$D_1^2 + D_1^2 \rightarrow He_2^3 + n + 3.27 \text{ Mev}$$

and the fusion of a deuterium and a tritium nucleus to form a helium nucleus and a neutron yields 17.6 Mev:

$$D_1^2 + T_1^3 \rightarrow He_2^4 + n + 17.6 \text{ Mev}$$

Per nucleon, the energy release in this $D^2 + T^3$ reaction is bigger ($17.6/5 = 3.52$ Mev) than either the $D^2 + D^2$ fusion ($3.27/4 = 0.81$ Mev) or the splitting of uranium or plutonium (about 1 Mev).

But before these nuclei can fuse, they must come within $5 \cdot 10^{-13}$ centimeter of each other. Since nuclei contain protons that repel each other, fusion of small nuclei to form larger ones can be achieved only if enough energy is provided to surmount this repulsion, which is proportional to the square of the number of protons contained in the two small nuclei. So this amount of energy is smallest when each nucleus has only one proton, such as hydrogen and its isotopes deuterium and tritium. It turns out that among these three elements the most advantageous combination is fusing deuterium and tritium together, a process which, as we have seen, rearranges the two protons and three neutrons into a helium nucleus (two protons and two neutrons), a free neutron that flies away, and 17.6 Mev of energy. One obstacle in releasing this energy is that both deuterium and tritium are gases at normal temperatures, and in order to store them it would be necessary to cool them down to a liquid state. This would indeed be a nuisance—a bomb that needs a huge refrigerator with it! However, one can dispense with bulky cryogenic machinery by using lithium deuteride LiD, a solid, as part of the "fuel" in a fusion bomb. When a neutron strikes a Li_3^6 nucleus, helium He_2^4 and tritium T_1^3 are produced; thus when it strikes a $Li_3^6 D_1^2$ nucleus, the process looks like this:

$$Li_3^6 D_1^2 + n \rightarrow He_2^4 + T_1^3 + D_1^2 + 4.6 \text{ Mev}$$

Then the T_1^3 and D_1^2 on the right-hand side of the equation fuse according to the process:

$$T_1^3 + D_1^2 \rightarrow He_2^4 + n + 17.6 \text{ Mev}$$

The only other ingredient needed to accomplish fusion is an enormous source of energy which, for a very brief period of time (measured in millionths of a second), squeezes the deuterium and tritium nuclei together until they fuse. In an actual weapon this energy is provided by fissioning a small mass of plutonium. So a typical fusion nuclear weapon looks something like the contraption in Figure 4. The energy generated by the splitting of the plutonium nuclei travels down the length of the weapon and fuses the deuterium and tritium. The fusion proceeds optimally when the two elements are heated to 1 billion degrees centigrade (10^9 degrees), but even at the slightly cooler temperatures generated by the fissioning of the plutonium (10^7 to 10^8 degrees centigrade) fusion occurs within a millionth of a second.

One of the results of this fast and intense fusion is that each neutron released in the process $D^2 + T^3 \rightarrow He^4 + n$ + energy has the appropriate energy to split the relatively stable uranium nucleus, U^{238}_{92}. So an ordinary fusion weapon will have a blanket of U^{238}_{92} around it. The uranium nuclei are split by the neutrons generated by the fusion process, and the energy they release adds to the energy produced by the bomb. Since U^{238}_{92} is very cheap, this combination is an inexpensive way to double the explosive yield of a nuclear weapon.

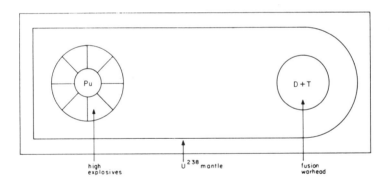

FIGURE 4. An idealized sketch of a thermonuclear weapon.

Now, let's get an idea of the physical size of a fusion weapon and roughly how much plutonium, deuterium, tritium, and uranium 238 it contains. It turns out (see Appendix B if you are interested in the derivation) that a

1-megaton nuclear weapon* contains a few kilograms of lithium deuteride and tritium, some kilograms of plutonium, and about 100 kilograms of uranium 238 (see Appendix B). (Certain fusion weapons, commonly called neutron bombs, do not have the U_{92}^{238} mantle, thus allowing fast, lethal neutrons to escape into the atmosphere.) Thus the total weight of a 1-megaton nuclear weapon would be at most a few hundred kilograms. So a few hundred kilograms of matter rearranged by the nuclear force releases as much energy as 1,000 million kilograms (1 million metric tons) of matter (TNT for example) rearranged by the electromagnetic force.

The immediate result of the fission-fusion-fission process, which is completed in less than a millionth of a second, is a seething, furiously expanding mass of radioactive nuclear fragments and newly created helium nuclei, all stripped of their electrons. This cloud of vaporized matter, at this point a few meters in diameter and possessing a temperature of many tens of millions of degrees, is what is often referred to as the fireball. What form does all the energy that has been released by the rearrangement of all these nuclei take? A large fraction of the energy released rushes out from the superhot fireball in the form of electromagnetic radiation. The rest is partly in the form of kinetic energy of the new smaller nuclei created by the fission of the small amount of plutonium and the larger mass of uranium 238, partly as kinetic energy of the helium nuclei created by the fusion of deuterium and tritium, and partly as kinetic energy of the neutrons that fly away. Most electrons are stripped from their orbits, and these also carry some kinetic energy.

Any object hotter than its environment emits energy in the form of electromagnetic radiation. The electromagnetic spectrum consists of gamma rays (which are waves with

---

* It has become customary to measure the amount of energy released by a nuclear detonation in terms of the weight of TNT that would release the same amount of energy if detonated. Each gram of TNT releases 1,000 calories when it explodes. A metric ton of TNT releases 10^9 calories. When we say that a fission-fusion-fission bomb releases a megaton of energy, we mean that its detonation releases energy equal to that released by 1 million metric tons of exploding TNT.

extremely high frequency and high energy), and in the order of decreasing energy, x-rays, ultraviolet radiation, visible radiation (which is about one millionth as energetic as gamma rays), infrared radiation, and then many of the things that we commonly refer to as waves: television waves, radar waves, radio waves. These are all electromagnetic waves, differing only in frequency (see Figure 5 on page 40). Electromagnetic radiation has an interesting property: The higher the temperature the higher the frequency of the majority of the waves and therefore the more energy, on the average, there is in the radiation waves the object emits. An iron that is a few hundred degrees hot gives out predominantly infrared radiation, so most of the waves that leave it carry a fraction of an electron volt (ev) of energy. A red-hot coil of an electric stove gives out mostly visible radiation which consists of waves that carry about 1 ev of energy. At even higher temperatures an object emits primarily ultraviolet light or even x-rays, each of which carries thousands of ev.

Although the fireball is completely "transparent"—i.e., it does not absorb any electromagnetic radiation (see Appendix C for the explanation of this effect)—and high-energy radiation thus escapes from the initial fireball, x-rays can't go very far because they get absorbed by air molecules. As the x-rays get absorbed by adjacent layers of undisturbed air, they heat up the air molecules to the point where the air around the original fireball becomes transparent enough to allow more high-frequency radiation to escape and heat up still additional layers of air farther out from the expanding fireball. On the one hand, this process removes energy from the interior of the fireball and uniformly cools it down. On the other hand, it makes the fireball expand at supersonic speed. As the temperature of the fireball decreases, the average energy of the electromagnetic waves that it emits also decreases. These waves now have on the average lower frequencies and are absorbed even more readily by the air. Thus, the distance they can travel decreases and the net effect is that the growth of the fireball slows down. As the expanding fireball cools, the radiation that escapes from it changes from mostly x-rays to primarily visible light, and eventually to predominantly thermal (infrared) radiation. When the fireball's temperature is reduced to about 300,000° C, the speed with which it grows by emitting radiation becomes equal to the speed of sound in the air. At that point two things happen. First, the superheated weap-

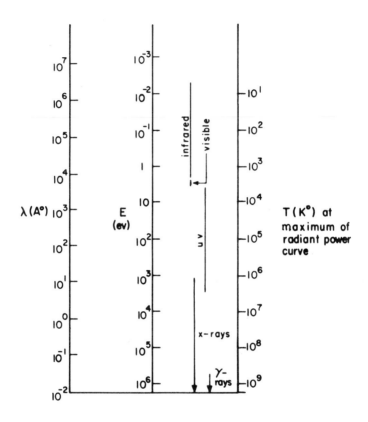

FIGURE 5. Relationship between the predominant wavelength and energy of electromagnetic radiation emitted by a body at the temperature shown in the rightmost scale.

ons debris (vaporized bomb material, bare nuclei, electrons) that was traveling inside the fireball with supersonic speed catch up with the outer edge of the fireball as it slows down. And second, a shock wave develops at the outer surface of the fireball that shock-heats* the air around the fireball, making it incandescently hot, and applies a devastating pressure on everything in its path.

Since hot air absorbs visible radiation, one cannot see the fireball until the gases around it have cooled enough to permit visible light to escape. That is called the "breakaway" point. The obscuring of the fireball by the shocked air is the cause of the characteristic "double flash" of light that a nuclear detonation in the air displays. This is, incidentally, the signal that monitoring satellites look for to detect atmospheric nuclear weapons tests.

The size of the fireball depends on the yield of the weapon and the place of detonation. For example, at breakaway, the fireball of a 1-megaton weapon that explodes on the ground will be about 800 meters in diameter.† The fireball keeps on growing after breakaway until it reaches its maximum size approximately nine minutes later. A 1-megaton weapon exploding on the ground will generate a fireball about 3 miles (4.8 kilometers) in diameter before it even begins to lift into the atmosphere. Figure 6 (page 42) gives the relationship between the yield of the weapon and the size and height to which the resulting cloud of hot gases and debris rises for ground-level explosions. For example, a 1-megaton weapon will develop a cloud with a 10,000-meter radius that will rise to a height of more than 25,000 meters.

The sudden release of a very large amount of energy in a very small volume of space creates other special effects: The atoms of the bomb debris and of nearby matter become ionized (stripped of their electrons) by the γ-rays generated by the explosion. The resulting stripped nuclei are slower and stay behind, while the much lighter electrons fly off in all directions, interacting with the radiation and the super-

---

* When pressure is applied suddenly on an object (for example, by hitting a piece of metal with a hammer), the process heats the object. When pressure is removed suddenly from an object (for example, when air is taken rapidly out of a tire), the object cools down. The shock wave heats the air exactly in the same fashion as the hammering heats the piece of metal. This is called shock heat.
† The radius in meters of the fireball at the instant of breakaway is $R = 40 \cdot Y^{.4}$ for detonations in the air and $R = 50 \cdot Y^{.4}$ for detonations on the surface of the ground where Y is the yield in kilotons of TNT.

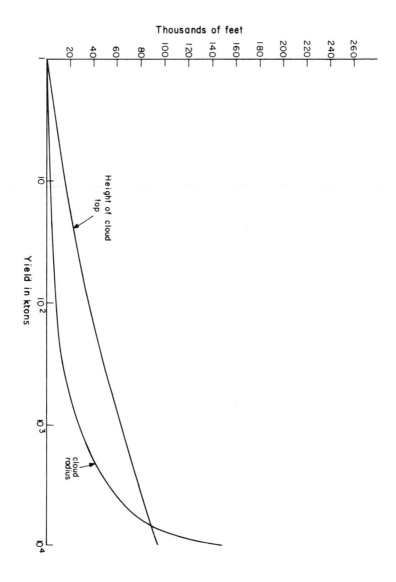

FIGURE 6. The size and the height reached by the mushroom cloud formed by a nuclear explosion in relation to the energy yield of the explosion.

heated gases of the fireball and, finally being absorbed by the ground underneath the explosion, or colliding and recombining with other ions. The new atoms created by the fissioning of the Pu^{239} and U^{238} nuclei are also completely stripped of electrons, fly off emitting gamma rays or electrons, and, in a ground-level explosion, stick to the vaporized particles of dirt that are lifted up by the ascending fireball.

Thus changes in the nuclei of a relatively small number of atoms create a number of catastrophic physical effects in the surrounding environment: After a very intense burst of neutrons and gamma rays generated by the fissioning of U^{238} and the fusion of deuterium and tritium nuclei, there is a silent wave of intense heat and a flash of light hundreds of times brighter than the sun. A shock wave of extreme pressure follows, slapping down on everything with crushing force. This shock wave travels outward from the point of detonation like an ever-expanding ring. It is followed by intense winds that reach speeds of thousands of miles per hour and die down slowly as the shock wave travels farther and farther away from the point of detonation. As the fireball rises from a ground explosion, it lifts with it millions of tons of vaporized dirt that cools, condenses, and starts falling toward the ground as the winds at the upper level of the atmosphere sweep the huge cloud downwind from the point of detonation. A billion billion billion million oxygen and nitrogen molecules in the air have been combined by the heat of the blast into nitrogen oxides and rise with the cloud to the upper levels of the atmosphere. An even larger number of free electrons start spiraling along the lines of the geomagnetic field of the earth. All of these events, be they at the nuclear, atomic, or molecular level, produce numerous larger physical effects, some momentary, some long-lasting, some limited to the blast site, and some encompassing our entire planet. In the next chapter, we will examine these effects of a single nuclear explosion.

3

THE PHYSICAL EFFECTS
OF A NUCLEAR EXPLOSION

THE MANY EFFECTS of a nuclear explosion differ drastically in magnitude and kind from those caused by the detonation of chemical explosives such as dynamite, not only because of the larger amount of energy released by a nuclear weapon but also (and more importantly) because of the much briefer time and the smaller volume within which the energy of a nuclear weapon is released. A nuclear weapon releases 99% of its total energy in about a billionth of a second, while a chemical explosive takes about a thousandth of a second to blow up. Modern weapons that can release energy equivalent to 1 million metric tons of TNT (1 megaton) weigh much less than a ton and can fit in a cone 50 centimeters in diameter and little more than a meter high. On the other hand, 1 million metric tons of TNT would fill a freight train 300 miles long. Traveling at 50 mph, this train would take six hours to pass in front of you.

As a result of these basic differences, the energy released per unit of mass of nuclear material is millions of times more than the corresponding energy density reached during the detonation of chemical explosives. As a consequence, the vaporized materials of a nuclear weapon have a temperature of millions of degrees centigrade immediately after the completion of the fission-fusion-fission process, compared to only a few thousand degrees for the products of a chemical explosion. This is crucially important, because how energy partitions itself inside a hot body depends on the body's temperature. At relatively low temperatures of a few thousand degrees, most of the energy goes into the motion of the atoms and molecules of the material, and a very small fraction is emitted as radiation. At temperatures of millions of degrees, which are characteristic of nuclear detonations, most of the energy goes into radiation and only a small portion goes into motion of physical matter. While the nuclear explosion is actually going on, most of the energy it releases (about 80% of it) is in the form of kinetic energy of the fission fragments and helium atoms the process generates. But about a millionth of a second after the fission and fusion processes cease, this energy has taken three forms: Most of it is being radiated out in the form of thermal (low-energy or soft) x-rays.* A small portion (about 10%) is stored as excited energy inside the newly generated nuclear fragments. The remaining energy is in the form of kinetic energy of the weapon debris, the vaporized remains of the bomb and the products of the nuclear processes, gamma rays, neutrons, and fission fragments. The difference in the temperatures created by a chemical and a nuclear explosion has one more very important consequence. At the low temperatures of a chemical detonation the radiation that leaves the explosion is in the form of visible light and infrared radiation or heat, but at the high temperatures of a nuclear explosion the emitted radiation is in the form of thermal x-rays.

Even though the neutrons and gamma rays take up no more than 5% of the energy generated by the nuclear explosion, they cause a number of serious effects, such as the electromagnetic pulse, and the prompt nuclear radiation which is lethal to humans. The excitation energy stored inside the nuclear by-products of the explosion eventually manifests itself as the lethal radioactive fallout that accompanies nuclear explosions on the ground. Both prompt and delayed nuclear radioactivity and the electromagnetic pulse are phenomena caused only by nuclear explosions and are totally absent from chemical-explosives detonations no matter how large they are.

In this chapter we examine the effects of the detonation of a single nuclear weapon in different environments: in-

---

* The exact fraction of energy that goes into x-rays is determined by the yield-to-mass ratio of the weapon and to some extent by its design.

side the atmosphere, underground, underwater, and in outer space beyond the earth's atmosphere. The initial partition of energy into x-rays, the kinetic energy of the nuclear radiation, and excitation energy stored inside the nuclear fragments is common to nuclear detonations in all of these environments. But the secondary effects that these different forms of released energy generate depend on where the weapon explodes.

When a nuclear weapon explodes in the atmosphere, about half of the energy initially emitted as x-ray radiation transforms itself, within a few milliseconds, into kinetic energy of the air molecules through the interaction of the x-rays with the atmosphere. (The remaining energy escapes as thermal radiation.) The collective motion of these molecules away from the point of detonation is one cause of the blast that follows an explosion. Much of the kinetic energy of the escaping nuclei and other atomic fragments also eventually contributes to the blast. So about a minute after the detonation, about 50% of the total explosive energy is in the form of a giant blast wave, about 40–45% (depending on the design of the weapon) is in the form of thermal radiation, and the rest, 5–10%, is stored in excited nuclei.

Thermal radiation, which is one of the most devastating aspects of a nuclear explosion, consists of photons—packets of low-frequency waves (infrared, visible, and even ultraviolet waves)—each of which carries little energy. The effects of thermal radiation on living beings and the environment depend on three properties of the source of the radiation: its intensity (that is, how many thermal radiation photons leave it every second), its temperature (that is, how energetic each photon is), and the length of time the radiation is emitted by the source. For example, a burning log in a fireplace emits many more thermal radiation photons per second than a lit candle. Put your hand the same distance from both and the log will singe the skin much more readily. The burn will be worse if the skin is exposed to a small acetylene torch rather than the flame of a candle since its flame is hotter than the candle (that is, its radiation photons are more energetic). Of course, with any of these three sources, the farther away your hand is, the less severe the burn will be, because the heating effect of any source decreases with the distance from it. And again, with any of these three sources, the greater the amount of time the skin is exposed, the worse the burn will be.

These principles apply just as well to radiation from nuclear detonations. A large nuclear weapon creates more intense thermal radiation than a smaller one; a large fireball also remains hotter for a longer period of time. So even though the radiation waves from a large nuclear detonation will have the same frequency (that is, carry the same energy) as those from a smaller one, the thermal damage will be more severe in a larger detonation because of both the increased intensity and the longer exposure. The intensity, of course, decreases as one moves away from the radiation source, and the effects will vary with the distance from the point of detonation. But in general, and as one would expect, thermal damage is proportional to the yield of the weapon.

The amount of thermal radiation an object receives depends on a number of factors. One factor already mentioned is distance. The radiation emitted from a detonating nuclear weapon spreads out uniformly in all directions. As the energy radiates over a larger and larger area, its intensity dissipates.* Furthermore, as the thermal radiation travels through the atmosphere, it is absorbed by air molecules and dust, and its intensity is additionally reduced. Less and less radiation is left to do damage. How much energy is absorbed by the atmosphere depends on the weather conditions. Heat from a nuclear detonation will travel much farther in the clear, crisp air of winter weather than in fog or rain. So the thermal damage a nuclear detonation can do to someone or something depends not only on distance but also on the prevailing weather.

Another important factor is that some of the radiation that

* The amount of radiation that hits a given area decreases with the square of the distance from the point of detonation. To illustrate this, imagine a huge spherical balloon of radius R centered at the point of detonation. The total surface area of the ballon would be $4\pi R^2$. If E is the total energy emitted by the explosion, each unit area of the ballon will receive the same amount of radiation equal to $E/4\pi R^2$. Thus at any distance R, the amount of energy is divided by R^2.

falls on a surface is reflected and some absorbed, the proportion of absorbed to reflected radiation depending in part on the nature of the surface. The absorbed fraction is what raises the temperature of the material and causes damage: skin burns, scorching or ignition. For example, 12 kilometers (7.4 miles) from a 1-megaton weapon ground burst on a clear day, the intensity of thermal radiation is about 6 calories (that is, 25 watts for 1 second) per square centimeter of surface, and a person's exposed skin will suffer some second-degree burns. At this distance, paper, dry leaves, and rotted wood will ignite spontaneously. Exposed persons 10 kilometers (6.2 miles) from the point of detonation will suffer third-degree burns from a radiation exposure of about 10 calories/cm² (40 watts for 1 second). Construction materials such as plywood and roofing tarpaper will ignite spontaneously about 7 kilometers (4.3 miles) from the explosion. Closer than 7 kilometers, materials will start melting, and everything within several hundred meters from the explosion will evaporate.

Every easily flammable object within a radius of approximately 10 kilometers from the point where a 1-megaton weapon explodes on the ground on a clear day will ignite and continue to burn. In many instances this massive holocaust, fed by flammable materials such as gasoline from broken tanks and gas from shattered gas lines—known as a "firestorm"—will continue to burn for a long time. Firestorms are a uniquely self-sustaining and highly destructive form of conflagration that can take place in cities that contain a lot of combustible material and can also be caused by massive conventional incendiary bombing—as in the Allied attack on Dresden in World War II. Thus the properties of firestorms are reasonably well known. The hot gases from the fire ascend rapidly, causing the air around the burning area to rush in at speeds of 100 mph or higher and feed the firestorm with necessary oxygen. Temperatures inside the firestorm often reach 2,000 to 3,000 degrees Centigrade. At the same time, the carbon dioxide generated by combustion, since it is heavier than air, settles into low-lying places like basements, air-raid shelters, and subway tunnels, asphyxiating anyone there. Temperatures in these places will reach many hundreds of degrees, so people that may have sought shelter there would be literally dry-roasted, since there would be no oxygen to support combustion. Consequently, whenever a nuclear weapon dropped on a city initiates a firestorm, it can be expected that all living things within the firestorm will perish.

Even in the absence of a firestorm, the thermal radiation from a nuclear detonation causes more immediate damage at a greater distance from the explosion than any other prompt catastrophic effect.* This is mainly because, compared to other prompt effects (such as blast shock wave and prompt nuclear radiation), the intensity of thermal radiation is attenuated more slowly with increasing distance from the explosion. An example of this property is retinal burn, that is, permanent damage to the eye, which is in fact the most far-reaching—though not necessarily lethal—prompt pathogenic effect of a nuclear weapon. (An additional reason that retinal burn takes place so far from the detonation point is that the eye focuses the light it receives, largely canceling whatever attenuation of intensity has occurred over distance.) Thus a 1-megaton weapon exploded at an altitude of 3,000 meters will cause permanent retinal damage to an unprotected eye looking at the fireball from 50 kilometers (31 miles) away during the day and from twice that distance at night. If the weapon is detonated at an altitude of 15,000 meters, the corresponding distances are 70 and 140 kilometers (43 and 87 miles) respectively.

The thermal radiation emitted by a nuclear explosion has delayed effects as well as immediate ones. An important one is the depletion of ozone in the stratosphere. Ozone is a form of oxygen gas molecule that consists of three rather than the ordinary two atoms of oxygen. At altitudes of 20 to 30 kilometers above its surface, the earth is surrounded by a thin layer of ozone generated by a complicated series of photochemical reactions. This layer is biologically very important because it absorbs most of the sun's ultraviolet ra-

* It is true, of course, that long-term radioactive fallout from a ground explosion of a nuclear weapon can travel over very large distances and that it is the most long-range pathogenic effect of the weapon, but its effects are not prompt. Depending on the amount of fallout, radiation sickness occurs at varying times after the explosion, and its effects develop slowly.

diation and thereby performs a protective function for life on earth. Ultraviolet light is easily absorbed by the skin, and even in modest doses causes sunburn and can damage the cornea of the unprotected eye. Snow blindness, an effect well known to skiers, is caused by ultraviolet light that is reflected off the snow.

When a nuclear weapon detonates, it heats enormous amounts of air. For each metric ton of TNT equivalent explosive yield, the weapon will heat a ton of air to above 2,000 C°. A 1-megaton weapon will thus heat to at least this temperature 1 million tons of air, and in the process convert about 1% of the heated air to nitric oxides. So a 1-megaton weapon generates about 10,000 metric tons (10^{32} molecules) of nitric oxides. Since nitric oxides combine easily with ozone and destroy it, numerous nuclear explosions might well create enough nitric oxides to deplete the ozone layer. A larger fraction of the sun's ultraviolet radiation would then reach the surface of the earth, causing extensive blindness among diurnal animals of all kinds. It is theorized that since the vast majority of these explosions would occur in the Soviet Union, the United States, and Europe, the ozone layer would suffer depletion predominantly over the northern hemisphere. (The depletion over the southern hemisphere is expected to be only a third to a half of that over the northern latitudes.) Even though the ozone layer would probably reform, it might take five to ten years to do so, and in the meantime the animals in the affected areas would have been blinded and many would have died.

There are several things we do not know about the phenomenon of ozone depletion. First, it is not entirely clear how the size of the explosion and the proximity of one explosion to another influence the rate of ozone depletion. For the nitric oxides to destroy the ozone they must reach an altitude of 20 to 30 kilometers. The mushroom clouds from explosions of a 1-megaton bomb will reach these heights, but clouds from explosions of smaller yields will not. On the other hand, several smaller explosions, if they occurred relatively near each other in rapid succession, might generate a combined cloud that would reach the ozone layer. Also, we do not know how much ozone is in the stratosphere and cannot be sure by what percentage it will be reduced as a result of, for example, 1,000 nuclear weapons going off in quick succession throughout the northern hemisphere. We also do not know how much ultraviolet light would prove damaging to the eyes of people or animals continually exposed to it. A very small increase over the present "normal" level might be damaging, or it might not. Finally, we do not know the differences in response of the various species of diurnal animals to an increase of ultraviolet light. But despite the many great uncertainties, it is clear that ozone depletion resulting from nuclear detonations can cause devastating and widespread damage to the global ecology.

Since only about half of the energy released by the explosion of a nuclear weapon escapes in the form of thermal radiation one may well wonder what happens to the rest. As mentioned earlier, a large fraction of the original energy of the weapon initially starts out as x-rays. The less energetic x-rays (sometimes called "soft") are absorbed by the air around the detonation after they have traveled only a few centimeters in it. As a result the layer of air that has absorbed them becomes very hot, which is the colloquial way of saying that the air molecules acquire lots of kinetic energy and move about quite violently. Those that happen to be moving outward toward the undisturbed air farther away from the detonation collide with the slower molecules of the cool air and in turn give them additional kinetic energy. The end result of all this is that some tens of millionths of a second after the detonation, a very large number of air molecules are rushing away from the point of explosion, forming a shock wave that moves at supersonic speeds. This collective motion forms a wall of compressed air crushing and sweeping everything in its way. This is the blast shock associated with all explosions.

Helping in the formation of this shock wave is the vaporized weapon debris that is moving out in all directions away from the point of detonation. As the air that had been heated by the x-rays engulfs more and more undisturbed air in the vicinity of the explosion, it cools down and the rate of expansion slows. Eventually, the weapons debris catches up with the shock wave and contributes its energy, by colliding with the air molecules, to the outward push of the expanding front.

The very high pressure of the shock wave is like a heavy weight, crushing everything in its way. But as the shock wave moves outward, it also sweeps everything in its path. Thus an object experiences two forms of pressure from the shock wave: a downward pressure, like the crushing force of a car tire running over your hand, which is called "static overpressure," and a pushing pressure, similar to what you feel if you put your hand out the window of a speeding car, which is called "dynamic overpressure." Dynamic overpressure is caused by the hurricane-force winds that accompany the shock front as it moves out from the point of detonation.

Since the amount of radiation which is created by a detonation, and which subsequently heats the air, causing the shock front, is proportional to the yield of the weapon, it follows that the pressure generated will be proportional to the overall energy yield of the bomb. But the pressure will also depend on the fraction of this yield that goes into radiation and kinetic energy of the bomb fragments. The fission process emits a lot of soft x-rays and also creates all the highly energetic fragments of the fissioned nuclei, while the fusion process creates high-energy nuclear radiation (γ-rays and neutrons) and no fission fragments. As a result, a fission weapon will create a more powerful shock front than a fusion weapon of the same explosive yield.

The pressure, of course, also varies with distance from the point of detonation. The closer to the explosion, the higher the pressure. The amount of pressure can be calculated according to the yield of the weapon and the distance from it. In order to be able to predict how much damage a nuclear weapon of a given yield will cause at a given distance away from its point of explosion, we must find how pressure varies with this distance. The important thing to remember is that the air molecules, when they absorb the radiation and start moving very fast, fly out in all directions, which means that at any moment after the detonation they form a continually expanding sphere. Using this simple physical fact, we can derive a formula that relates pressure, yield, and distance for detonations that occur at the surface of the Earth.* (This formula is only valid for values of P > 100 psi, however.) For example, the static overpressure P at .5 nautical miles from the point of detonation of a 1-megaton weapon is

$$P = \frac{16.4 \cdot 1}{(\frac{1}{2})^3} = \frac{16.4 \cdot 1}{\frac{1}{8}} = 16.4 \cdot 1 \cdot 8 = 126 \text{ psi}$$

The dynamic pressure (that is, the pressure experienced by a surface perpendicular to the direction of motion of the shock front) is related to the overpressure at that point (see Appendix D). Table 1 (page 54) shows the magnitude of the dynamic pressure and the corresponding wind speed at given values of P, the static overpressure.

What are the effects of such pressures? The blast wave will be felt as a crushing and shattering blow followed by a powerful gust of wind. Overpressures of 2 psi will shatter shingles and wrench wooden sidings from the outside walls

---

* Since about half of the energy yielded by the detonation is transformed into kinetic energy of air molecules, we have $Y/2 = (1/2) MU^2$, where Y is the yield of the weapon, M is the total mass of the air inside the expanding sphere, and U is the average speed of the air molecules that fly out. Now we have to find how much M is. Well, if the radius of the sphere is R, its total volume V is $(4/3)\pi R^3$, and since the mass of an object is equal to its density ρ times its volume, we have $M = V \cdot \rho = (4/3)\pi R^3 \rho$. So now we have $Y = (4/3)\pi R^3 \rho \cdot U^2$. But density multiplied by velocity squared is the effective overpressure (P, the crushing pressure) at the surface of that sphere, so

$$Y = (4/3)\pi R^3 P$$

When we put in the proper units this becomes

$$P = \frac{16.4Y}{R^3}$$

where P is measured in pounds per square inch (psi), Y in megatons of TNT equivalent (that is, the energy released by the explosion in millions of tons of TNT), and R is traditionally given in nautical miles. This relationship allows the prediction of the overpressure a given distance R from the explosion on the ground of a weapon of yield Y. This formula is exact only for large overpressures; it is only approximate for overpressures under 30 psi. If the weapon explodes at some altitude above the earth, the distance at which a given overpressure under 30 psi will occur is larger than that given by this formula. This is because of the manner in which the shock front from an air burst propagates along the surface of the earth after it slams down on it.

TABLE 1

WHERE THE STATIC OVERPRESSURE P IS (IN PSI)	THE DYNAMIC PRESSURE Q IS (IN PSI)	THE WIND VELOCITY IS (IN MPH)
200	330	2,078
150	222	1,777
100	123	1,415
72	74	1,168
50	41	934
30	17	669
20	8	502
10	2.2	294
5	0.6	163
2	0.1	70

of houses. Brick houses will be destroyed by 3–5 psi; windowpanes will shatter at 5 psi. Concrete or cinderblock walls will be demolished by 1.5–5 psi overpressure. All trees will be uprooted by the following wind where the overpressure is 3–4 psi. Roof water tanks will be destroyed by overpressures of 4–8 psi. An overpressure of 10 psi will not destroy the concrete-and-steel skeleton of a high-rise building but will probably sweep everything in between the concrete floors out into the streets: walls, furniture, and inhabitants. At about 100 psi overpressure, the steel structures themselves will collapse.

The body of a person subjected to the blast wave from a nuclear explosion is quickly squeezed inward from all directions. This damages the lungs and disrupts the circulatory system. Severe lung damage occurs at overpressures between 20 and 30 psi, with some damage caused by pressures as low as 10 psi. Eardrums rupture at 5 psi. About half of the people exposed to 50 psi will die just from the squeezing effect of the overpressure. Even more probable, however, is death or injury from being thrown against walls or objects by the wind, or by being struck by flying debris. At 17 psi, the winds from the explosion will hurl a person at 100 kilometers per hour. Where the overpressure is 5 psi, near any window there will be about 400 pieces of glass per square foot of surface (each weighing 5 grams on the average), flying at speeds of 60 meters per second or 200 kilometers per hour. So there is little chance of avoiding injury from flying debris even in situations in which the direct effects of the overpressure are minimal.

Prompt nuclear radiation (that is, neutrons and gamma rays emitted within the first minute after detonation) is another immediate effect of a nuclear explosion. It causes little physical damage to structures and equipment, but it can injure living organisms because its biological effects are similar to those produced by x-rays, electrons, and alpha particles. Collectively these are known as "ionizing" radiation, because what they do, in effect, is remove electrons from the atoms that form the molecules of the cells of our body tissues. This is the mechanism that ultimately gives rise to radiation sickness.

The most important biological effect of ionizing radiation is the destruction of molecules, due to their ionization, inside the cell. The destruction of molecules causes in turn the death of the cell, especially if many molecules are damaged or destroyed at the same time. Our body has mechanisms capable of repairing irradiated molecules, but only at a limited rate. If the damage produced by the radiation occurs faster than the rate at which the repair mechanisms of the body function, then "radiation sickness" sets in. Thus there are two factors which determine the degree of damage: the dose, which is the number of ionizing particles or waves that enter the body, and the period of exposure. For example, a particular dose received over a day or two may lead to death within one to two weeks. If received over a period of months, it may cause genetic damage or, eventually, cancer, but not any of the symptoms or effects of radiation sickness. If received over a lifetime, it may have no noticeable clinical effects.

Radiation doses are measured in units called rems. As is usually the case with units, one has to look at the history behind the rem in order to understand what it means. The basic unit of ionizing radiation is the roentgen, after Wilhelm Roentgen, the discoverer of x-rays, and it was originally devised as a measure of gamma-ray or x-ray radiation. A roentgen is the amount of radiation that will produce $2.08 \cdot 10^9$ ion pairs (that is, separated electrons and positively charged atoms) per cubic centimeter of air.* So the roentgen is a measure of the radiation to which an object or a living creature is *exposed.* But damage is proportional to the amount of radiation *absorbed* by a person or an object. Since radiation damage is caused not only by gamma rays and x-rays but also by absorbed electrons, neutrons, protons, and alpha particles, a new unit, the rad, was invented to quantify such damage. A rad is the amount of absorbed radiation that will deposit 100 ergs of energy in each gram of absorbing material.

Now it so happens that exposure to 1 roentgen of x-rays and gamma rays generated by a nuclear detonation will result in just about 100 ergs of energy deposited per gram of body tissue, so, in general and with little error, we can equate an exposure to 1 roentgen to an absorbed radiation of 1 rad. However, the biological effects of various types of ionizing radiation vary, depending on the type of the particle and the type of damage under consideration. For example, 1 rad of neutrons would cause much more severe biological damage than 1 rad of x-rays. Or, 1 rad of alpha particles absorbed by the bones will cause cancer much more readily than the same dose of the same particles to the skin. So in order to describe more precisely the biological effects of different kinds of ionizing radiation, the dose had to be multiplied by an empirically established factor that described its specific biological effect—that is, by the RBE or "relative biological effectiveness" factor. The product of an absorbed dose in rads multiplied by the appropriate RBE is the rem. In other words, rem = rad × RBE. For neutrons and gamma rays that are emitted within a second or so from the instant of a nuclear detonation, the RBE is very close to unity, and therefore we say in this instance that 1 rem equals 1 rad.

The effects of different doses of radiation received by a human being in a period briefer than a day are of most interest to us in considering prompt nuclear radiation. Although there are few visible effects at doses less than 100 rems, there are significant effects nonetheless. The systems

* That is equivalent to releasing 88 ergs (2.1·10⁻⁶ calories) of energy in 1 gram of air.

of the body that manufacture the various components of our blood are seriously affected. For example, at about 100 rems the body stops making the various types of white cells that protect the body from infection. After two weeks or so the body recovers and the blood contents return to normal, but in the meantime the irradiated individual is more susceptible to infection and more vulnerable to the effects of burns. At about 150 rems, one starts losing hair and will probably be nauseous and vomit for several days. At doses of about 200 rems most individuals will suffer from severe radiation sickness and a few will die. At 450 rems, 50% of the exposed population will die of radiation sickness, and at 600 rems practically everyone will die.

Radiation affects most seriously the cells that multiply rapidly, like blood-making cells and the cells that line the mouth, stomach, and the intestinal tract, particularly the small intestine. At levels up to 600 rems these cells are not killed, but can no longer multiply. Since the body normally sloughs off such cells at a high rate, without rapid replacement the intestine is quickly denuded, so that it can neither absorb foodstuffs nor retain water in the body. As a result, the victim of radiation sickness develops diarrhea, dehydration, and infection of the intestinal tract, eventually dying from starvation or by collapse of the circulatory system.

Radiation affects rapidly multiplying cells by damaging the DNA molecules within them. Because these long, complex nuclear molecules control mitosis, the doubling process by which nearly all cells reproduce, irradiated cells lose their ability to replicate themselves exactly, or at all. Even though the cell has two sets of two copies each of the DNA, with higher radiation doses the probability increases that all four will be damaged. Although each cell can potentially repair DNA damage, it seems that once radiation doses exceed a given level, the damage is more than the cell can repair within its lifetime, and so it is sloughed off. This accounts for the particular vulnerability of cells which naturally reproduce quickly. It may also explain why such a modest increase in dosage (from 200 to 400 rems) has such an enormous difference in the mortality rate (from practically no fatalities to 50% of the exposed population dying).

The effects of prompt nuclear radiation from a ground

burst are similar to those from an air burst, except that the doses of radiation are reduced by a factor of two for a given distance because of the configuration of the burst. This modification does not make a significant difference, however, and the lethal area from prompt radiation will be essentially the same as that given by an air burst, about 8 square miles for a 1-megaton weapon. In addition, the ground immediately surrounding the blast becomes highly radioactive because the many high-energy neutrons emitted in the explosion activate nuclei in substances on the ground. This is called "neutron-induced radioactivity," and can contribute significantly to the ambient radiation when elements such as sodium are involved, since, when they are neutron-activated, they emit high-energy gamma rays. This radiation is confined to a small area, and since most of the neutron-activated radioactive nuclei have a half-life of less than a day, neutron-induced radioactivity does not contribute to the contamination of large areas of land.

Another important effect of prompt nuclear radiation is the electromagnetic pulse or EMP. About 0.3% of the energy released by a nuclear detonation is carried by energetic gamma rays that knock electrons from their orbits around atoms of the surrounding atmosphere. These electrons move more or less in the same direction as the gamma rays, that is, outward from the point of explosion. Each carries roughly half the energy of the gamma ray that stripped it from its atom. Since most of these prompt gamma rays have energies of about 1 Mev, the electrons fly out with energies of about 0.5 Mev. As they fly through the air each electron strips about 30,000 additional "secondary" electrons off other atoms. So within 10 nanoseconds after the explosion a very large number of electrons have rushed away from the point of detonation, leaving behind an equally large number of slower, positively charged ions. (Since an atom has a neutral charge—having the same number of protons in its nucleus as it has electrons orbiting around it—when an electron is removed from its orbit the atom is left with an unpaired proton in its nucleus and therefore is positively charged.)

If the weapon is detonated on or near the ground, all the gamma rays that strike the ground are absorbed and do not produce any fast, primary electrons. But those gamma rays that move into the atmosphere generate lots of fast electrons, creating, in effect, a powerful electric current moving upward from the surface of the earth. This current creates giant electric and magnetic fields that spread out for tens of kilometers. Attracted by the positive ions left behind, the slow secondary electrons start moving back toward the point of detonation, creating an electric current flowing in the ground. In effect, then, we have electric currents both in the air and in the ground, each producing an electric and a magnetic pulse that travel together away from the point of detonation as a single electromagnetic pulse (EMP). Electric fields of tens of thousands of volts per meter and currents of up to 10,000 amperes accompany this pulse. The total energy of such an EMP from a 1-megaton weapon is about a hundred thousand million (10^{11}) joules. Since even a small fraction of a joule is sufficient to damage solid-state electronic devices if it flows through them, and about 1 joule can burn out relatively sturdy electrical equipment such as telephones and life-support systems in hospitals, the EMP—even from a ground burst—will cause widespread and indiscriminate damage to all electrical and electronic equipment within a distance of 10 to 20 kilometers from a ground nuclear detonation.

The EMP generated by a high-altitude (between 50 and 300 kilometers above the surface of the earth) nuclear explosion is vastly more damaging. When a 1-megaton weapon is exploded at an altitude of 300 kilometers, those gamma rays that travel toward the earth penetrate the atmosphere and knock large numbers of electrons off the atoms they encounter. The stripped electrons in turn create 30,000 times as many secondary electrons in a pancake-shaped volume of atmosphere 800 kilometers in radius and 50 kilometers thick, about 60 kilometers above the surface of the earth. This "deposition area" (so called because that's where the gamma rays "deposit" their energy by knocking electrons off atoms) now becomes the source of an electromagnetic pulse that spreads down to the earth and out to the horizon in all directions, as far as 1,700 kilometers.

The extraordinary strength of the EMP from a high-altitude nuclear burst is the result of the combination of several physical phenomena. One is that when charged particles are slowed down or travel in a curved path they radiate off an electric field that spreads over long distances. This is particularly true for particles of little mass—like electrons. Also, since above the atmosphere* there is little air to stop the electrons, they travel for hundreds of kilometers. As they do so they are forced by the earth's magnetic field to travel in circular paths, a motion that makes them radiate away the electric field portion of the EMP. Because these electrons travel far and do so for several minutes, the EMP they generate is both long-range and persistent. The electric field's strength is not diminished substantially as it travels out to this distance, so the field will still be 20,000 volts per meter—about three times the strength of the field over an electric wall outlet—as far as 1,500 kilometers from the point of detonation. Some low-frequency components of this field bend around the horizon and affect essentially the entire earth. (That effect, incidentally, can be relied upon in detecting and confirming nuclear tests in the atmosphere or in outer space.)

The implications of the EMP effect are dramatic. One large high-altitude explosion in the middle of the United States could bathe the country from coast to coast in an EMP that would be picked up by power lines, antennas, and the wires and circuits of all electrical equipment, damage the most delicate computers and electronic communications devices, and even disrupt the sturdiest electrical power generation and distribution equipment. It is quite probable that such an EMP would cause a total electric blackout and incapacitate the communications network of the United States. In addition, even though the military have been making efforts to reduce the susceptibility of the command and control system that ties the various units of the armed forces to their commander and ultimately to the

---

* The atmosphere is traditionally broken into four layers: the lower atmosphere, which extends a few thousand meters above sea level; the troposphere, which ranges between 6 and 18 kilometers thick; the stratosphere, 50 kilometers thick; and the mesosphere, about 30 kilometers thick. By legal convention, the top of the atmosphere is 100 kilometers above sea level.

national command authority, it is most probable that the EMP from one or more nuclear detonations would disrupt that system to an unknown and probably unknowable degree. For this reason alone, there is a great risk that a nuclear war would rapidly become uncontrollable, as the military units of a country would be forced to make decisions about the use of nuclear weapons in near-total isolation from their national command authorities.

The presence of an EMP can also disrupt the launch and flight of intercontinental ballistic missiles. An electric field of 20,000 volts per meter generates an electric potential of 200,000 volts across a missile 10 meters long. This potential in turn causes an electric current of about 20,000 amperes to flow on the surface of the missile. Such a flow can induce smaller, but still disruptive, currents inside the missile, burning out the electronic circuits of the missile's guidance system or the arming and fusing mechanism of its nuclear warheads. As a result, one nation can "pin down" the land-based ballistic missiles of another by detonating a nuclear weapon 200 to 300 kilometers above the opponent's missile silos every fifteen minutes or so.

We come now to examine the fate of the portion of energy released by a nuclear explosion that is stored as excitation energy inside the fragments of the fissioned plutonium and uranium nuclei. In the typical fission-fusion-fission nuclear weapon that we have been examining, about half of the released energy comes from the fissioning of the U^{238} nuclei that form the mantle of the weapon. But uranium and plutonium nuclei usually fission into two new nuclei, one with an atomic weight of about 100 and the other of about 140, and two or three neutrons. Sometimes, however, a uranium nucleus will fission into two very uneven new nuclei. The result of the fissioning of the vast number of uranium nuclei is a collection of new nuclei that contains practically every nucleus and every isotope of every nucleus of all known elements. As we noted, about 10% of all the energy created by the explosion is stored as excitation in these nuclei. Thus the key characteristic of all these new nuclei is that they are either excited or they contain too many neutrons, or both.

Immediately after the end of the explosion process, these nuclei begin to shed some of their excess energy in the forms of gamma rays and to convert some of their excess neutrons to protons by emitting an electron. The actual de-excitation of any one individual nucleus is a random process, but each species of nuclei has its own characteristic time for returning to a stable and unexcited configuration, ranging from a few seconds to millions of years. Consequently, this collection of nuclei keeps on radiating electrons and gamma rays, although at a decreasing rate as fewer and fewer nuclei remain excited with the passage of time. For every sevenfold increase in time, the rate of radiation decreases by a factor of ten. For example, seven hours after detonation, the total radioactivity of the collection of nuclei generated at the instant of the explosion will be one-tenth what it was one hour after the explosion. It will be a hundred times less forty-nine hours after the explosion.

The pattern of dispersal of all these radioactive nuclei depends on the location of the detonation. If the weapon explodes high enough above the ground for the fireball not to touch the surface of the earth, all the radioactive nuclei are carried to a high altitude, 60,000 to 80,000 feet for a 1-megaton weapon. There they are picked up by the jet stream, which in the northern hemisphere blows west to east, and are sent several times around the globe before they slowly drift down to the surface of the Earth. This dispersal spreads the radioactivity generated by the explosion over very large areas. Therefore the resulting radioactivity at any one point on the earth is very small, perhaps no more than twice the natural radioactivity that the earth receives from the sun and other sources in the galaxy.

A very different situation arises, however, when the weapon detonates near or on the ground. A 1-megaton weapon exploding on the ground will excavate in ordinary wet soil a crater about 400 meters in diameter and 70 meters deep. Much of this dirt will be vaporized by the intense heat and carried, together with the radioactive nuclei, to high altitude by the ascending fireball. As the fireball cools, some of the vaporized dirt condenses back to solid form and starts dropping back to earth as small particles of dust.

Many radioactive nuclei become attached to these dust particles, returning to earth rather quickly. About 50% to 70% of the radioactive nuclei are associated with the relatively large particles that return to the ground in large concentrations in less than a day. The remainder, which amounts to about one-third of the radioactive nuclei generated by an air burst, becomes global fallout. Meanwhile, however, the prevailing winds at the point of detonation carry the sedimenting dirt particles and their attached radioactive nuclei along with them. As a result, large doses of radioactivity can blanket the area immediately downwind from the point of explosion (as shown in Figure 7 on page 64).

Radiation damage from this early fallout constitutes the main catastrophic contribution from the radioactive nuclei produced in the fission process. Sophisticated models have been proposed to predict the patterns of radiation doses resulting from early fallout, but since atmospheric conditions are highly variable, the only reliable estimates are those of the total land area affected. Most models predict distribution of radioactive fallout following cigar-shaped contours like those in Figures 7 and 8, but in an actual situation fluctuations in wind patterns and crosswinds make these contours more irregular.

TABLE 2

Areas inside contours defined by the accumulated dose in Figure 8

ACCUMULATED DOSE LARGER THAN (IN RADS):	AREA (km^2)	
	AFTER ONE DAY	AFTER ONE WEEK
1,000	415	650
300	1,145	2,000
100	2,730	5,980
30	6,500	17,160
10	12,480	35,100
3	20,020	62,400
1	24,400	101,400

Figures 7 and 8 indicate how the fallout patterns develop over time. When the burst occurs, the total activity of the

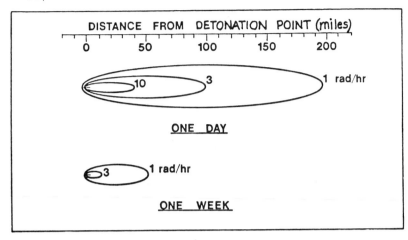

FIGURE 7. Idealized dose rate contours for a 1-megaton surface burst for one day and one week after the explosion resulting from the model described. A 15-mph wind is assumed.

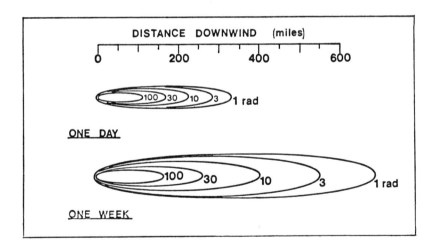

FIGURE 8. Theoretical accumulated dose contours resulting from a 1-megaton surface burst, given by the model described. The dose is in rads. The areas inside these contours are given in Table 2. A 15-mph wind is assumed.

cloud is at its peak, but the cloud is very localized. The winds carry the radioactive cloud along, so the radiation dose rates in the areas downwind rise as the dust continues to fall. After all the fallout is deposited, the dose rates begin to decrease, because the intensity of the radioactivity decays with time. Figure 7 shows the dose still received after one day and after one week for a given distance from the blast. Figure 8 shows the total dose that would be accumulated by then.

The lethal area (that is, the area within which an individual would be exposed to over 400 rems in one day) is approximately 1,000 square kilometers for a 1-megaton ground explosion. The number of fatalities can be predicted by multiplying the population density by the lethal area. Population densities in the United States range from 40,000 people per square kilometer in metropolitan areas during business hours to less than 2 per square kilometer. A single ground burst of a 1-megaton nuclear weapon could kill, by delayed radiation alone, anywhere from 5,000 to 10 million people, depending on the time and location of the explosion, the weather conditions, the degree of advance warning of the impending fallout, and the protection from radiation available to the affected population.

Those who escape death would be unable to return to their homes for a long period of time, because the ground would be contaminated with radioactive particles. They would have to wait until the combined effects of radioactive decay, rain, and snow reduced the activity to acceptable levels, a process known as the "weathering" effect. With a maximum acceptable dose defined in peacetime as 2 rem per year, the amount of land that would remain unfit for human use for a particular time period can be determined from Table 3 (page 66). If all the contaminated land were previously cultivated, 1 million acres of land would be removed from cultivation for seven years.

The figures given in Table 3 indicate that larger areas of the land would be affected for relatively shorter but still socially disruptive amounts of time. Over 50,000 square kilometers would be uninhabitable for one month, which could necessitate massive dislocations of several hundred thousand or even millions of people. In an attack that in-

volved the use of several weapons, the cumulative radioactivity would almost certainly contaminate a large number
of factories and workplaces, causing billions of dollars of
economic losses for industry in addition to the agricultural
losses.

TABLE 3

Area that becomes uninhabitable for a given time
assuming the maximum allowable dose is 2 rem per
year. Surface-burst case, 1-megaton weapon, 15-
mph wind.

TIME UNINHABITABLE	AREA (km²)
1 week	80,600
2 weeks	67,600
1 month	54,600
2 months	44,200
6 months	13,000
1 year	3,120
2 years	390
3 years	145
4 years	90
5 years	30
10 years	5

Radioactive fallout, characteristic only of nuclear explosions, is the most disturbing long-term effect of a nuclear
detonation, since it contaminates large areas of land far removed from the point of explosion for disruptive periods of
time. It has been estimated, for example, that an attack
against the missile silos in the northwestern United States,
involving about 2,000 1-megaton weapons, would produce
enough radioactive fallout to kill between 5 million and 20
million inhabitants of states east of the targets and would
remove from cultivation vast areas of land. Consequently, a
person or a nation surviving the immediate effects of a nuclear attack would still be threatened by the long-term effects of radioactive fallout, either directly from lethal doses
of radiation deposited far away from the detonation, or in-
directly from starvation, since contaminated food cannot be

consumed with impunity, and the generation of new food supplies would be hindered by the contamination of fields and pastures downwind from the explosions within the first twenty-four hours after the attack.

Since the fallout is deposited on open surfaces, its adverse health effects are more moderate inside houses and buildings; the walls absorb some of the radiation. The nature of radioactive fallout is such that inside an ordinary frame house the radiation is about four times less than outside and inside a concrete apartment building between ten and a hundred times less. Thus the population of a contaminated area could find some protection from the radioactivity hazard by staying indoors. The problem then, of course, is the duration of confinement. In relatively distant areas removed from the point of explosion, a few days of confinement indoors might prove adequate in avoiding radiation sickness. But in areas closer to the explosion, where the fallout would be initially heavy, it might require weeks of confinement indoors to avoid dangerous exposure. Worse, survival might depend on complete and rapid abandonment of the entire contaminated area. Because the extraordinary preparations needed for such evacuation would be so disruptive and costly to peacetime society and the results so uncertain, there has been little effort to prepare against the hazards of radioactive fallout.

Finally, we examine the physical phenomena generated by nuclear explosions underground, underwater, or far above the atmosphere in outer space. By negotiated agreement among the nuclear powers, peacetime nuclear explosions in outer space and underwater are forbidden. But in time of war such explosions may occur, and that prospect indicates that they merit at least a brief description.

The amount and initial forms of the energy released by the explosion of a nuclear weapon are the same no matter where the weapon detonates. But what happens to that energy and how it interacts with the environment are crucially dependent on the properties of the medium in which the explosion occurs. Very different things happen depending on whether the weapon is detonated deeply underground, underwater, or very high up above the atmosphere in outer space.

The energy released in the first instants of the explosion of a deeply buried nuclear weapon is almost completely absorbed by the surrounding rocks and dirt. The amount of energy is so large and is released so suddenly that it doesn't have time to spread out. So it melts or vaporizes the rock around the point of detonation, creating a large cavity.* The pressure inside this sphere of rock vapors rises suddenly to many millions of atmospheres, and under this enormous pressure, the vapors expand and create a shock front that moves out in all directions, crushing the rock farther and farther out. If the soil where the weapon detonates contains a lot of water, the heat from the explosion will turn the water into steam and add to the pressure pushing against the surrounding rock.

The part of the shock wave that moves upward reaches the surface of the earth above the point of detonation. What the effect of this part of the pressure wave will be depends on the depth of burial and the yield of the weapon. In general, if the depth is greater than $100 \cdot Y^{1/3}$ meters, where Y is measured in kilotons, then the shock wave will not break through the surface, which means that most of the wave's energy reflects back into the ground. (As a rule, underground nuclear detonations are set off far enough beneath the surface that the pressure wave never breaks through.) When the wave moves back down, it stretches, rather than crushes, the rock as it goes through. As a result, the crushed and molten rock above the cavity collapses downward, creating a cylindrical chimney (Figure 9).

While the chimney and crater are caused by the portion of the shock wave that moves upward toward the surface, the rest of the shock wave keeps traveling in the ground away from the point of detonation, in an ever-expanding spherical pressure wave, losing strength and speed until it becomes an acoustical wave. Acoustical waves can have many forms. Some are a series of alternating compressions and rarefactions along the direction in which the wave trav-

---

* The radius of the cavity, R, is equal to $10 \cdot Y^{1/3}$ meters, where Y is the size of the weapon measured in kilotons.

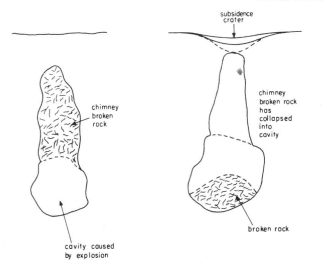

FIGURE 9. Sketch of the process of formation of a subsidence crater by an underground explosion.

els. Others are like a "shear wave," which makes matter oscillate up and down as the wave passes through it. Sometimes the shock wave from an underground nuclear detonation can set in motion a series of waves on the surface of the earth that roll like the waves of the ocean, although their height is too small to detect without special equipment. Whatever form they take, these waves can travel over very long distances—essentially around the earth—and therefore can be detected with special seismographs thousands of miles away from the point of the nuclear detonation. Thus, regardless of the site of underground nuclear explosions, their existence and the magnitude of their yield can be measured with considerable confidence and accuracy. This fact has provided the method by which the United States and the Soviet Union verify that the other country is abiding by their treaty agreement to limit the yield of underground nuclear explosions to less than 150 kilotons.

The effects of an underwater nuclear detonation (currently forbidden by treaty) depend not only on the yield of the weapon but also on the depth of the detonation and the distance to the bottom. The energy from an underwater explosion is quickly absorbed by the surrounding water, which turns into very hot steam. The temperature is so high (several thousand degrees centigrade) that the steam becomes incandescent and actually forms a small fireball, a rapidly expanding underwater bubble that glows brightly through the water. The pressure inside this bubble rises to millions of atmospheres and pushes the surrounding water so violently that it generates a shock wave similar to those in atmospheric and underground nuclear detonations. The portion of the shock wave that travels upward reaches the surface of the water and literally shatters it into tiny droplets. The droplets, pushed by the shock wave, rise hundreds of meters into the air and form a bell-shaped dome of spray. Eventually the pull of gravity and the friction of the water droplets with the air stop the expansion of this dome and the droplets of spray begin to fall back toward the surface of the water. Behind the shock wave that caused the dome of spray comes the bubble of incandescent gases that rises, eventually catching up with and breaking through the expanding spray dome, releasing the pressure inside it. This in turn causes millions of tons of water to be sucked up behind the fireball bubble. From a distance, the effect is of a solid column of water rising from the surface, capped by the dome of spray (see Figure 10).

Eventually the spray and the hot steam condense into a cloud that rises above the column of water, forming a perfect mushroom of water and steam. Slowly all this water either falls back down or is carried away by the prevailing winds in the form of a cloud that is highly radioactive from all the excited fission fragments produced by the weapon.

Meanwhile a series of waves formed on the surface of the water run concentrically away from the point on the surface above the detonation. As the waves move out, their height decreases slowly. A 20-kiloton underwater explosion creates waves 30 meters high at 300 meters from the point of explosion; that height is reduced to 3 meters at a distance of 4 kilometers from the explosion.

Since water is not nearly as compressible as air, it tends to transmit pressure without attenuating it significantly. So

FIGURE 10. Picture of the condensation cloud formed by an under-water explosion. Note the effect the shock wave has on the surface of the water as it travels outward.

peak overpressures from underwater explosions are much higher at the same distance from the point of detonation than the corresponding overpressure in the air. For example, a 1-megaton weapon 10 kilometers away will cause a 500 psi overpressure in water, but less than 1 psi in air. Even so, underwater nuclear detonations are not especially damaging to submarines, because these boats are built to withstand the tremendous hydrostatic pressures they encounter when deeply submerged. A submarine designed to operate at 1,000 meters depth can withstand at least 14,000 psi and probably twice that. Therefore, the hull of a submarine 300 meters below the surface can sustain at least 10,000 psi overpressure without damage. Overpressures of this magnitude occur about 1 kilometer from the point of detonation of a 1-megaton weapon. Only if the nuclear weapon exploded closer than 1 kilometer or if the submarine was submerged well below 300 meters would its hull be crushed. But the overpressure shock would be felt by a submarine like a blow. Even if this blow did not crack the hull of the submarine, it could cause havoc because the shock would be transmitted inside to the various pieces of equipment and the crew. Because of the inertia of heavy objects, the bolts that hold machinery to the ship's frame might shear as the frame moved under the shock. Sensitive electronic and inertial guidance equipment might very well be severely damaged. Proper design and installation might prevent such damage up to a certain shock overpressure, but it could not eliminate the danger altogether. Therefore, the distance at which an underwater nuclear explosion would render a submarine inoperable might be several times larger than the distance at which the explosion would literally crush the craft.

When a nuclear weapon is detonated in shallow waters near the coastline, it generates a rolling wave, which, like a tsunami, travels in the ocean, rolls onto the sloping coast, and crashes on land. Although only a few percent of the energy released by the nuclear detonation is carried by this Van Dorn wave (so called after the physicist who first studied the phenomenon), it can reach many feet in height. The exact size of the wave depends on the explosive yield of the nuclear detonation, the distance of the explosion from the coast, and the way the bottom of the ocean slopes away from land at that point. On the eastern coast of the United States, megaton-sized weapons detonated several miles from the beach could generate a huge tidal wave able to devastate houses and other structures on the coast. However, this would be a very inefficient way to attack coastal cities. A Van Dorn wave could damage submarines lurking over the continental shelf by rolling them on their side or even upside-down, but otherwise, a shallow-water detonation has little strategic importance.

We have yet to explore the effects, other than the generation of an EMP, of a nuclear weapon exploding higher than 50 miles over the earth, where there is hardly any atmosphere and very little matter to absorb the thermal and nuclear radiation that the detonation releases. At these altitudes, the earth's geomagnetic field plays an important role in the ultimate fate of the energy that leaves the bomb. This occurs because the weapon debris and the fission products are highly ionized and therefore behave like positively charged particles. Propelled by the kinetic energy it acquired during the brief fission-fusion-fission process of the weapon's explosion, the ionized bomb debris tends to stretch the geomagnetic field lines in front of it the way a falling body would stretch a safety net. Eventually the geomagnetic field stops the motion of the charged debris, but not before the debris has traveled for hundreds of miles. Those particles that speed toward the earth heat the air, forming a fireball that rises back into the upper atmosphere, emitting thermal radiation in the process. And the charged debris that moves away from the earth either escapes into space or travels along the lines of the geomagnetic field and reenters the earth's atmosphere hundreds or thousands of miles away.

The x-rays, which inside the atmosphere are the main cause of the fireball, are not affected by geomagnetism. They can therefore travel unimpeded over very large distances in the upper atmosphere. Those that travel toward the earth contribute to the formation of a fireball at the top of the atmosphere, but those that move away from it travel for large distances before they interact with the rare molecules of air and ionize them. The geomagnetic field determines how long these positive ions and freed electrons will travel and how they will eventually recombine into neutral molecules. The result is that the number of electrons in space, at a distance of 200 to 400 miles over the earth, increases temporarily. Many of these electrons travel very great distances, spiraling around lines of the geomagnetic field, colliding with more air molecules and ionizing them. Apart from this source of ionization, the radioactive debris that has flown into space returns to its unexcited state by emitting neutrons, gamma rays, or electrons. These also ionize the rare molecules of air in outer space.

This sudden surge in the density of electrons in the ionosphere would have drastic effects on the transmission of radio and radar waves. Since the flux of energetic electrons traveling along magnetic field lines is known to damage electronic equipment on satellites, a high-altitude detonation could play havoc with communications, radar operations, and satellite-borne electronic equipment, even though no direct destructive effect from such a nuclear explosion reaches the surface of the earth.

4

THE PHYSICAL EFFECTS
OF A NUCLEAR WAR

IN PREVIOUS CHAPTERS we have examined the physical phenomena that are caused by a single nuclear detonation and their physical effects on the natural and man-made objects around it. We saw how the energy is released from inside the fissioned nuclei, and how it produces a destructive blast wave and other less violent but equally destructive effects such as the electromagnetic pulse, delayed radioactive fallout, and the generation of nitrogen oxides that destroy the protective ozone mantle above the Earth. The effects of a single nuclear detonation on human beings and their habitat and society, though massive, are not completely irreversible, as we have seen in the cases of Hiroshima and Nagasaki. The destruction of these cities and of hundreds of thousands of their inhabitants represents what we hope will be a unique tragedy in human history. Yet within days after the nuclear attacks against them, these cities marshaled a semblance of organized activity. The survivors were treated and cared for. Rudimentary public services, such as the supply of food, water, power, transportation, and medical care, were reestablished. A centralized authority directed the entire effort, at first toward survival, and then toward recovery.

But the experience of these cities cannot give us a true measure of the impact of a nuclear war on human life. Nor can they provide us with information that would allow us to conclude whether a nation can survive a nuclear war and recover after the termination of hostilities. Simply put, there is no precedent in history for the widespread, simultaneous, perhaps irreversible destruction that a large nuclear attack would cause to a nation. We can perhaps imagine the effects of one nuclear explosion on one city by extrapolating from the relatively small-scale attacks on Hiroshima and Nagasaki. We can gain an appreciation of the radioactive fallout caused by a few detonations of nuclear weapons in the atmosphere by recalling the radioactive contamination of parts of the United States during the early tests of nuclear weapons in Nevada. But nothing in human memory even distantly approximates the conditions caused by the attack that I will describe here. History can teach us very little about what we can anticipate at the end of a nuclear war. We cannot learn much, for example, from the devastation of Germany toward the end of World War II. The total explosive energy of all the bombs that fell on Germany in the last four years of the war was less than a millionth of the energy a modest nuclear attack would visit upon the United States. The destruction that the bombing of Germany caused was local and spread over a span of years, which permitted both the population and the war effort of the country to adjust and take remedial measures. And most important, in Germany there was no radioactive fallout to impede activities in or near the bombed cities or deny the use of land. So we must attempt to imagine how things would be after a large-scale nuclear war without even any vaguely familiar images to help us. In doing so one fact must be constantly borne in mind: The destruction would be widespread and simultaneous, so that one region of a nation would be unable to aid another.

I do not think that using the example of an attack on the United States will diminish the general validity of the conclusion we will arrive at. It is true that nations are different from one another in political, economic, and social institutions. But as different as societies are around the world, the needs of human beings for food, shelter, clothing, and medical care remain basically the same. The effects of a nuclear war on a nation would be so pervasive that whatever differences exist between nations, the outcome of a large-scale nuclear attack on any one of them would be virtually identical. Nuclear war would destroy the very means of survival —food, shelter, and health facilities—and these are universally crucial for sustaining human life. It might also destroy the physical bases for reconstructing the institutions and patterns of cooperation which make human society possible.

Many long-term effects of a large-scale nuclear attack are a result of the pervasiveness and abruptness of the destruction such an attack would cause. A small fleet of intercontinental ballistic missiles carrying nuclear explosives could, in a matter of minutes, destroy an entire country. This kind of destruction would have very different long-term effects than the slow and sporadic destruction brought about by a conventional nonnuclear war. The United States and the Soviet Union today possess many more nuclear weapons with intercontinental range than are needed to destroy both countries quickly and completely. So in contemplating the possible outcome of a nuclear war we must bear in mind that the expected level of destruction would not be limited by want of nuclear bombs.

The long-term outcome of a nuclear attack on the United States or the Soviet Union in a nuclear war between them would be influenced by the fact that one country would, in all probability, attack the other's land-based missiles. Since such an attack would require exploding nuclear weapons on the ground, it would generate very large amounts of radioactive fallout. Thus, serious radiation hazards would occur for extended areas downwind from the points of detonation. This effect was largely absent from the attacks on Hiroshima and Nagasaki, which were both airbursts.

Finally, some of the long-term effects of a nuclear war would occur simply because of the enormity of the cumulative results of a few thousand nuclear detonations. For example, a single 1-megaton nuclear weapon exploding in the air would generate as many electrons as there are normally found in the ionosphere around the earth. A few hundred nuclear explosions would create as many nitrogen oxide molecules as all the ozone molecules in the stratosphere. Clearly, some effects of a nuclear war have global proportions.

In order to assess the long-term effects of a nuclear war, let us examine the effects of a large-scale nuclear exchange consisting of about 3,000 large nuclear weapons exploding on the United States within a matter of hours or days. It is reasonable to assume that the Soviet Union would use somewhat under half its strategic weapons (the Soviet Union has about 7,000 nuclear weapons capable of reaching the U.S. mainland) in an all-out war. For one thing, the reliability of Soviet missiles is not perfect and a number of missiles would not launch upon command. Furthermore, not all of the Soviet weapons would be ready for use or would reach their intended targets. Some of the Soviet bombers, for example, would almost surely be shot down before they delivered their weapons. Perhaps most important, about 3,000 warheads is currently the number needed to successfully attack all the land-based intercontinental missiles, strategic airfields, and ballistic missile submarine pens in the United States, and destroy 80% of the thirty-four most important manufacturing sectors of the United States and 97% of the U.S. petroleum-refining capacity, steel production, primary smelting facilities, engine and turbine manufacturing capacity, and electrical distribution equipment production—in short, to obliterate the military capability of the United States and the ability of the country to recover. This is known as a counterrecovery attack. (There is little reason to suspect that Soviet planners think any differently from their American counterparts, who since the dawn of the nuclear era and the cold war have targeted the U.S. nuclear arsenal against the Soviet Union with the same purposes in mind.)

Consider now the specific targets of such an attack. The United States has 1,052 silos, each containing an intercontinental ballistic missile. It is likely that the Soviet targeteers will devote two ½-megaton weapons to each. They would want the first one to detonate in the air as close to the silo as possible but without digging up a crater, and the second to detonate on the ground. This would be done so that the first detonation would not generate debris that would destroy the second warhead aimed at the same silo. This means there would be 2,104 ½-megaton weapons detonating in the American silo fields, which are located in Montana, North and South Dakota, Kansas, Arkansas, Missouri, and Nebraska. Three weapons would be targeted on each of the forty-six strategic Air Force airfields for a total of 138 weapons, and finally two weapons each over the two existing ballistic submarine bases, as well as the two now under construction, for a total of 2,250 ½-megaton weapons targeted against U.S. nuclear weapons, of which at least 1,052 would explode on the ground.

It has been calculated that to destroy 80% of the manufacturing capacity of the United States, the Soviet targeteers would need the equivalent of 436 1-megaton weapons against seventy-one major industrial complexes in the United States and 264 100-kiloton weapons against specific facilities: 75 against petroleum refineries, 60 against steel mills, 54 against primary smelting facilities that produce aluminum, zinc, and other important metals, 15 against factories that make internal-combustion engines and turbines, and 60 against industrial plants that manufacture electrical power production and distribution equipment.

The attacks could come with near simultaneity or could be divided into two phases: a counterforce attack against silos, air fields, and submarine pens followed by counter-recovery attack. The important point here is that the results of such a concerted nuclear attack would, in the end, be very nearly the same regardless of its details. An unknown but some claim large fraction of our land-based missiles—and a larger fraction of the bombers on the ground—would have been destroyed. At the most, one-half of the ballistic-missile-carrying submarines would also have been put out of commission. The counterrecovery attack would have achieved the objectives outlined above.

In human terms, the loss of life would be staggering. Even though such an attack on the United States, and an at least equally devastating attack against the Soviet Union, would probably not extinguish human life throughout the northern hemisphere (or even throughout the two warring countries), it would kill a very large number of people and profoundly alter the way of life of the survivors. In order to assess these effects we will examine in some detail the impact of such an attack on six determinants of human survival: medical care, food supplies, shelter, energy, life-support systems of the physical environment, and the socioeconomic infrastructure that makes life as we now know it possible. Most of these factors of survival are interdependent: Food production and availability to city dwellers, for example, depends on energy supplies, and the general health of a population depends on both adequate food supplies and shelter.

In examining these six factors, we will assume that the course of events after an all-out nuclear attack will be more or less the following:

The actual attack will take at most a few hours, probably much less. This will be followed by an early post-attack period of a few days to a week during which the immediate effects of the nuclear detonations will still be the dominant factor. Fires will still be burning, and radioactivity levels will still be accumulating, though at a decreasing rate. The unattended injured will still be alive but rapidly dying; people who may have sought protection in some kind of shelters, basements of houses and large public buildings, may still be alive if the firestorm has not killed them. Then there will come a period of a basic struggle for survival which will last at least a year. This will, with luck, be followed by a period of recovery that may last at least ten years and finally a period of slow evolution toward what was the normal state of things before the nuclear attack, which may take as long as fifty years but almost certainly not less than half that time. It is expected that we will never return to the same physical, social, economic, and political structures and institutions that we are familiar with now, but probably what will eventually evolve out of a nuclear catastrophe will be similar.

What about human casualties? The attack against industrial facilities, which are usually located within large urban centers, will cause the immediate or near-term death of 65% of the urban population of the United States, which now amounts to 132 million people. So 86 million people will be dead within a week after the attack. In addition, the counterforce attacks will kill between 5 million and 20 million additional people, depending on the prevailing winds, time of year, and other environmental conditions. So about 100 million Americans or roughly 45% of the entire country will be dead. Additional millions will be injured from the prompt effects of the detonations: burned by the heat, wounded by the effects of the blast, or irradiated by prompt nuclear radiation. Many survivors will be subject to additional irradiation from the fallout caused by the 1,052 ½-megaton bursts against the silos.

All the survivors will find themselves in grim surroundings. The seventy-one urban centers attacked with 1-megaton weapons will be in shambles, with most houses either totally destroyed or uninhabitable. Electricity, telephone, radio and television, police and fire stations, food stores, oil-storage facilities, gas lines, and warehouses will be destroyed, burned, or heavily damaged. Water will not be running because the pumping stations will not have electricity to operate.

But even worse, under these conditions, there will be little opportunity to provide medical assistance to those who need it, because the attack will have destroyed most medical facilities and killed most doctors. Most of the hospitals, and therefore the majority of the doctors, are located in the center of urban areas. Consequently it is expected that about 70% of the doctors and a comparable number of hospital beds will be destroyed outright by the nuclear detonations. As a result it has been estimated that on the average each surviving physician will have 1,000 patients to take care of in a post-attack environment. Assuming it takes him fifteen minutes to diagnose and treat each such patient and that he works ceaselessly sixteen hours a day, it will be two weeks before he will have a chance to see each of these 1,000 injured people for the first time. But this scenario is unlikely because many surviving doctors will themselves be injured. In addition, they will not be able to reach many of the wounded because of high radiation levels. Even if they could reach them, doctors will have few supplies and little equipment to work with: drugs, plasma, blood, dressings, instruments, diagnostic facilities, operating rooms will have been destroyed by the blast and fire. What hospitals remain standing will have no electricity, running water, medical supplies, or even working sewage. The EMP will have destroyed most electrical equipment. The large supplies of drugs and medical equipment will be in wholesale drug warehouses that in all probability will have been destroyed or will be inaccessible because of the debris, radioactivity, or loss of functioning transportation and fuel. So most of the injured, probably as many as 80%, will die unattended, without even an injection of a narcotic to relieve their pain—narcotics are not stored in the great quantities that would be needed to reduce the suffering of 40 million severely burned or injured people. So medical care will be rather ineffectual and cannot be counted on to reduce the mortality rate among the injured or even to lessen the misery and pain of the dying.

The most serious medical problems in the immediate post-attack period will be dehydration, infection, and starvation. It will become increasingly difficult for survivors to obtain uncontaminated water. This is especially true for those survivors who are obliged to remain indoors because of the ubiquitous radioactive fallout. In those cases where mild exposure to radiation causes vomiting and diarrhea, dehydration will become an acute and even fatal problem.

The survivors will be much more susceptible to infection immediately after the attack, as well as during the survival period, because the direct effect of nuclear radiation will be to reduce the immune response of individuals. Thus burn and injury victims who might have survived even without any medical care will frequently succumb to infection because of the weakening of their biological defenses from radiation (one-twentieth of the lethal dose will double the mortality of burn victims), the lack of medical care and drugs, and finally the lack of water, food, and adequate shelter, especially if the attack comes during the cold winter months.

During the subsequent survival period the chief medical problems will come from infection, communicable diseases, and epidemics. The surviving population will encounter hard and primitive conditions accompanied by undernourishment, need for exhausting labor, and probably inadequate and unheated shelter. Thus the surviving population, especially since it has not been exposed previously to many pathogenic organisms and thereby permitted to develop natural resistance, will be extremely vulnerable to infectious diseases such as typhoid, cholera, smallpox, diphtheria, and streptococcal infections. Sanitation will be virtually nonexistent during this post-attack period, and the very large number of unburied, decomposing corpses will probably promote an uncontrolled increase in insects, which in turn will greatly facilitate the transmission of disease among the survivors.

Many diseases endemic to the United States which are now kept under control by public health efforts will probably become pandemic within the first year after the attack, and they will affect not only the population of the attacked or radioactive areas but the inhabitants of those parts of the country spared any direct destructive effects of the war. Cholera, malaria, plague, shigellosis, typhoid fever, yellow fever, tuberculosis, hepatitis, influenza, and meningitis will be rampant. Particular concern has been voiced about tuberculosis and the plague, because the post-attack conditions will be particularly favorable for the unchecked transmission of these diseases among the members of a population weakened by radiation, hardships, and malnutrition. There have been estimates that as many as 35% of the post-attack survivors—almost 45 million people—may die during the one-year period following the attack because of the spread of infectious diseases. A much larger fraction of the survivors will contract one or more of these diseases, but survive.

The medical problems in the recovery and redevelopment period will primarily take the form of increased cancer incidence among the survivors and genetic disorders and abnormalities among their offspring. Tragic and regrettable as those may be, they will pale in magnitude and importance compared to the medical problems of the early post-attack and survival periods.

For those surviving disease, the great obstacle to survival will be the problem of obtaining food. A massive nuclear war will generate a precipitous and prolonged reduction of food supplies to the population of the attacked areas immediately, and to the entire nation during the early post-attack years. Since the average American urban family shops for food once a week, or more frequently, an average home will have food supplies for no more than a week or two, assuming that they have not been destroyed or burned. Since there will be no electricity, all perishables will spoil, and there will be some difficulty in cooking the remaining foodstuffs. After the first post-attack week the survivors will have to forage for food in neighboring stores and food warehouses.

But finding food in stores will become increasingly difficult everywhere, because the food-retailing system of the country will collapse. Food production is a specialized industry concentrated in a few states—California, Florida, the Midwest, and Texas. Furthermore, the food chain depends on processing, storage, and transportation of food supplies to large consuming centers (like industrial and urban complexes) at an uninterrupted rate. Thus at any one time there is only a one-to-two-week supply stored in the retail stores and food warehouses of a large urban center. In addition, it must be expected that a large fraction of the warehouses and cold-storage facilities will be destroyed, or rendered inoperative by the lack of electric power. Therefore, it is reasonable to expect that, in metropolitan areas, the available food will be reduced by at least the same percentage as the population, and that the survivors will have at best a two-week supply of food, most of it housed in undestroyed stores and warehouses in outlying areas of the attacked cities.

The survivors will have great difficulty in reaching these supplies, however. Not only will many of them be injured, but the radioactivity in many areas will be too high to permit lengthy treks and forays in search of food. In addition, very few people know where to look for food beyond their local grocery stores and supermarkets. The majority of the surviving population of attacked areas will thus face starvation within two to four weeks after an attack, unless food supplies are brought into the stricken areas, or the survivors abandon their domiciles and migrate into the countryside in search of food.

The probability of fresh food supplies arriving into attacked areas within a month after the attack is very small, for a number of physical reasons. There will be no fuel to move the trains, trucks, or barges needed to transport the food. Gasoline and diesel fuel stores and the refineries that could produce more will have been destroyed in the attack. Coal-burning transportation systems for which there would be fuel have all but disappeared. The prompt effects of nuclear detonations will have destroyed or impaired electrical power generation and distribution. The radioactive fallout will not allow repairs to be performed for quite a while, even if skilled labor were alive and willing to work rather than look after family members or search for food. Even though there is, on the average, seventy days' worth of food for the entire population stored in the grain-producing areas of the United States, the disruption of transportation, lack of fuel, absence of personnel, and radioactive fallout will prevent its distribution.

Conditions cannot be expected to improve significantly as time passes, since the food supply in the United States depends critically on the availability of oil and the chemical companies that use it to produce fertilizers and pesticides. With 95% of the refining capacity of the United States destroyed, and its distribution system disrupted, we cannot assume that the food production, processing, and transportation chain that now takes up about 4% of the total oil consumption in the United States will receive the energy it needs to move the farm equipment, pump water, milk the cows, process the food, package it, store it, and transport it. Furthermore, the radioactive fallout from the nuclear attack will have contaminated that year's grain crop, and killed millions of head of cattle and other animals as well as a substantial portion of the farm labor in the Midwest. Finally, the lack of fertilizers and pesticides will handicap the production of food in subsequent years.

It is true, however, that after the attack the country will need much less food than at the present. The consuming population will have been reduced by about 50% to 60%; the American food-production chain, which is both excessively energy-intensive and wasteful, could probably function with much less available energy. At some point, perhaps a few years after the war, demographic adjustments will bring an equilibrium between supply and demand for food. Additional millions of survivors will die of starvation, for example, and a migration of many survivors from useless and uninhabitable industrial centers to the farmlands of the Midwest will solve the labor shortage there and the food shortages in the attacked areas. We must expect, then, that for several years after the attack the population of the country will go on decreasing while an even larger percentage of the survivors return to farming the land inefficiently.

Compounding the difficulties created by the medical and food problems that the survivors will have to overcome will be the lack of shelter for a substantial number of those that survive the prompt effects of a nuclear war. The large urban and industrial centers of the Northeast and Central states will have about 60% to 70% of the dwelling units of their metropolitan areas destroyed or severely damaged. The severe winters that these areas experience will make this destruction an additional cause of disease and death, since malnourished and overstressed people will be less able to survive winter conditions in damaged and unheated living quarters. Reconstruction will require both building materials and fuel to move construction equipment, but these supplies will be lacking. Therefore, the most probable response to the destruction of shelter will be the migration of survivors to areas where housing has remained undamaged, and the orderly or violent sharing of this housing with its lawful proprietors.

In fact, the physical difficulties of reconstructing cities and industrial facilities ravaged by a nuclear attack and contaminated by fallout are such that the task seems very difficult and certainly of dubious cost-effectiveness. Therefore, we should expect the permanent abandonment of the destroyed and damaged areas of the urban-industrial complexes of the northeastern third of the country. The population shift that will be imposed by post-attack conditions will have profound socioeconomic and political effects. It may be, for example, that the absorption of millions of homeless, starving, and sick survivors from the urban centers by the rural communities of the country will be carried out in an orderly, cooperative manner. But it may also be that in a country of proprietary and privately armed individuals, the migration will take the form of diffuse and anarchic civil strife. Again, in the long run, these difficulties will be sorted out in one fashion or another, but it will probably be ten or more years before society returns to a period of relative order and normalcy.

Energy is by far the most important short- and long-term factor that will affect the ultimate fate of the individual survivors of the nuclear attack as well as the fate of the country as a whole. Half of the energy requirements of the country are now satisfied by oil, of which 60% is produced locally and 40% is imported. Of all the oil used in this country, 88% is refined locally. Another 25% of the energy needs of the country are met by natural gas and about 20% is met by coal, which is used mainly in the production of electricity.

In the early post-attack period there will be no energy available to the attacked regions and electrical power will be cut off in the entire country because of the disruptive effects of the EMP. Oil supplies not destroyed will be rapidly consumed, and since the attack will have destroyed all refineries, the entire internal-combustion-engine–driven transport system of the country—meaning aircraft, trucks, diesel locomotives, and barges, in addition to farm machinery, earth-moving equipment, and construction equipment—will halt. It is quite likely that a year after the nuclear attack there will be no more liquid fossil fuels, no means of transporting whatever food supplies may exist in the food-producing areas, and no way to mine or transport coal, of which we have ample supplies but which requires electricity for its mining and diesel fuel for its strip-mining and transportation. Transportation of needed supplies, materials, and equipment around the country will cease. We must expect then that daily life as we know it will cease to exist, even in areas not destroyed by the nuclear attack. The continental scale of the economy, for example, will, because of the lack of transportation, shrink to a fragmented aggregate of local economic activities with unavoidable inefficiencies, dislocations, and scarcities characteristic of medieval times in Europe.

The restoration of energy supplies will be a slow, gradual process. Because the natural-gas supply will remain largely intact and the pipelines that carry it could probably be repaired within a year, natural gas will probably be the first major supply of energy available for use in restoring the energy-production and transportation facilities back to an adequate level. Eventually, by restoring the damaged electrical power network and the electrical power plants, it will be possible to provide the undamaged areas of the country with electrical power. But since the attack will have destroyed 97% of the industry that manufactures the necessary power production and distribution equipment, it may be many years before such restoration takes place. In the absence of electricity the cities will lack water supplies and suffer from the absence of sewage-treatment plants. It is not inconceivable then that the lack of energy will be an additional reason for massive migrations of urban dwellers (even of unaffected cities) to the countryside in search of a life that does not require energy-dependent support systems.

An alternative answer to the energy problem of the country is massive imports of refined oil products from abroad. If the attack had destroyed the major ports such help would be very difficult to receive. But even with the ports intact such help would be improbable. With no industrial products or food to sell, the United States will lack the funds to purchase the fuel it will need. With a decimated labor force scattered away from urban-industrial centers, it is questionable whether the marginal industrial capacity of the country could be raised to a level that would produce not only the massive quantities of the myriads of products that will be needed for the survival of the population and the reconstruction of the country itself, but in addition create a surplus that could be sold abroad in exchange for energy. It is even questionable whether there will be enough surplus capital for reconstruction, since the country's remaining resources will be devoted to consumption. It is conceivable, of course, that the United States will be able to coerce oil-producing countries into sending to this country refined oil products by threatening a nuclear attack. But it seems unlikely that such a policy could be practically implemented.

About 45% of the U.S. energy sources will survive a massive nuclear attack. It would seem, since about 45% of the population is also expected to survive, that this will be an adequate supply of energy. But nearly all of the intact energy sources will be coal or natural gas, causing severe difficulties for an economy dependent on liquid fuels. In addition, the inability to strip-mine and transport coal, and the damage to the natural gas pipeline and pumping systems will allow only a very small percentage of the available energy resources to reach the ultimate consumer in a post-attack situation. For example, in principle, if the underground coal mines receive the necessary electrical power, they can provide high-quality anthracite for further electrical power production. But in reality the probability is very small that the surviving supply of coal stored at the yards of power plants will be used to produce electricity distributed primarily to coal mines. Even if this organizational and managerial feat is accomplished amid the chaos of a nuclear post-attack situation, the mined coal could not be transported to the power plants for use. Coal-burning locomotives are as rare as hand-operated gasoline pumps in this country, and those that exist could not be marshaled to the necessary locations because of the general breakdown of communications that will follow a large-scale nuclear attack.

It is quite possible that the result of a large-scale nuclear attack on the energy network of the United States will reduce the per capita available energy to levels characteristic of the era before the industrial revolution. The surviving population will then have to resort to wood-burning for heating and cooking, and any industrial activity will have to depend on makeshift power that relies also on wood or falling water, as did industries of the late seventeenth and early eighteenth centuries.

Given the destruction of cities and productive capacity, the widespread diseases and epidemics, the starvation deaths of a large fraction of the survivors, and the unknown genetic effects of the radioactive fallout there is some question about when, if ever, the birthrate in the country will exceed the deathrate, and what the political and economic fate of this nation will be if it does not. It is, of course, possible that shortly after the termination of the nuclear hostilities, massive and persistent infusions of food and fuel supplies into this country from abroad will stabilize the surviving population. It is questionable, however, whether countries like Japan, Australia, Argentina, and Saudi Arabia will rush to the aid of a demolished, unproductive, and politically and militarily useless United States. It is more probable that countries unaffected by the immediate results of a U.S.–U.S.S.R. nuclear exchange will have their own dislocations (radioactive fallout, and lack of industrial products, chemicals, fertilizers, drugs, and food imported from the industrialized United States and Soviet Union) to cope with and will scramble for world ascendancy in the vacuum left by what to all intents and purposes must be considered the demise of the two superpowers.

The disintegration of many features of modern life will be a pervasive aspect of the socioeconomic environment facing the survivors of a nuclear war. It is important, however, to make a distinction between the surviving dwellers of attacked areas and the inhabitants of unaffected rural areas, towns, and villages. The very fact that a nuclear war will probably create two drastically different classes of citizens will be the root of some of the difficulties of the post-nuclear-war era. Peacetime contemporary life and economic activity rest on the successful integration of highly specialized production activities, the existence of central and local authorities, and the undisrupted functioning of an infrastructure of public and private services such as police, fire and medical facilities, telephone, radio and television, and the entire complex and interrelated network of retail services and banking. While some of these cornerstones of contemporary life will survive and continue to function immediately after a nuclear attack in the majority of rural localities, they will be totally destroyed or disrupted in areas of direct attack or heavy radioactive fallout.

Consider the situation confronting a family of survivors in an urban suburb. Their house will have been destroyed or damaged beyond use; shortly after the attack they will face problems of food, water, and, if injured, medical supplies and services. They will have no means of knowing what the local radioactivity level is and how it will change in the days to come, and probably no means of communicating or receiving instructions and information. They will find themselves without any physical security, since there will be no police, military presence, or organized authority. They will, all the same, be forced to forage for food and water while thousands or millions of others are competing with them within the same general area for scarce or nonexistent resources.

The popularity of firearms in American society guarantees that many of these hungry, desperate, disoriented people will be armed. In the absence of a central authority to impart a sense of confidence and security, the survivors will have a heightened inclination to acquire the essential needs for survival by looting or violence. Since this social chaos will be taking place in a ravaged environment, filled with the dead and dying and incapable of supporting the living, it is quite probable that physically able survivors will at least attempt to leave the attacked metropolitan areas and migrate haphazardly to the countryside in search of food, water, shelter, and fuel supplies in the form of wood. It is to be expected that such treks, especially if attempted in wintertime, will take a heavy toll of the children and the elderly among the survivors, so it is possible that the countryside immediately surrounding the metropolitan areas will be filled with roving bands of armed adults struggling to survive by looting and plundering.

But even migrating families and unarmed survivors will impose an enormous strain on the rural communities that they eventually reach. Contrary to the desperate, homeless, starving, and sick metropolitan refugees, the rural communities will have retained intact most of their organized social and administrative functions and institutions. Police, fire, and medical services will be more or less functional. Even though, however, local means of production will be intact, the occupations of most inhabitants will not be available to them, because of lack of energy. Their homes and their water supply will continue unimpaired but they will experience food shortages. Yet these people will be entertaining more or less the same expectations and sense of values about property, privacy, and individual freedoms and rights that they maintained before the war. In light of these values and the limited resources available, they will see the invading victims of the nuclear attacks as a threat to *their* survival.

It is quite possible, then, that the two groups of post-nuclear-war citizens will clash, the urban refugees trying to survive, the indigenous rural population trying to hold on to their houses, their food, and their ability to live their lives as before. Since both populations will be well armed, it is almost certain that there will be numerous violent clashes that will be mitigated only by the eventual depletion of ammunition supplies. There is no reason to expect that a central, federal, or even state authority will be able to impose order in this post-attack chaos, since there will be no manpower, transportation, or communication facilities to effect such order. This period of strife for survival will eventually subside, but not without additional substantial loss of life and considerable delay in the initiation of the process of recovery and reconstruction.

Information as to the location and extent of destruction and of the availability of surviving stocks of material will be very difficult to gather. Managing the recovery process, even with such information, will be such a slow, inefficient, and halting affair that there is serious question whether enough productivity could be restored to meet basic needs by the time existing stocks have run out. In the physical, social, and economic chaos that will follow a nuclear war, this crucial goal may not be achieved. If not, and if supplies cannot be replenished faster than they are consumed, the country will enter a descending spiral of inadequate resources insufficient to maintain the population, which in turn will result in a further diminution of this population and consequently an even lower productive capacity.

On the other hand, the resiliency and instinct of survival of the human race may overcome the adverse physical conditions, the scarcity of energy and material, and the climatological changes to be discussed later. For one thing, there will be rural communities that will escape the destructiveness of war and the socioeconomic strain of migrating refugees, and, if not plagued by long-term radioactive fallout, they may very well manage to survive, grow, and prosper. Quite possibly these areas may become the seeds of a renewed society that will slowly evolve back from a predominantly agrarian economy to the diversified, specialized, highly technological industrial society that we live in now.

There has been intense and at times acrimonious public debate on the contribution a large-scale civil defense effort could make toward the certainty and pace of recovery from a nuclear attack. Proponents argue that given advance warning of a nuclear attack (between seventy-two and ninety-six hours before it occurs), and with carefully prepared and rehearsed evacuation of the inhabitants of large urban centers to public and private dwellings in rural communities, a properly funded civil defense policy can save millions of civilian lives from the prompt effects of nuclear detonations in the metropolitan areas of this country. Such an effort would be of truly monumental proportions. Twenty-five million tons of food would have to be stocked in the period between the time the federal government notifies local authorities of an impending evacuation and the beginning of nuclear hostilities. In addition, 7.5 billion tons of uncontaminated water must be stored and space equal to a billion square feet must be found to house up to 100 million refugees for two weeks. All these resources must be in addition to the needs of the local people who will host the evacuees from the urban and industrial centers.

Those who question the efficacy of civil defense point out that the assumption of such early warning of an enemy attack is unrealistic. They also calculate that adequate and realistic preparations for such massive evacuations will be fantastically disruptive of peacetime activities and will cost tens of billions of dollars annually. They further claim that physical and life-sustaining assets of the attacked cities, such as housing, industrial plants, hospitals, universities, energy-producing and managing facilities, and so on will be destroyed anyway, exacerbating the difficulties of post-attack existence. Finally, they point out that a determined opponent can detonate so many nuclear weapons on the ground, and so blanket the country with such a high level of long-lived radioactivity, that it would not be possible to sustain the survivors long enough in shelters to avoid the effects of the radioactive fallout.

The most serious flaw in a civil defense program that depends on seventy-two hours' warning lies in the fact that it can be defeated by the opponent at no real cost to him. Presumably advance warning of an attack will be the mobilization of the opponent's nuclear forces in a time of deepening international crisis. By continuing to escalate the crisis and making preparations for an all-out nuclear attack, the opponent can convince U.S. civil defense authorities to commence evacuation of the urban population. Optimally, this evacuation will take about three days to complete. At that time, the opponent can de-escalate the crises, and reduce the level of readiness of his nuclear forces. Eventually, this will induce the U.S. government to call off the evacuation and return the urban population to its cities. Then the Soviets can attack by surprise.

Thus, civil defense evacuation plans that require advance warning have three serious flaws. First, the enemy can attack without warning. Second, the enemy can fake the warning and catch the urban population after they have returned to their cities, at a time when they would not be ready to believe government assurances that an attack is again imminent and evacuation is again necessary. Third, "advance warning" is so poorly defined that it is difficult to imagine how the responsible authorities will recognize what does, and what does not, constitute assured warning of an impending attack. It is quite clear that the population will not be willing to evacuate twice, so the civil defense authorities must interpret the behavior of the opponent correctly. It is also possible that once the urban population of the United States has been evacuated, the U.S. government may feel itself under political pressure to begin a nuclear war in order not to lose credibility with its citizenry.

It is indeed true that a large-scale civil defense program, properly organized and funded, and given adequate tactical advance warning, can both increase substantially the surviving manpower pool and minimize the immediate post-attack-period medical problems. On the other hand, the survival of additional millions of people will leave essentially the same amount of undestroyed resources and supplies to be shared by a larger number of survivors. Consequently, post-attack consumption requirements will be much higher than they would be in the case of an unprotected population, and therefore, the accumulation of sufficient surplus supplies to avoid the downward spiral of the economy in the post-survival era will be that much more difficult. Also, those civilians who would have died in the cities in the absence of a massive evacuation will die of starvation and disease sometime after the attack, since the supplies available won't be enough to support the extra survivors. Massive transportation of people into communities that cannot absorb them over the long term or provide them with productive occupations or other means of subsistence after the nuclear war will exacerbate social and economic strains between urban refugees and rural inhabitants. For these reasons, it seems that, aside from the difficulties pointed out by the opponents of a civil defense, a civil defense plan, even if perfectly executed, can merely postpone the problems rather than solve them. Probably it cannot even achieve that much because an opponent can, if faced with a civil defense protection plan, overwhelm it by changing the tactics and nature of the attack.

In the final analysis, all efforts at survival and recovery will be limited by the effects on the environment of a large-scale nuclear attack against the United States. This attack, and presumably one of similar magnitude occurring almost simultaneously against the Soviet Union, will produce discernible and possibly even permanent catastrophic changes of the physical environment of three different kinds: (1) the deposition of radioactive debris more or less uniformly over the middle latitudes of the northern hemisphere, beyond the areas of local deposition; (2) the change of the climate caused by the injection of 100 million tons of fine dust into the atmosphere; and (3) additional climatological and ecosystem changes caused by the depletion of ozone in the stratosphere over the northern hemisphere.

The dust and debris that the fireballs of ground-burst weapons carry into the stratosphere will be very radioactive. Large tracts of arable land, mainly in the Midwest used for grain production, will be contaminated by the fallout caused by these counter-silo explosions. In an area of at least 400,000 square miles (see Figure 11 on page 96), the size of France, Germany, and England combined, all livestock and the year's crop will be lost, and it is doubtful whether any of that land area could be put back into use the next growing season. All conifer trees in this area will die. Downwind from each collection of silos, the radiation will be so high that all fruit trees and other deciduous plants will die in areas of as much as 10,000 square miles.

Since the areas of radioactive contamination will be so extensive, it will be impossible for the inhabitants to abandon them until the radioactivity level subsides below harm-

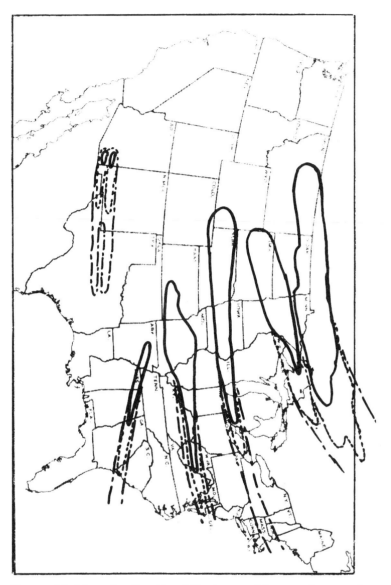

FIGURE 11. Map of radioactive fallout caused by a nuclear attack on the Minuteman and Titan missile silos.

——————— 1,450 rems

– – – – – 600 rems

— – — Strontium 90 over $2\mu C/m^2$, the current ERDA limit for agricultural use of land

ful levels. So it must be expected that the largest portion of the farm labor force in these areas will perish, and the survivors will not be able to use the land for several years because of the high level of radioactivity. This is particularly damaging because many of the affected areas downwind from the silos are important sources of food. Iowa, for example, is only 2% of the land area of the United States, yet produces nearly 10% of the U.S. food supply; it produces 20% of the national corn production and has the largest livestock industry of any state. Depending on the exact wind direction at the time of a counter-silo attack, anywhere between 40% and 100% of Iowa will be covered with about 1,000 rems of radiation within the first four days after the detonations. No one can be expected to survive under this condition. Additionally, at least 600 rems of radioactivity will accumulate during the same period in North and South Dakota, Nebraska, the northeastern half of Kansas, Illinois, Minnesota, parts of Michigan, Indiana, Ohio, Tennessee, Kentucky, Virginia, West Virginia, and smaller regions of New Mexico and northwestern Texas. The entire country east of Montana, Wyoming, and Colorado and north of the Arkansas-Mississippi-Alabama-Georgia line will be covered with enough radioactive strontium 90 (more than 2 microcuries per square meter) to render the land unsuitable for cultivation according to the current ERDA standards. Strontium 90 decays slowly; it will take twenty-eight years to decrease by half the radioactivity of the strontium deposited in these areas. So there may be several years before even the least contaminated areas can be returned to safe agricultural use.

Much worse contamination of the land will occur if the enemy decides to attack, with nuclear weapons, our nuclear reactors and the high-level radioactive waste storage pools associated with them. A reactor contains about 2,000 times less radioactivity than the radioactivity generated by the detonation of a 1-megaton weapon an hour after the explosion. But the radioactive material from the nuclear reactor loses its radiation much more slowly, so land contaminated with the contents of a nuclear reactor will remain unusable for ten to a hundred times longer than land contaminated only by the fallout from nuclear weapons explosions on the ground. The radioactive wastes in the storage tanks have radioactivity even more persistent than the nuclear reactor.

If a nuclear weapon explodes at a reactor, it will evaporate both the reactor core and the radioactive wastes from the storage pools, and carry that radioactive debris to heights of 40,000 to 60,000 feet. Then as the cloud cools, the prevailing winds will spread the contents of the reactor and the waste pods downwind from the destroyed reactor site. A month later, 12,000 square miles of land downwind from the reactor will still have enough radioactivity to make anyone there sick. A hundred years later there will still be 2,000 square miles that remain uninhabitable by the criteria of the U.S. Environmental Protection Agency.

Some fine particles of dust on which radioactive nuclei have congealed as the fireball cooled will stay in the atmosphere for quite a while, perhaps for years. This portion of the radioactive fallout will return to earth over a period of time in two ways. Some of the dust will be carried back by rainfall. This will create unpredictable radioactive sites perhaps thousands of miles away from the location of the explosions as storms and the jet stream distribute the dust over the northern hemisphere. The remaining dust will slowly settle back to the surface, forming a more or less uniform mantle of long-lived radioactive nuclei such as iodine 129 and strontium 90 over the entire middle band of the northern hemisphere.

Except in rare cases, this long-term radioactive fallout will not amount to doses that will cause radiation sickness. But since its presence will be long-term and pervasive, it will find its way into the food, drink, and air of the inhabitants of the northern hemisphere. Day in and day out, these people will be ingesting and breathing in small amounts of radioactive nuclei. Since these nuclei are long-lived, their effects inside the body will be cumulative, especially since the metabolic activities of the body tend to segregate different substances to different parts of the body. Iodine, for example, is stored in the thyroid gland, and strontium is amassed in the bones. So even though the amount of these radioactive nuclei may be small per square kilometer of the surface of the northern hemisphere, accumulations of these radioactive nuclei can form "hot spots" inside the organs of the bodies of animals and humans and inside plants. The data is not complete on the effects of such hot spots, but there is strong evidence that they cause cancer, abnormalities in babies born of mothers exposed to such chronic radiation, and an increased rate of miscarriages.

At the very least this diffuse radioactivity will cause sickness in additional millions of people, many of whom will die. It will also reduce the birthrate of many plant and animal species, raising the possibility of extinction of entire species, man among them, in the attacked countries. The problem really is that we do not know, and in fact cannot imagine, what the totality of the effects of long-term radiation can be. The ecosystem is quite delicate, but also quite resilient. For example, about 60 million years ago an unknown event happened on earth that released enormous amounts of energy and caused massive clouds of dust that wiped out thousands of species in the northern hemisphere, among them the dinosaurs. This did not end life on the planet, but it certainly altered it profoundly. The sudden release of thousands of megatons of energy in a nuclear war and the subsequent long-term and ubiquitous radioactivity may also cause significant changes in the ecosystem.

The injection of well over 100 million tons of dust into the atmosphere will cause another significant physical effect: Less sunlight will reach the surface of the earth, because the dust will scatter and absorb it on the way. The northern hemisphere will live in a haze for a year or two. A similar effect occurred in 1883, when the volcano Krakatoa literally blew up, sending about 10 million tons of dust into the stratosphere. As a result, the average surface temperature on the earth was lowered a few tenths of a degree for about a year. The following winter was colder and wetter in the northern hemisphere than the average. So we can expect that the first winter after the nuclear war will be a particularly cold one, and the cereal crops in Canada, the United States, and the Soviet Union will probably fail that year as a result. But in the long run the dust will settle and the temperature of the earth will be restored to its present level.

The so-called ozone depletion effect will be a significant by-product of a nuclear war. The nitrogen oxides that will be generated by all the nuclear detonations will be lifted by the fireballs into the part of the stratosphere that contains the ozone. This will result in a rapid depletion of about half the ozone layer over the northern hemisphere, a reduction that could last several years. It has been estimated that a 50% reduction of the ozone layer will increase the ultraviolet light on the surface of the northern hemisphere anywhere between ten and one hundred times. This additional light might change the heating pattern of the atmosphere, which can affect tropospheric air circulation patterns and thus the overall weather of the entire hemisphere. Heating of the upper levels of the atmosphere will cause a reduction of the average surface temperature of the earth by about 1° C, a change that may last a few years. Coming on top of the cooling caused by the dust suspended in the atmosphere, this cooling could have more permanent and drastic effects, not only on the chances of the survivors to stay alive, but on the entire ecosystem that will be burdened anyway by the effect of ozone depletion upon animal and even plant life.

It is expected that a tenfold increase in the amount of ultraviolet light that reaches the earth will kill some plants outright, harm others to an unpredictable degree, kill light-colored animals, and cause severe and abrupt sunburns to exposed skin of humans. By far the most serious threat of such an increase in ultraviolet is its effect upon the eyes of a large number of animal species. Ultraviolet light burns the surface of the eye, causing scar tissue on the cornea that blocks light from entering the eye. The damage occurs slowly, but it accumulates to the point that the exposed animal becomes blind. And for many animals sight is crucial to survival. Short-lived animals such as insects will probably not be affected because they don't live long enough for the damage on their eyes to accumulate and blind them. Nocturnal or aquatic animals will not be affected. But a massive blinding and death of thousands of diurnal species such as mammals and birds, together with the destruction of many plant species, could cause imbalances among species populations leading to the collapse of the ecosystem in the northern hemisphere.

As improbable as such far-reaching consequences might

seem, one cannot escape a feeling of apprehension that the synergy of all these effects—the lowering of the earth's temperature, persistent radioactivity, the blinding and death of numerous species of animals, the destruction or stunting of many plant species, and the myriads of ways in which these mutually reinforce each other—will cause some unprecedented catastrophe that is beyond calculation or prediction. There is just no way of accurately estimating these effects, nor, therefore, the extent of such a collapse. We are simply ignorant of the full gamut of the effects of a large-scale nuclear war, and to conceal our ignorance would be not only unscientific but irresponsible. Yet not to admit that we have the power to inaugurate events totally beyond our control represents an equally egregious and ultimately far more terrifying error.

5

INTERCONTINENTAL
BALLISTIC MISSILES

T HE UNITED STATES, the Soviet Union, Great Britain, and France have each placed a large number of their nuclear weapons on ballistic missiles that can carry them, within a few minutes, to targets many thousands of kilometers away and land within hundreds of meters from target. The uses to which such missiles can be put depend on their accuracy. A ballistic missile consists basically of two parts: a booster rocket that may have one or more stages, and a structure on top of the booster rocket that contains the "payload." In early ballistic missiles the payload consisted of one nuclear weapon inside a "reentry vehicle," which is a cone-shaped object specially designed to reenter the atmosphere at very high speed without damaging the weapon inside. In contemporary ballistic missiles, the payload is a "bus," a structure so named because it is maneuverable and carries several reentry vehicles, each with a nuclear weapon inside. The bus therefore carries both fuel and its own small rockets so that it can change its speed and direction of motion.

Each stage of the booster rocket consists of a fuel supply and a thruster engine that burns the fuel and directs the jet of hot gases generated by the burn. The lowest stage ignites first, pushing the entire missile upward. When the fuel of that stage is exhausted, the stage drops off—there is no reason to carry useless weight along—and the second stage ignites, providing propulsion to the remaining part of the missile. When no more propulsion is needed, the payload is separated from the last stage and starts coasting.

The rocket engine of an intercontinental ballistic missile

burns for only a small portion of the total flight time. After the engine shuts off, the missile coasts under the influence of gravity, tracing an elliptical trajectory that takes it well above the atmosphere. The missile is actually in the atmosphere (and therefore subject to friction with the air) only during the first few minutes of its ascent and the last two minutes of its descent to the target; for most of its flight it moves in the vacuum of space.

Boosters have two types of propulsion systems: solid-fuel engines and liquid-fuel engines. The latter type is much like an oil-fired burner of a home-heating system, where kerosene or diesel fuel is mixed with air and burned. In a rocket, however, the liquid fuel, usually kerosene, is burned with an oxidizer, since there is no air (and therefore not enough oxygen for combustion) when the missile rises above the atmosphere. How much fuel is burned and therefore how much thrust the rocket engine generates is controlled by valves in the pipes that carry the fuel and oxidizer to the combustion chamber of the rocket engine.

Inside the missile the fuel and oxidizer are in separate tanks; they are not yet combined, and therefore there are no exhaust gases. When the engine is turned on, exhaust gases are formed in the thruster chamber, pushing at its walls in all directions with the same force. Now, if the chamber is completely closed, nothing will happen (Figure 12a on page 104). The force of the gas pressure pushing at the upper end of the chamber is neutralized by the equal and opposite force at the lower end. But if a hole is opened at the lower end, the gases pushing downward go out and do not push against the bottom of the thruster chamber. This leaves a net force pushing at the top of the chamber, which makes the thruster chamber move upward. Since the chamber is firmly attached to the rest of the missile, the entire missile moves (Figure 12b). Whenever a body is acted upon by a constant force, it accelerates, that is, changes its velocity. Once the fuel stops burning in the thruster, there are no more gases being exhausted, and no net force pushing the missile. The missile stops accelerating, which means that the instant after the cutoff of the thruster, the missile has reached its maximum velocity.

In liquid-fuel rockets the amount of thrust can be con-

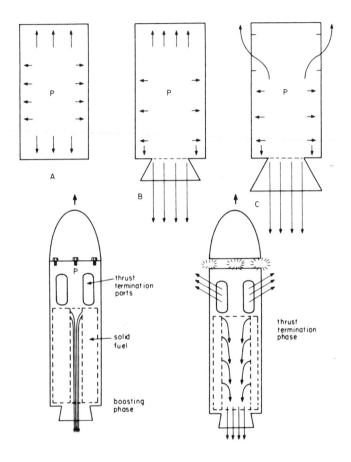

FIGURE 12. Illustration of the working principle of a solid-fuel thruster. The exhaust gases from the burning fuel push the entire missile forward. In order to stop the thrusting and release the payload, the thrust termination ports are opened and the explosive bolts that secure the payload to the booster are blown away.

trolled by a throttle mechanism. But in solid-fuel missiles, the rocket engine consists of a cylinder that contains a rubbery solid (consisting of a combination of fuel and oxidizer) with a hole running along its center. The fuel burns along the surface of this hole until it is entirely consumed. There is no way to control the rate of burning or to stop it. To prevent the thruster from further accelerating the missile, four windows, with a total area bigger than the hole at the bottom of the thruster, are popped open at the upper part of the thruster chamber. Thus the exhaust gases that were pushing against the top of the thruster chamber can now escape through these windows (Figure 12c), and acceleration ceases. At the same instant, the bolts that attach the payload to the rest of the missile are blown apart; the booster falls away and the payload begins its unpowered ballistic coast in the vacuum of outer space.

The question now is, how is the missile guided toward its target—how does it navigate there? Anyone who has thrown a stone or a ball or a dart has made use of the working principle of a ballistic missile. Although there are significant differences between the flight of a dart that weighs a few grams and has a range of a few meters and the flight of a ballistic missile that can weigh up to 100 million times as much as the dart and can travel 10,000 kilometers, the physics of motion is the same for both.

Consider what happens when a player throws a dart at a dartboard. The player sees the board, therefore knows the direction and distance to the board, and mentally calculates how hard and in what direction he must throw his dart if he wants to hit the bull's-eye. By holding the dart firmly as he swiftly moves his arm, he gives the dart the same speed as his moving hand. When he releases the dart, the player gives it not only speed but also a direction toward the board. Where the dart goes after it is released depends totally on the speed and direction—the velocity—with which the player released it. After release, the dart moves toward the board in an arc caused by gravity, which draws it continuously towards the ground. If the player has not thrown it vigorously enough (that is, has not given it enough speed), the dart will fall to the ground under the influence of gravity before it reaches the board. If the player has given it exactly the right amount of speed but has not released it in the proper direction, the dart will miss the board. There are only two important points here. First, all the player can do to make the dart hit the bull's-eye is to give the dart the right velocity the moment he releases it. Second, after it is released, the player has no more control over its motion and the dart moves only under the influence of the force of gravity (if we ignore any air currents in the room) that draws it to the ground (actually to the center of the earth). These are the two basic elements of ballistic motion.

After an initial push that imparts a given velocity to a projectile (a dart, a stone, a cannon shell, a ballistic missile), the projectile follows a trajectory toward the target under the influence of gravity alone. Sometimes one can influence both the magnitude and the direction of the release velocity, as in the case of stones released from a slingshot, for example, or arrows from a bow. In other cases, only the direction can be varied and the magnitude is fixed. For example, identical cartridges fired in the same rifle always give their bullets the same push; all the bullets have the same speed as they leave the rifle barrel, but they can be made to hit different targets by giving them different directions. Liquid-fuel rockets allow control over both the speed of the missile and its direction. Solid-fuel rockets allow control over only the direction of the rocket thrust.

The motion of the missile and of the reentry vehicle (or vehicles) depends on the forces acting upon them. What are these forces? First is the force of gravity, which acts on the missile from the moment it is launched to the moment the payload reaches the target. Then there is the propulsive force, always equal and opposite in direction to the impulse of the hot exhaust created by the booster rocket. Finally, there is the drag that the missile experiences as it ascends through the atmosphere, followed by the drag that the reentry vehicle experiences as it crashes through the air on its way to the target during reentry. Of these forces, only the rocket thrust can be controlled, and it is therefore the only means available to determine the trajectory of the missile from launch to target. Since the booster engine burns for only about one-sixth of the duration of the missile's flight, it is necessary to calculate, or guess, ahead of time what the subsequent motion of the reentry vehicle will be so that, by working backward from the target, the necessary terminal velocity can be determined. Without knowing the motion of the reentry vehicle after it leaves the missile, there is no way of determining what the appropriate terminal velocity of the missile should be at the moment of separation.

The process of predicting the motion of the reentry vehicle after release begins with determining what the reentry vehicle will do as it crashes through the atmosphere. If we know the shape and weight of the reentry vehicle, its velocity 50 kilometers above the earth's surface, and the angle at which it reenters the atmosphere (about 25° to the horizon), it is in principle possible to calculate the forces of drag and lift that will affect its motion and therefore to predict its trajectory in the atmosphere. Practically, however, this is a difficult task. Winds near the surface of the earth can deflect the reentry vehicle from its theoretical trajectory. Changes in the density of air that come with the change of barometric pressure, or the presence of rain, snow, or clouds over the target, also affect the reentry vehicle. They change the aerodynamic forces of lift and drag, and can alter the expected flight path of the reentry vehicle.

A reentry vehicle is shaped like a slim aerodynamic cone in order to pass quickly and smoothly through the atmosphere. Such a vehicle gets red-hot as it collides with air molecules on its way to the target. So it must either be given a blunt shape to move slowly through the atmosphere, creating a bow wave that protects the rest of the vehicle from overheating, or it must be covered with a material that gradually peels and burns off, carrying away the excess heat. But the density of the atmosphere affects the rate at which this protective shield burns off, or ablates. This ablation changes the shape of the reentry vehicle and creates some resistance to its motion, both of which can change its trajectory. We should therefore expect that a number of unpredictable physical effects during reentry will influence the trajectory of the reentry vehicle and degrade the accuracy with which it descends upon the target.

The motion of the reentry vehicle before it enters the

atmosphere is in the vacuum of outer space. Between the time the reentry vehicle leaves the missile at booster shut-off and its entry in the atmosphere, it coasts on an elliptical trajectory influenced only by the force of gravity. In order to calculate its motion we must know the exact value of the pull of gravity at each point along its trajectory. This value, in turn, depends mainly on the exact value of the gravitational field of the earth, which varies from point to point. Topographical variations and local concentrations of heavier elements create local gravitational anomalies that cannot be easily mathematically accounted for in precalculating the ballistic trajectory of the reentry vehicle after its release. Despite all the unknown variables, by taking all the predictable factors into consideration, it is theoretically possible to compute a standard elliptical trajectory which, together with the theoretical trajectory inside the atmosphere, is of sufficient accuracy to determine the missile's required velocity—that is, the velocity it must have at the moment of thrust termination.

A more difficult question is how to ensure that the missile has exactly the required velocity at the point in space where the payload of reentry vehicles is released. This is actually a formidable technical problem, considering that a missile is a massive object anywhere between 10 and 200 tons in weight that is accelerating toward the end of its boosted flight at about ten times the acceleration of gravity. It therefore reaches speeds of more than 7,000 meters per second in five minutes from a dead start. After it has traveled only one-tenth of the distance to its target, it must have an error in its terminal velocity of less than 0.001% if it is to land within 500 meters of its target. There is a striking contrast between the massive size and propulsive power of an intercontinental ballistic missile and the exquisite precision with which it must be guided.

The remarkable and precise navigation of a ballistic missile is achieved by a method called inertial guidance. It utilizes a totally self-contained system of instruments carried on board the missile. Once it is given the position of the target with respect to the launch point and the initial position, velocity, and acceleration of the missile in its silo, the inertial system can guide the missile during the powered portion of its flight so that the payload acquires the precise required terminal velocity for a trajectory that terminates at the target.

Inertial sensing is based on Newton's second law, that a body of mass m subjected to a force F will acquire an acceleration a, such that $F = m \cdot a$. We know from elementary physics that the product of acceleration and time is the velocity of a vehicle, and in turn the velocity multiplied by time gives us the distance the vehicle has traveled. So if there's a way for the missile to measure its own acceleration, then with the aid of a very precise clock the missile can know what velocity it has and where it is with respect to its launch point.

The instrument which does that is an accelerometer. It consists of a very precisely measured test mass and a mechanism that accurately measures the force experienced by the test mass because of the propulsive action of the booster. There are many ingenious ways to measure that force. One such mechanism could be compared to a small spring scale placed between a driver's back and the seat of a car. As the car accelerates, the driver's back presses against the seat with a force proportional to the acceleration of the car. By reading the scale, one can measure what force that represents.

It is important to realize two things about accelerometers. First, their output is a number, and therefore they must be calibrated before they are used. Second, acceleration, having both magnitude and direction, is a *vector* quantity. (By contrast, a *scalar* quantity, like the temperature of an object, has only magnitude.) So an accelerometer, which measures only the size of the force, is not enough by itself.

René Descartes, the celebrated French mathematician and philosopher of the early seventeenth century, who enjoyed spending his mornings in bed, realized one such morning, as he was staring at the point where the ceiling of his room met two walls at a corner, that a vector quantity such as a force or an acceleration could be described completely if one knew the size of its projections on three axes perpendicular to each other. So by this principle the total acceleration of the missile, whatever it may be and in whatever direction, can be known completely by measuring its components along three mutually perpendicular axes. An accelerometer can be made to measure acceleration only along *one* direction (hence the name, single-axis accelerometer). So if three such accelerometers are placed on the missile, so that the direction along which each one measures is perpendicular to the other two, then the size of the missile's acceleration along each of the three axes will be known and therefore, according to Descartes' discovery, the *total* acceleration of the missile including its total size and direction can also be known.

The most convenient choice of these three directions would be along the x, y, and z axes of Figure 13. Since the direction of the line that joins the launch point to the target and the direction of the local vertical at the launch point are known, it is easy to align the missile with three mutually perpendicularly aligned accelerometers in a manner such that each accelerometer will measure the missile's acceleration along the x, y, and z directions of that convenient frame of reference. As a matter of fact, that's exactly what is done when a missile is placed in its silo: It is aligned precisely so that one accelerometer is lined up with the line of a plumb bob and a second along the launch-point-to-target line. The third is aligned perpendicular to the plane formed by the other two lines. It is quite a task to complete this alignment but, as we shall see, it is crucial to the accuracy of the missile. (This alignment is, as one might expect, much less precise for missiles launched from submarines.)

The next problem is how to maintain this alignment once the missile starts moving. As a missile rises, it slowly tilts toward the target. During its launch, the missile also rotates around its long axis as it rises above the surface of the earth. How does it keep track of its original frame of reference? To avoid losing track of the direction along which each of the accelerometers is measuring, each one is rigidly mounted on a platform stabilized by a gyroscope and suspended in gimbals (see Figure E.1 in Appendix E). As the missile rotates and turns, the accelerometers maintain their original direction with the help of special motors that rotate each platform by an amount equal but opposite to the rotation of the missile sensed by the gyroscopes.

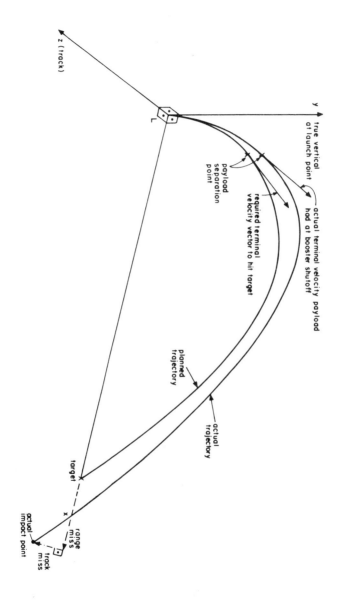

FIGURE 13. The three-dimensional system of coordinates in which the missile is guided to its target.

The complete unit of three accelerometers on mutually perpendicular platforms, suspended in gimbals and stabilized by gyroscopes, is called an "inertial measuring unit" or IMU. This is the key instrument in the missile's guidance system. The output of the IMU consists of six signals, three for the instantaneous value of acceleration along the x, y, and z directions and three for the angular motion (yaw, pitch, and roll about its long axis) of the missile. These six signals are fed into the on-board guidance computer of the missile, which, with the aid of a precise clock, continuously calculates its velocity and the distance the missile has traveled. Since the accelerometers cannot measure the acceleration the missile experiences due to gravity, the value of gravitational acceleration at each point of the missile's path is stored in the computer's memory. With this information the computer calculates the force of gravity on the missile and adds it to the force exerted on it by the booster rocket. Then the computer calculates the velocity (and then distance traveled by the missile) by multiplying the total rocket and gravitational acceleration the missile experiences by the length of time it has been flying.

The missile navigates—that is, knows where it is, how fast it's going, and in what direction—on the basis of the accelerometer output signals. At the beginning of its flight the missile is preprogrammed to fly through the dense portion of the atmosphere in such a way as to encounter the least resistance. When the missile reaches the top of the atmosphere its velocity is not anywhere near the required velocity that must be reached before the payload is released. Since the job of the guidance system is to steer the missile so that its velocity gradually reaches the terminal velocity, it must change both the speed and the direction of the missile appropriately. To do that, the guidance system generates commands that control the direction of the rocket thrust. (The laws of physics dictate that outside the atmosphere the direction of a change in the velocity of a missile is exactly opposite to the direction of the thrust. So by changing the thrust direction, one can change the direction of motion of the missile.) In liquid-fuel missiles, changing the direction of the thrust is done by turning the entire rocket engine. In solid-fuel missiles, the exhaust gases from the rocket engine are deflected by blowing some compressed gas on the exhaust, or by providing the missile with small control jets.

In modern missiles, the required terminal velocity is continually recalculated by the guidance computer on the basis of the initial conditions of motion of the missile, the predetermined trajectory of the reentry vehicle both in space and in the atmosphere, and the velocity and location of the missile at every instant during its powered flight. The actual velocity of the missile and its position are constantly revised by the computer, using the output signals from the IMU and the time from the accurate on-board clock (see Appendix E for a detailed analysis of the IMU).

Using this information, the guidance system determines what changes are needed in the direction of the propulsive force in order to reach the required terminal velocity. In this manner, if everything works right, components of the missile's velocity along the x, y, and z axes, $V_M(x)$, $V_M(y)$, and $V_M(z)$, will become equal to the three components of the required terminal velocity, $V_R(x)$, $V_R(y)$, $V_R(z)$, at the same instant. If and when this happens, the computer signals the thruster to cut off, since the necessary required terminal velocity has been reached and no more changes in velocity (that is, no more acceleration) are needed. At this point the rocket engine ceases to propel the missile, and the payload separates from it and proceeds on its ballistic trajectory. The extinguished rocket with the rest of the missile tumbles back to earth.

The simultaneous passage of the quantities $V_M(x) - V_R(x)$, $V_M(y) - V_R(y)$, and $V_M(z) - V_R(z)$ through zero at the same instant is a sure sign that everything has worked properly so far and that the payload is on the right trajectory. When this happens, the weapon on the missile is armed and is now ready to detonate on a signal from its fusing mechanism.

But how well does such a guidance system really work? What kind and magnitude of errors can occur, and how sensitive is the trajectory of the missile to such errors? In short, what is the probable effectiveness of such a guidance and navigation system?

The expected performance of a ballistic missile can be

tested in a number of different ways. One: We can get an idea how well these systems work by examining the performance of ballistic missiles that carry satellites into space. Two: It is also possible to test a ballistic missile by firing it from one point on the surface of the earth to another, with reentry vehicles containing dummy rather than real nuclear warheads. Or three: We can simply calculate the target miss distance a given missile malfunction will cause, as we shall do in this chapter.

In space travel we use the same type of booster rockets and the same type of inertial guidance as in intercontinental ballistic missiles. Judging from the precision with which NASA can place a satellite in orbit or send a vehicle to the moon and back or a space probe to Saturn, we might conclude that boosters with inertial guidance work pretty well. We must not forget, however, that in space-related activities, the launch of the rocket is often postponed, and last-minute malfunctions are repaired. That will not be possible in the case of ballistic missiles carrying nuclear weapons that have to be launched quickly. Either the missile leaves its silo when the launch keys are turned or it doesn't. So we should expect that in a sizable number of cases last-minute difficulties that cannot be fixed will prevent the real missile from functioning properly. It is difficult to predict how often this will happen, but existing ballistic missiles have reliabilities said to be between 70% and 90%. Another difference between space-related uses of boosters and nuclear ballistic missiles is that after a space vehicle is launched, one can correct its orbit or trajectory by observing its velocity and position with powerful radars and then ordering it with radio signals to change its motion by selectively firing small jets on the space vehicle. In manned space travel, like the trips to the moon or the space shuttle, human operators can effect the necessary changes. So space-related uses of rockets and inertial guidance are not a good analogy to ballistic missiles carrying nuclear weapons.

The second method to measure the performance of ballistic missiles is to actually test them (as both the United States and Soviet Union do) over ranges comparable to those that they would have to fly if actually used in war. U.S. ballistic missiles are tested from a launch site at Vandenburg Air Force Base in California to a target area in

Kwajalein, an atoll in the Marshall Islands group in the central western Pacific. Tests are, of course, performed without detonating nuclear warheads at the target. Still, the overall performance of the missile's guidance system can be evaluated. But as a result of differences between the test trajectories and operational trajectories, estimates of a weapon's accuracy derived from this method contain significant uncertainties (see also Chapter 6).

Based on the results of tests and the expected performance of the guidance and propulsion systems of the missiles it is possible to calculate the expected performance of a ballistic missile. To do that we have to imagine what can go wrong during the flight of a missile and by how much it would, most probably, affect its accuracy.

Analyses of this sort have identified six different classes of errors:

1. The instruments on the inertial measuring unit may malfunction during flight. They may have been improperly manufactured or installed.

2. Since the inertial guidance system does not measure the force of gravity, the value of this force must be given to the computer for every point along the missile's trajectory. But the gravitational field along operational trajectories is not always accurately known. So the wrong values for the gravitational field may be used.

3. The implementation of the commands of the guidance computer to the thruster motor may be imperfect. Thrust termination, for example, may not take place at the precise instant the on-board computer commands. Or since the missile is not perfectly rigid, its body and the thruster may move with respect to the IMU (which is located in the payload).

4. Since the IMU can only measure *changes* in the motion of the missile, the initial conditions of motion* at the instant of launch must be determined separately and fed into the guidance computer. This information may be wrong.

5. The actual reentry trajectory of the weapon may not

---

* "Initial conditions of motion" include the velocity of the silo with respect to the center of the earth (which is equal to speed of rotation of the surface of the earth) and the initial acceleration of the missile (which is equal to the acceleration of gravity).

be as calculated. Weather conditions over the target different from those assumed in calculating the hypothetical trajectory, or a sudden gust of wind, or unforeseeable rain or snow can alter the actual trajectory of the reentry vehicle.

6. Finally, the target may not actually be where the guidance computer has been told it is. The position of the target with respect to the launch point is determined via an elaborate process of photographing the earth from space and carefully recording the position of the satellite when each picture is taken. By putting all the data together, maps are prepared that indicate the distance between launch point and the target. But these maps can and do have errors. So the guidance computer can compute a trajectory, which the payload may faithfully follow without terminating at the target.

Let's see how big these errors probably are for contemporary ballistic missiles and what effect they can have on the overall accuracy of the missile. Clearly, our prediction will depend on the exact construction of the missile, the actual implementation and instrumentation of the inertial guidance principle, on the precise trajectory of the missile, and on the distance from the launch point to the target. But a general impression of the average size of each of these six effects can be gained by imagining a specific trajectory over a 10,000-kilometer range that requires boosting the missile for 300 seconds.

To begin with, five things can go wrong with the actual instruments on the IMU.

1. One or more of the accelerometers may have been incorrectly calibrated. This will result in an error which is a fixed percentage of the acceleration shown by the accelerometer. Even if this error is as small as one part per million it will result in a 40-meter range error (that is, error along the x-axis in Figure 13). (See Appendix F for an explanation of this and all subsequent error values.) There will be no "track error"—that is, no miss along the direction perpendicular to the line that joins the launch point to the target (which in the reference frame that we are using means no miss along the z-axis).

2. The accelerometers may not be aligned perfectly perpendicular to each other. An original alignment error of

only one millionth of a radian* will result in 20 meters of range error. If the accelerometers are jarred only 5 millionths of a radian out of alignment by the violent vibrations from the burning fuel in the rocket engine, this will cause a 70-meter range error and 30-meter track error.

3. The accelerometer may be sensing a force other than the actual propulsive force of the rocket. A spurious force of a tenth of a dyne,† such as the weight of a particle of dust, on an accelerometer test mass of 10 grams will cause large errors. In this case I assume a 45-meter range error and a 7-meter track error.

4. The gyroscopes, unless perfectly constructed, will not be able to keep the accelerometer platforms perfectly aligned with the original reference frame. If they allow the platform to drift, say, a constant 2 thousandths of a degree per hour, the resulting errors will be a 45-meter range miss and a 13-meter track miss at the target.

5. The performance of the gyroscopes is degraded by the fact that as the thruster emits the exhaust gases the missile both accelerates and vibrates. Gyroscopes tend to drift away from their original alignment because of the acceleration they are subjected to. So if the gyroscopes drift 2 thousandths of a degree per hour for every 1 g of acceleration‡ they are subjected to, the resulting miss at the target will be 70 meters in range and 20 meters in track. Similar gyroscope drift can result from the strong vibrations caused by the exit of the exhaust gases from the thruster engine. The size of these errors can be comparable in size to the errors resulting from gyroscope drifts caused by the acceleration of the missile.

The important thing to keep in mind is that the miss at the target is always proportional to the size of the error source. The proportionality constant depends on the details of the missile construction, its inertial guidance implemen-

---

* This is equal to the angle between two wires joined at one end and attached to the two ends of a cigarette placed 62 miles (100 kilometers) away.

† A dyne is the force that will impart one thousandth the acceleration of gravity to a mass of 1 gram.

‡ One g of acceleration is equal to the acceleration of gravity, or 980 cm/sec². An acceleration of 2 g would be 1,960 cm/sec², and so forth.

tation, the trajectory, and the range. (For the 10,000-km trajectory described here, the proportionality constants are listed in Appendix F, Table F.l.)

Now, how do these errors actually cause the miss? Because of the malfunctioning of accelerometers and gyroscopes, the indicated missile velocity is *not* the actual velocity of the missile. So the computer "thinks" that the missile has achieved the required velocity when it is actually flying with a slightly different speed in a slightly different direction. So the *actual* velocity with which the payload begins its ballistic trajectory is not the required velocity that would get it to its intended target.

Consider now the second possible source of error: inaccurate values for the force of gravity fed into the missile computer. The errors caused by inaccurate gravity values are significant only during the first couple of minutes of flight. For one thing, as the missile gets farther from the earth, the influence of gravity on the missile's motion diminishes (inversely as the square of the distance of the missile from the center of the earth). Once the missile has gone some distance from the earth, errors in the value of gravitational acceleration become relatively unimportant. In addition, the error in the trajectory of the missile caused by using the wrong value for the force of gravity multiplies its effects with the passage of time. If the wrong gravity strength is given to the computer early in the missile's flight, it will have a long time to influence all subsequent computer calculations responsible for the missile's trajectory. But if the error occurs late in the missile's flight, its effect won't have time to influence significantly the subsequent trajectory of the missile. Therefore unexpected anomalies of the gravitational field near the launch point of a missile can cause considerable target miss distances, whereas such anomalies near the top of the missile's trajectory or near the target will have a small effect. Miss distances of, say, 50 meters in range and 15 meters in track at the target could be caused by unaccounted-for gravitational anomalies along the missile's trajectory.

The third class of potential malfunctions is improper execution of the guidance computer commands. For example, the manner in which the thrust is terminated and the payload separated from the missile can dramatically affect the accuracy of the missile. An error of one thousandth of a second in stopping the propulsion will cause a range miss of almost 700 meters. Improper or late separation of the payload from the thrusting missile can change in unpredictable ways the direction of the payload at the start of its ballistic trajectory. To minimize these errors, designers have provided the missiles with little vernier jets that coax the payload slowly into the required terminal velocity after the main thruster has been shut off.

A fourth source of inaccuracy results from errors in establishing the missile's initial conditions of motion. These errors can cause very large target misses. For missiles launched from silos on land it is generally easy to determine the exact geographic location and altitude above sea level of the launch point. But for missiles launched from submarines, determining the exact position at the instant of launch is quite difficult. The missile's velocity at the instant of launch must also be provided to the computer. The initial velocity of a silo is equal to the velocity that the earth's rotation gives its position on the earth. This can be easily computed. But the true velocity of a submerged submarine subjected to underwater currents and tides is quite difficult to determine. While target miss caused by initial position and velocity errors of a land-launched missile can be 70 meters in range and about 60 meters in track, the corresponding errors for sea-launched missiles can be as large as 500 meters in range and 100 meters in track.

Additional inaccuracy at the target can be caused by improper alignment of the missile and incorrect determination of direction of the true vertical at the point of launch. A missile has to be physically aligned with a reference frame and the true local vertical has to be determined. These are delicate and difficult operations, the latter further complicated by the possible presence of local anomalies in the gravitational field. The situation is even more difficult in the case of submarine-launched missiles, since the launching platform is not fixed in space. Hundreds of meters of track miss can occur as a result in submarine-launched missiles.

The last two sources of inaccuracy, reentry effects and

the location of the target, affect the calculation of the required terminal velocity. Clearly, if the exact distance between launch point and target is not known very precisely, the missile, even if guided perfectly, may well land at a point other than the target. Even though satellite photography and geodesy have significantly improved the accuracy of distance measurements compared with older ground-based methods, errors of tens of meters over distances of 10,000 kilometers (that is, errors of some parts per million) cannot be confidently excluded.

Reentry, during which the reentry vehicle is buffeted by strong aerodynamic forces and sustains extreme mechanical and thermal stresses, is the most unpredictable portion of the weapon's voyage to its target. The free-fall trajectory the reentry vehicle follows in the vacuum of space is abruptly changed by the high drag forces it experiences as it enters the denser portions of the atmosphere. These changes can be theoretically predicted given a set of assumptions about the barometric pressure, crosswinds, and other meteorological conditions over the target. Any unexpected change in these assumed conditions will substantially change the actual trajectory of the weapon, and will also invalidate the previously calculated value of the required terminal velocity. As a result, it is easy for misses of 100 meters in range and about 50 meters in track to occur.

Additional difficulties exist. The weapon must be made to detonate by fusing it appropriately. If it is to detonate on the ground, a contact fuse is used and the weapon goes off when it hits. But if the weapon is to detonate at some altitude over the target, the fuse must be based either on a timing mechanism that makes the weapon explode a given time after payload separation from the booster, or on an altitude-sensitive device such as a radar altimeter. Time-of-flight fusing can cause very large misses because of the very high speed of the reentry vehicle as it approaches the target. A thousandth-of-a-second error in timing can cause a several-hundred-meter miss. Radar altimeters, on the other hand, could be jammed by a determined opponent. Therefore, the very fusing and detonation mechanisms of the weapon can add to its inaccuracy.

The figures used here as examples to describe the magnitude of the sources of error and the resulting miss at the target (see also Appendix F) can mean a cumulative range miss of nearly 200 meters and a track miss of almost 100 meters. These numbers do not apply to any specific missile but are typical of the inaccuracies to be expected in guiding a modern missile from its launch point to a target 10,000 kilometers away. These translate into a CEP of 170 meters for a hypothetical weapon. The CEP—"circle of equal probability" or "circular error probable"—is a measure of error equal to six-tenths of the sum of track and range error (see page 139 for a fuller discussion of the CEP).

How near to reality are these estimates, and what are the limits to the accuracy of an intercontinental missile that uses an inertial guidance system? Experts claim that CEPs of only about 30 meters are possible in principle if the reentry vehicle is guided all the way to the target during its flight through the atmosphere. But what about the currently deployed missiles in their real-world context, in which usually very little works perfectly? One can imagine how such errors as those that come from thrust termination or the calculation of the missile's velocity can be made smaller than those described above. Perhaps the values of position and velocity at launch can be determined somewhat more precisely and the process of alignment be made more accurate. Even the performance of individual accelerometers and gyroscopes might be expected to benefit from adjustments made during many thousands of hours of operation, while the missile is waiting in a silo or a submarine firing tube.

But unguided reentry will remain a major source of target miss, as will unexpected effects when the missile is sent to fly over untested trajectories. Target misses measured in the low rather than the high hundreds of meters have no doubt been achieved over test trajectories such as the Vandenberg-to-Kwajalein test range. But even in these tests the performance of missiles often deviates unexpectedly from statistically established levels of accuracy. So the optimistic CEP value that has been calculated here may be plausible under assumed perfect conditions, but might be quite removed from the performance of actual operational missiles launched over untested trajectories to targets surrounded by unknown meteorological conditions at locations mapped only by satellite and determined through recourse to elaborate mathematical calculations.

With this background, we can now examine a number of other points about ballistic missile operations that have been widely publicized. One is that modern intercontinental ballistic missiles, which carry many nuclear warheads, can aim each one of these warheads at a separate target with an accuracy comparable to the accuracy of a missile with only one warhead. These MIRVed (for "multiple independently targetable reentry vehicle") missiles were introduced by the United States in 1970 and by the Soviet Union five or six years later. The payload of a MIRVed missile is a "bus" that holds several reentry vehicles. It is equipped with a low-thrust booster and a guidance system of its own. After the bus separates from the rest of the missile, it is preprogrammed to perform sequentially a number of changes of its velocity. After each change a single reentry vehicle is released, thereby beginning its free-fall trajectory with the velocity the bus had at the instant of the release. Thus each warhead, released in a slightly different trajectory, reaches a different target. These targets cannot be arbitrarily distant from each other. Their maximum allowable spread depends on the amount of fuel the bus carries, which in turn determines how widely different are the velocities that the bus can impart to each of the reentry vehicles. The length of the area over which the reentry vehicles can be spread is at most a few percent of the total range of the missile, and its width is always much shorter than its length. So the "footprint," i.e., the area over which a MIRVed missile can spread its warheads cannot be much larger than 150 kilometers along the missile's trajectory and 50 kilometers wide.

There is, in fact, no reason why the accuracy of a MIRVed missile should differ substantially from a single-warhead one. What was said earlier in this chapter about the possible sources of error apply in the case of MIRVed missiles as well. The difference in velocity from one MIRVed warhead to another is no more than a few tens of meters per second, while the bus after separation from the missile has a velocity of very nearly 7,000 meters per second. So a given error in the velocity change necessary to send each reentry vehicle to a different target will be minuscule compared to the basic velocity of the bus. The overall accuracy of the missile determines the accuracy of the individual reentry vehicles.

An especially significant military application of ballistic missile and inertial guidance technology is submarine-launched intercontinental ballistic missiles. Submarines that carry sixteen missiles were first developed by the United States and later by the Soviet Union and France. More recently, much larger submarines carrying twenty-four larger and heavier missiles, which can fly farther and transport bigger payloads, have been constructed both in the United States and in the Soviet Union. Fundamentally, these new submarines with their new, larger missiles do not incorporate any new principles. So what I will say about submarines and their ballistic missiles applies to both the earlier and the more recent incarnations of these systems.

The most significant thing to know about these submarines is that once submerged in the ocean they are extremely difficult to detect and locate, and therefore hard to destroy. It is virtually impossible, at least with the current and foreseeable technical means at our disposal, to find and destroy within a short period of time an entire fleet of thirty or so submarines, all hiding in some ocean or other. Consequently, we can conclude without knowing anything else about these weapon systems that submarine-carried ballistic missiles are not subject to destruction by a surprise enemy attack and will assuredly survive any conceivable nuclear exchange. As long as a country has submarines with ballistic missiles deployed in the oceans of the world, it will be able to retaliate against any enemy that attacks with nuclear weapons. For this reason, submarines are considered an assured retaliatory force that deters all but insane enemies from attacking. But launching a ballistic missile from a submarine is somewhat more difficult than launching one from a silo. After the submarine missile is launched, it behaves exactly the same way as any other missile. The difficulties stem mainly from two fundamental properties of the submarine: It is a mobile rather than a fixed launcher, and it is submerged in the ocean when it fires its missiles.

Because the submarine is submerged, it is very difficult to determine precisely its position and velocity at the instant of launch without some outside source of information. Yet, as we saw, these quantities are part of the initial conditions of motion that must be read into the guidance computer of the missile before launch. A missile guidance computer needs the latitude and longitude of the submarine's position when it launches a missile, the altitude (that is, the submarine's depth below sea level), the direction of the local north and the local vertical, and the speed and direction of the submarine at the instant of launch.

The submarine could surface, and by observing the position of a star in the sky or a landmark, or even by receiving radio signals from land-based or satellite-borne stations, it could determine its position very precisely. This, however, is not a good solution to the problem, since it is desirable to have a submarine travel for very long periods of time without surfacing. That way there would be no chance of being detected.

By using a large shipboard inertial guidance system called SINS (for "ship inertial navigation system"), a submarine can know where it is in exactly the same way a missile can. The location of the submarine is read into the SINS computer before the ship leaves port. Then the inertial system, by determining the acceleration given to the submarine by its propulsion system, can calculate the sub's velocity and position at any instant thereafter. The significant difference between the operation of the inertial guidance system on a missile and on a submarine is that in the former case the system has to work only for five minutes or so but handle tremendous accelerations, while in the latter the acceleration of the ship is quite small and the system has to work for days and weeks. But gyroscopes tend to drift even with no vibrations and no high acceleration loads. So even if the gyroscopes of SINS drift only by a thousandth of a degree per hour, the error in the position of the submarine moving at 20 knots will build up at a rate of about 60 meters per hour, so after only one day the location of the submarine determined by SINS will be about 1.5 kilometers in error. Such error in initial location when fed into the guidance computer of the missile will contribute a target miss of equal size to a missile fired from the sub. The submarine will have to surface or find some other way to update the indications of the SINS navigator at least several times a day, because the longitude of the submarine's position is totally arbitrary, since it is measured with respect to an imaginary line that passes through a suburb of London called Greenwich. So it must be provided by some kind of physical observation from the submarine in order to correct the SINS navigator. When the submarine is completely still with respect to the surface of the earth, even when submerged its inertial system can provide the necessary data for determining true vertical and the local north, which together are sufficient to calculate the latitude of the ship.

Several schemes may come to mind that would allow a submarine to know where it is without surfacing. One could, for example, plant sonic markers at carefully surveyed points in the ocean. If a submarine locates a known marker (by listening for it) and positions itself exactly over it, it would know its precise location. That is not a very safe method, however, because there is a good chance that an enemy submarine, which could also locate the marker, could be permanently stationed nearby. One can counter this danger by proliferating the number of markers to the point that the enemy won't have enough attack submarines to stake all of them out.

A variation of the same approach is to survey the bottom of the ocean very carefully, identify easily recognizable features like mounts or ridges or underwater hills, and determine their position accurately. Then submarines that want to find out exactly where they are can locate these features and so determine their exact underwater position.

Yet another approach is to use gravity gradiometers to map the change in the local gravitational field from point to point over the ocean basins. A gravity gradiometer is an instrument that can detect and measure minute *changes* in the direction and size of the local force of gravity between two points on the earth. With its help one can make very accurate maps of the force of gravity. A submarine could "read" these maps with the help of a gradiometer and know where it is. Gravity gradiometers are not small enough or robust enough to be carried by a missile to measure the gravitational force along the missile's trajectory, but they could be used on submarines, not only to improve the inertial guidance of the submarine, but also to determine the location of the ship with the aid of a detailed map of the earth's gravitational field.

So far, we have examined techniques that can be employed to improve the ability of submarines to determine their location accurately the instant they fire their ballistic missiles. An entirely different approach to the problem of making submarine-fired ballistic missiles accurate is now possible. It is based on the idea that it doesn't really matter how big the error in the location of the submarine is as it fires its missiles, provided there is a way to measure it and correct for it *after* the missile has left the submarine and is in its boost phase. There are two ways to do that: by stellar guidance, or by using the forthcoming Global Positioning System of navigation satellites (GPS) now being put into orbit around the earth. Stellar guidance utilizes a small telescope on the missile which measures the angles an identified star of known position makes with the coordinate axes of the guidance system. The correct values of these angles when the missile has reached the required terminal velocity can be calculated ahead of time and stored on the memory of the missile's guidance computer. The difference between the actual angles measured by the telescope during the missile's flight and these stored values indicates the size of the error that has accumulated up to that point of the missile's journey. Those accumulated errors that are caused either by the drifting of gyroscopes or by incorrect initial conditions can then be corrected by the missile's guidance system: It commands the missile to turn so that the angles formed between tracked star and the axes of the coordinate system on the missile have the same values as those calculated and stored in the computer. This technique can correct the location errors inherent in submarine launches, but it cannot correct errors caused by accelerometer malfunctions.

The other method of correcting launching-platform position errors uses the GPS. This system, when completed, is designed to consist of twenty-four satellites, eight each in three orbits 20,000 kilometers above the surface of the earth. In addition, the system has four ground-based monitoring stations and one master control station, also on earth. Each satellite will carry a very precise clock and a high-frequency radio transmitter. With the help of these instruments all satellites will emit coded signals at exactly the same instant of time (within a millionth of a millionth of a second). At the same time each satellite will broadcast information about its exact location in the sky.

These signals are coded in such a way that a receiver will recognize from which satellite each signal is coming. All radio signals travel at the speed of light, so signals emitted simultaneously from the satellites will arrive at different times at a given point on the earth. The signal from the satellite nearest that point will arrive first and the signal from the satellite farthest away will arrive last. Special receiving equipment can recognize which signal comes from what satellite and correlate the time of arrival of each of the signals with the information each satellite sends about its exact location. That way the receiving equipment can rapidly calculate the distance of its location from each satellite. Since the position of each satellite is well known with respect to some fixed coordinates on the earth, the position of the receiver in this coordinate system can be calculated with an accuracy of 10 meters or better. If the receiver is on a moving vehicle, the velocity of this vehicle can also be calculated to a few centimeters per second (see Appendix G). A ballistic missile equipped with such a receiver could determine its actual position and velocity toward the end of its powered flight; on the basis of this information the guidance computer can give the proper commands to correct any errors in the actual velocity of the missile and make it match exactly the required terminal velocity. This combination of inertial guidance with location and velocity information from the GPS would decrease the target error of the missile, even when launched from a submarine. Some military planners worry, however, that the system of satellites or the monitoring and control stations of the GPS could be destroyed during a nuclear war and thus installing GPS receivers on ballistic missiles would be useless. They insist that the only war-worthy guidance systems are those like the inertial guidance system, which do not depend on external information for their operations.

Theoretically there is still one more way to ensure that a reentry vehicle from a ballistic missile will hit its target, even if it is launched from a moving submarine. This method is, quite simply, to guide the reentry vehicle onto its target after it has begun to reenter the atmosphere. Controlled guided reentry, used to compensate for unexpected atmospheric effects on the reentry vehicle, requires a guidance system on the reentry vehicle and some mechanism to influence its trajectory. Either movable aerodynamic control fins, or small precise gas jets, or some movable weight inside the reentry vehicle offset from the vehicle's center of gravity can be used to change its direction of flight. The guidance could be provided either by a miniaturized inertial guidance system similar to the one described earlier in this chapter or by some form of optical device that searches the terrain underneath the descending reentry vehicle and recognizes the target.

There are severe technical difficulties in implementing such a "maneuverable reentry vehicle." First of all, current guidance and control systems would occupy considerable volume and add weight to the reentry vehicle. So the nuclear weapon carried by the reentry vehicle will of necessity be smaller or the reentry vehicle must be made bigger, so fewer could be carried on a missile. Second, it is very difficult to implement either of the two guidance schemes listed above. If the reentry vehicle is made to descend at a steep angle toward its target it will be buffeted by such strong forces that an inertial guidance system would probably malfunction. A steep descent also creates a sheath of hot gases around the reentry vehicle that come from the burning ablative shield. Such a sheath would block visible and radar waves and in effect blind the system's sensors. The reentry vehicle could not "see" the target, much less recognize it and have time to maneuver. If the reentry vehicle is made to glide for an extended period of time in the atmosphere on its way to the target, so that it has time to "look down," find the target, and maneuver, the guidance system will have great difficulty keeping the errors caused by the rigors of reentry at a minimum. So even though developing a reentry vehicle that glides toward its target seems to be a good idea, the technical problems it entails are formidable. At this time, stellar guidance and the GPS system seem the most promising ways to minimize the inaccuracy of submarine-launched ballistic missiles.

How do ballistic missiles compare with other delivery systems for nuclear warheads? Ballistic delivery of weapons is superior to delivery by aircraft or cruise missiles and rockets over very short (measured in the few kilometers) and very long (measured in the many thousand kilometers) ranges. For short ranges we use artillery shells, for long range we use ballistic missiles. Militarily they are better because there is no way to stop a reentry vehicle or a cannon shell from reaching its target once it has been launched properly. Also, ballistic missiles guided by inertial guidance and launched from submarines are the most invulnerable nuclear weapons system a country can have. So ballistic missiles are an important military asset and an important measure of a country's ability to transport nuclear weapons to targets in an enemy country.

6

THE CALCULUS
OF COUNTERFORCE

I N MOST PEOPLE's minds, nuclear weapons are associated with visions of devastated cities and smashed industrial complexes lying in ruins after a nuclear attack. Yet, in reality, the largest portion of the U.S. nuclear arsenal has always been targeted against military and industrial targets in the Soviet Union. Traditionally, only about 10% of the American nuclear weapons are assigned civilian targets. This, of course, does not mean that in a nuclear war the Soviet population will not be devastated. Not only are 900 warheads (10% of our strategic arsenal) more than enough to destroy all Russian cities over 100,000 in population, but many of the military or industrial targets are near or in cities and so attacking them would destroy the cities as well.

Since a city can be seriously damaged by relatively low overpressures and low levels of thermal radiation, the radius of destruction is much larger than the distance by which the missile could miss the center of the city. A 1-megaton weapon aimed at the center of a large city like Boston or Detroit or Washington would destroy the city even if it landed up to 1,000 meters away from its intended point of detonation. Therefore, accuracy is not important for weapons aimed against "soft" targets like cities, refineries, and airfields. The destruction would be so extensive and the cities are such large targets that it wouldn't really matter exactly where the weapon landed.

On the other hand, if the weapon is intended for use on a small "hard" target, such as a missile silo, its accuracy is of primary importance: Unless it landed very near the target, it would not destroy it. Until recently, ballistic missiles did not have guidance systems accurate enough to attack such fortified targets as concrete underground bunkers or the silos that house missiles. Accordingly no one contemplated using them in that fashion. But more recently, things have changed. The United States and the Soviet Union have installed such highly accurate guidance systems on their ICBMs that many experts believe these weapons could attack and destroy silos. But others believe that such an attack would be not only useless, since only a fraction of the nuclear arsenals of the United States and the Soviet Union are in silo-based missiles, but also neither technically nor operationally feasible.

This chapter describes a silo and how it protects a missile. It also describes the destructive effects a nuclear weapon can have on a silo, and how these effects depend on the accuracy, the yield, and the reliability of the weapon. With this background, we will look at the ways in which experts try to *predict* the results of a hypothetical nuclear attack against all the missile silos of a country. Finally, we will see why these methods of prediction do not take into account a variety of physical and operational factors, and how as a consequence their results are more theoretical than real.

Missile silos are made of reinforced concrete and steel and are designed to protect the operational readiness of intercontinental ballistic missiles (ICBMs) from nuclear attack. A ballistic missile, as we saw in Chapter 5, is a vehicle that carries a number of delicate electromechanical devices that can easily be disrupted by unexpectedly large shock and/or high levels of electromagnetic or nuclear radiation. Therefore, intercontinental ballistic missiles deployed on unprotected, aboveground launchers would be vulnerable to a preemptive nuclear attack.

The first nuclear strategic ballistic missiles were, in fact, deployed aboveground. They were liquid-fueled, required lengthy preparation for launching, and therefore could not be launched in response to a surprise attack. This combination of unprotected deployment and protracted launching procedures made the early strategic missiles vulnerable to preemptive attack, since the nation that attacked first would have an excellent chance to destroy the opponent's nuclear arsenal on the ground even with relatively inaccurate missiles. Underground silos, first constructed by the United States and the Soviet Union and later by China and France, eliminated this vulnerability. Protected in a modern silo, a strategic ballistic missile has a high probability of surviving the effects of a nuclear attack, and until recently, it was generally agreed that a significant fraction of the land-based missiles of the United States or the Soviet Union could survive an all-out nuclear attack.

A missile silo (Figure 14) is a vertical reinforced-concrete cylinder closed at one end and buried in the ground so that its upper, open end is flush with the surrounding ground surface. The interior of the silo is somewhat longer and wider than the missile it houses. The extra space permits the emission of the hot exhaust gases of the rocket motor during the first seconds of the launch before the missile clears the silo top (something not necessary for missiles, such as those in submarines, which ignite their engines after they have been popped out of the hold). The space also accommodates an elaborate suspension and isolation system that supports the missile and minimizes the transfer of motion from the walls and floor of the silo to the missile itself. The top one-third of the silo cylinder is completely surrounded by a multistory structure that houses the maintenance and launch facilities.

The silo cylinder and the structure around it are covered by a massive sliding door designed to withstand the airblast overpressure and the intense radiation that a nuclear explosion causes; the cover is designed to sweep away debris from a surface nuclear detonation as it slides open, to prevent it from falling onto the missile. The cover and its support surfaces are known as "headworks." In modern silos the headworks are constructed in such a manner as to transmit the vertical load of the airblast overpressure to the supports of the cover rather than to the vertical body of the silo, thereby minimizing the chances of a structural failure of the silo. In order to prevent damage to the missile caused by a nearby nuclear detonation on the ground, the missile is encased in a rigid frame held in place by a special suspension system. This set of springs and shock absorbers is

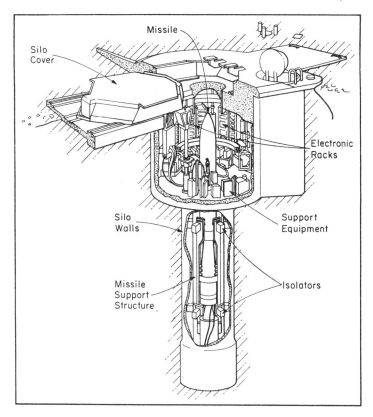

FIGURE 14. Diagrammatic sketch of a missile silo *(courtesy Boeing Corporation).*

designed to do two things: prevent the missile from rattling inside the silo as its walls shake during a nuclear explosion, and soften the shock to the missile from the explosion. If a strong shock were allowed to reach the missile, its delicately aligned guidance system and other sensitive components could be damaged or disrupted.

The missile is stored in the silo unattended. The functions of monitoring the missile's condition, testing its components, targeting, verification of the targeting, and finally launching the missile are performed remotely from an underground command post removed from the silo, where Air Force officers are ready around the clock to launch the missile. The support electronics and power supplies necessary for all these operations are housed in the structure that surrounds the silo. Information is communicated from the launch control facility to the silos and vice versa via underground cables and/or secure radio channels. Each launch control facility controls a number of silos (ten in the case of the U.S. Minuteman force), which can be spread out over an area 150 kilometers long and 50 kilometers wide. Each missile is connected to two separate and far-removed launch control centers. Especially worrisome for the security of the missile system are the considerable lengths of cable involved in all these interconnections. Cables, of course, are subject to physical damage from a surface explosion, but more important, they can act as efficient receiving antennae for the electromagnetic pulse (EMP) unless properly protected. They could, therefore, be one of the more vulnerable components of a missile force based in silos.

Given such a ground-based missile system, which nuclear explosion effects would be most effective in rendering the missile inoperative? Since the silo has no significant aboveground components, there is little concern for the effects of dynamic pressure and the high winds that would follow the passage of the overpressure shock wave. And since concrete conducts heat rather poorly, it is improbable that thermal radiation would cause the temperature inside the silo to rise enough to damage the most temperature-sensitive components of the missile. The same thing can be said about the prompt nuclear radiation generated by a nuclear detonation. One meter of concrete reduces the intensity of nuclear radiation by a factor of a thousand. Therefore the silo affords good radiation protection to the missile and its equipment. Those gamma rays that could reach the electronics of the missile might create a sudden but brief current pulse that could momentarily incapacitate the circuits in the missile's computer and control electronics. But these circuits can be, and probably are, designed to shut down rapidly when they sense this extraneous current pulse, and to "recover" shortly afterward.

Neutrons from a nuclear explosion would also be absorbed by the silo's concrete walls and the surrounding soil. Those that did penetrate into the silo and reach the missile could cause permanent damage to the solid-state electronics of the missile. But careful selection of the semiconductor material out of which these circuits are made and redundant circuitry in the missile could preserve the ability of the missile to function even after it had received neutron fluxes as high as 10^{13} neutrons per square centimeter. A 1-megaton weapon would create such a flux at an unprotected point as much as 2,000 meters away from the point of detonation. But even if the detonation occurred 100 meters away, the shielding of the silo would provide sufficient protection. However, there are other effects of a nuclear explosion, especially at such short distances, which would assuredly be much more destructive than neutrons.

The electromagnetic pulse could have unpredictable yet severe effects on a single missile in a silo or on an entire group of missiles in neighboring silos. The detonation of a nuclear weapon near a silo would induce large currents in the conductors of the missile electronics and the support equipment inside the silo. For example, a 1-megaton weapon could induce a 1,000-amp current in a wire thousands of meters away. By shielding the wire, grounding the shield, and enclosing the equipment in special shielding cages, this current can be made smaller, but not eliminated altogether. The steel rods that reinforce the concrete of the silo offer a measure of protection from the EMP, and special electrical and magnetic isolators may also improve protection. However, the efficacy of such measures is a function of the frequency of the EMP. The frequency depends on the precise mechanism of the pulse's generation, which is determined by the altitude of the explosion and other factors. Therefore it is impossible to predict with any confidence that a missile would not be damaged by the EMP of a nearby detonation. Worse, the network of wires that carry the commands from the manned command posts to the unmanned silos could act as antennae to receive the EMP and transmit its induced currents directly into the missile. Radio communication with missiles in silos would be affected by the EMP of a high-altitude nuclear detona-

tion for periods of time as long as several minutes, unless fiber-optic cables were used instead of the ordinary
cables.

By far the most predictably destructive effects for a silo
are those created by the airblast shock wave. The airblast
of a nuclear weapon could cause a number of things to
happen to the missile inside a nearby silo. If the weapon
exploded very near, the silo would tumble into the crater
and get crushed with the missile inside it, or it would be
covered completely with a thick layer of soil and rocks dug
up from the inside of the crater. In either case, the missile
would be lost. Even if the explosion was too far from the
silo to cover it with debris, the overpressure could crush or
crack the silo walls, shatter the cover, or damage the equipment inside. As the ground was pushed by the airblast
shock wave and the subsequent static overpressure wave,
the soil would press against the walls of the silo and crush
it. Also, as the ground moved, the silo would tend to stay
put, and the relative motion of silo and ground would cause
friction that could break the walls of the silo. This relative
motion could literally lift the entire silo up from its original
position, causing havoc inside it. If the weapon detonated
even farther out, the silo might remain intact but the missile inside might be damaged.

The most damaging effects of a nuclear explosion close
to a missile in a silo that remained otherwise intact could
be caused by the ground motions that the explosion would
produce. Although the missile is isolated by elaborate suspension systems from the surrounding structure, miscalcu-
lations in, or inadequacy of, the construction of these
systems could result in serious damage. The problem is that
the complexity of ground motion and stress caused by a
nuclear explosion, with its strong dependence on the geological features of the terrain around the silo, permits only
approximate predictions. If the springs that keep the missile suspended from the silo walls are too soft, they would
permit the missile to rattle inside the silo and be crushed.
If the springs are too stiff, the motion of the silo walls would
be transmitted directly to the missile and damage or jar its
guidance system out of alignment.

So even if the silo showed no visible structural damage,

the missile inside it might be damaged or its guidance system might be rendered nonfunctional. It is reasonable to assume that a land-based missile that had been subjected to the jarring effects of a nearby nuclear detonation would not remain accurate enough to attack an enemy missile silo with any significant degree of accuracy. Even if the missile managed to take off and achieve required terminal velocity, the initial alignment of the missile's guidance system could have been disrupted in a decisive manner. At the very least, careful and time-consuming realignment and testing would be required before the missile could be fired toward its intended target with anything like its original degree of accuracy. Therefore, although a surprise attack against the silo-based missile force of an opponent would perhaps not destroy a significant portion of the enemy's missiles, it most probably would render the majority of them unsuitable for countersilo attack (which requires a high degree of accuracy), unless the missile was given the means to literally "find its bearings" again after it was launched—as will be the case with the latest version of the U.S. ballistic missiles. As we saw, this can be done by using techniques such as stellar guidance and the Global Positioning System now being installed by the United States.

Thus, the most assuredly damaging effects of a nuclear detonation for a silo all come from the shock-wave overpressure caused by the detonation. They can destroy or damage a missile inside a silo farther from the point of detonation than any other effect. Consequently, in attempting to predict the probability that a nuclear weapon of a given explosive yield will destroy a silo, it is sensible to use the overpressure generated by such a weapon as a measure of its ability to do so. It is customary, in fact, to indicate the ability of a silo to survive a nuclear attack by the amount of overpressure it can sustain before it collapses. For example, a silo is said to be 2,000 psi strong when it can withstand a blast overpressure of 2,000 pounds per square inch (psi). This implies that the silo's designer has made sure that the silo is constructed in such a fashion that all the other nuclear explosion effects—heat, radiation, EMP —are attenuated by the silo to levels that in theory cannot hurt the missile inside. But it ignores the most important point: The shock wave can damage or destroy the missile without collapsing the silo. The implicit assumption of this predictive method is that if the silo survives the overpressure, the missile will survive as well. This is, as we have seen, a questionable assumption, since the acceleration of the ground caused by a nuclear explosion can damage the missile while leaving the silo intact.

Let us now examine the methods by which the military analysts attempt to predict the outcome of an attack on a silo of a given strength by a nuclear weapon of known characteristics. In order to do that, we need first to consider some general properties that apply to all weapons. From these we can appreciate the reasons for the particular tests, observations, and calculations that are needed in predicting the vulnerability of silos to nuclear weapons.

Whether an explosive charge, be it conventional or nuclear, destroys a target depends on three factors:

1. How strong the target is, or in modern military terminology, how "hard" it is. (The hardness of a target is a measure of how much energy it takes to destroy it. The distance within which a given explosive charge will destroy a given target is called the "kill radius" of the weapon for that target. The stronger the target, the smaller the kill radius of a given weapon against it; the more energy released by a weapon, the larger the kill radius against the target.)

2. How much energy the detonation of the explosive releases.

3. How close to the target the weapon explodes.

For example, a nuclear warhead would have a large kill radius against an airfield, since it could damage the aircraft there even if it exploded 2 kilometers away. The same warhead would have a small kill radius if it was used against a very resistant hard target, like a bunker made of reinforced concrete buried in the ground. Such a structure would not be damaged by a nuclear blast 2 kilometers away, but would be by a blast 100 or 200 meters away. Therefore the kill radius of a nuclear weapon against hardened targets is of the order of a few hundreds of meters.

Even when a weapon is navigated toward a target by some kind of internal or external guidance mechanism, it doesn't always land on it, especially if the target is very small. A bomb aimed at a bridge will probably not land directly on it, but some distance away.

All one can do is predict what is most likely to happen, and the way to do that is to calculate what will happen on the average. Thus military theorists are forced to resort to making statements about the *probability* that a weapon launched against a given target will land within a given distance from the target and cause a given amount of damage. For example, they say: "The probability that this bomb will fall within 50 meters of a target when released in such-and-such a way is 50%." Or "The probability that the bomb will land within 100 meters is 90%," and so on.

By "accurate" we mean a weapon that has a high probability of destroying its target. But the accuracy of a weapon is a relative concept that depends on both the precision of its guidance system and the kill radius of its warhead. A common measure of precision (not "accuracy") is the CEP or "circle of equal probability." CEP is a distance that is determined experimentally for each ballistic weapon. A target point is chosen and the weapon is fired many times against the target. Each time it is fired the weapon lands at a different point, and after many shots there is a distribution of landing points near the target. CEP is the radius of the circle, centered at the center of the distribution, that contains 50% of the landing points of the weapon.

As an example, suppose you fire 100 shots at a target. After recording the points where the shots land, you end up with a pattern like the one shown in Figure 15a (page 140). Most of the shots have landed quite close to the target, and on the average they have missed by the same amount on all sides. We would say that this weapon is precise— that is, it has a small CEP. If instead many of the shots land far from the target, as in Figure 15b, we would say that the weapon is less precise; it has a large CEP. Finally, if most of the shots have landed to one side of the target, as in Figure 15c, rather than distributing themselves symmetrically about the target, we say that the weapon has a "bias," which is the distance between the target and the center of the distribution. So a small CEP, by itself, does not ensure that the weapon would be lethal against the silo.

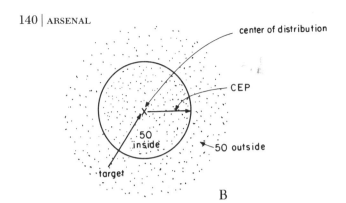

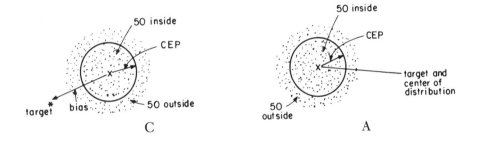

FIGURE 15. Illustrations of the definitions of CEP and bias.

Another way to illustrate the same concept is to plot the number of times the weapon lands within a series of concentric rings placed at regular distances from the target (see Figure 16a). Suppose, now, that having fired 200 weapons at the target we find that 60 have landed within 100 meters of it, 48 between 100 and 200 meters, 32 between 200 and 300, 24 between 300 and 400, 18 between 400 and 500, 12 between 500 and 600, 4 between 600 and 700, and 2 between 700 and 800. If we plot them we would get the curve

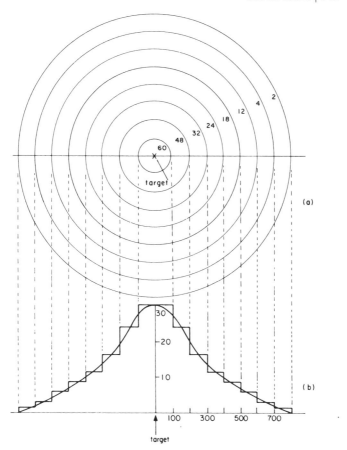

FIGURE 16. Illustration of the concept of normal distribution.

in Figure 16b. We can say that the probability that the next weapon we fire will land within 100 meters of the target is 60/200, or 30%; the probability that it will land within 200 meters is 108/200 (that is, the probability that it will fall within the first 100 meters plus the probability that it will fall between the 100-to-200-meter band), or 54%; and the probability that it will land within 800 meters of the target is 100%. The CEP of this weapon is a bit smaller than 200 meters.

How confident one can be in these probabilities depends on the number of test shots. The larger the number of tests, the greater the confidence that the future performance of the weapon can be predicted. What we must keep firmly in mind here is that this prediction is valid only if the conditions under which the weapon would be used in battle are exactly the same as those that prevailed during the tests.

In order to determine the CEP and the bias of a missile, military engineers fire several of them against a prearranged point several thousand miles away and record the points at which the weapons land. The weapon will have the same CEP no matter what its target, since the CEP depends mainly on the technical characteristics of the guidance system (see Chapter 5), which determines how consistently and precisely we can guide a weapon toward its target. The bias, on the other hand, depends on the precise knowledge of the location of the target, on how much and in what direction influences encountered along the way will alter the missile's original speed and direction, and on the ability to correct for these influences. But most important, the bias depends on being able to predict correctly *all* the influences that the missile will encounter. We can at least attempt to counter influences that we know about. But if we are not aware of something that affects the trajectory of a ballistic weapon, we cannot correct for it, and it will contribute to the bias error of the weapon. The bias therefore remains unpredictable, since the influences that would affect a ballistic trajectory are different for each target and even differ with time.

So four specific quantities have to be known in order to predict whether a missile armed with a nuclear weapon can destroy a silo. Three of them can be determined relatively easily. The CEP can be measured as I described, the yield of the warhead is known from its design, and the hardness of the silo can be inferred from its construction. But the bias is unknown, because it cannot be measured during the testing of the missile. If we assume that the bias of the missile is zero, we can proceed to calculate the probability that a missile of given CEP, carrying a warhead of known yield, will destroy a silo of known strength (using the formula in Appendix H). The result tells us at least that accuracy is much more important than the yield of the weapon when it comes to destroying silos. We must remember however that variations—in CEP, hardness, and yield—of 20% or more are not improbable. This must be taken into consideration when predictions of the outcome of a countersilo attack are made.

In order to have a method of predicting what will happen if, for example, the United States attacks Soviet silos, military strategists make the assumption that the bias is zero, just as we did. But in reality this is not a very good assumption, because the bias may at times be even larger than the CEP of the weapon. Using this method to estimate the outcome of an attack produces a very optimistic prediction from the attacker's viewpoint (see Appendix H).

Besides ignoring the bias of the missile, however, the formula fails to consider the effects of the soil between the point of detonation and the silo. The overpressure that could shatter the silo door is independent of the soil that surrounds the silo (or the soil's condition). But the pressure that the silo walls experience, and the displacement and acceleration that the silo and missile feel due to the detonation, depend very sensitively on the properties of the intervening soil. Where, for example, is the water table in relation to the silo? Is the soil wet or not; is it stratified or not? All of these conditions influence the progress of the shock wave through the soil, with the result that the pressure that the silo walls experience is somewhat unpredictable. In addition, the effects of the pressure wave on the silo walls are equally unpredictable. Finally, the response of the system of springs and shock absorbers that isolates the missile from the silo is again unpredictable to an extent. So in reality, the uncertainty of what will happen to a silo attacked by a nuclear weapon is quite large, and this uncertainty is not reflected in the formula commonly used to calculate the probability that a silo will be destroyed. Sometimes this formula underestimates the probability that a missile will be damaged by a given weapon, because it is based on a criterion for damage—the physical collapse of the silo—which is not necessary for the deactivation of the missile. Other times, the formula may overestimate the kill probability, because it neglects to take into account the bias, which may be significant, and which is totally unpredictable for missile trajectories that have never before been tested. Another factor that does not appear in this simple formula, but which could be introduced relatively easily (see Appendix H), is the reliability of the missile—the probability that any given missile will perform as expected when the launch button is pushed.

The question becomes: If we cannot predict the performance of one missile against one silo with the kind of precision the formula for calculation implies, what if anything can we say ahead of time about the outcome of an attack against, say, 1,000 silos with warheads carried by several hundred missiles? Can we, in fact, predict with any confidence what a surprise all-out attack by the United States against Soviet missile silos would achieve? Can we know with any confidence what would happen to U.S. silo-based ballistic missiles if the Soviets attacked suddenly?

The last two questions are similar, but our ability to answer them is not the same. Through repeated tests, we know what the CEP and reliability of our missiles are, and we know what the bias of our missiles would be against a target that we have extensively tested. And we know, although not as well, what the CEP of Soviet missiles is, since we have observed their test launches and landings, just as they have observed ours. But we have no way of knowing what their bias is, simply because we do not know where the Soviet missiles are aimed when tested.

So the military can know approximately what the CEP and yield of their own weapons are by testing them, and they can know what the bias of these weapons was during the tests, but they cannot know how big the bias will be when launched against real targets. Also, they can know something about the CEP (or precision) of the enemy weapons and also something about the yield of these weapons, but it is improbable that they would know anything about the bias of the opponent's weapons.

All of these uncertainties affect the formula used for predicting the vulnerability of a silo attacked by one or more warheads. Additional untestable assumptions must be made in order to calculate the physical vulnerability of an entire silo-based national ballistic missile force. The reason is that one must introduce all the uncertainties inherent in the very complex operation of launching, in a timely sequence, hundreds of missiles that carry thousands of warheads cross-targeted on a large number of silos. No two missiles will behave the same way. Some will behave better, some worse, and some much worse than we might predict. Perhaps even more uncertain is the human factor. Such an all-out attack can be rehearsed up to a given point, but it can never be practiced to give the human operators who will have to launch all these missiles the needed exquisite timing. Besides, these people will be under extreme psychological stress when actually ordered to fire their missiles, knowing that their actions may well bring an end to civilization. Of course, all of these uncertainties must be considered, regardless of which side's missiles are being launched.

It is simply not possible to mathematically account for all the relevant uncertainty factors that enter into calculations of the outcome of an all-out attack, nor to predict reliably the magnitude of statistical fluctuations of decisive quantities such as CEP. Even if one could achieve this analytical feat, the result undoubtedly would be that a considerable number of silos would survive any attack, because malfunctions do not average out. Any departure of a missile's performance from the anticipated performance would diminish its reliability and its effectiveness against a silo. Any unpredicted change in weather would decrease the accuracy of the reentry vehicles systematically.

Knowing that some silos might survive a nearby nuclear detonation, an attacker might use more than one warhead against a silo. If the first one somehow failed to destroy its target, subsequent ones could accomplish the silo's destruction. However, this is complicated by the fact that the effects of the detonation of the first warhead would interfere drastically with the trajectory of the second and subsequent warheads arriving soon after. This effect is known as "fratricide." Furthermore, the attacker could not wait a long time before sending a second warhead against a silo, because if the first one had not damaged the missile, this missile would soon be launched, leaving the second warhead with only an empty silo to destroy. Since fratricide would interfere with the second warhead if it arrived immediately after the first, timing becomes a very delicate and chancy process that further increases the uncertainty of the final outcome.

To conclude, then, we can say that we have available a mathematical formula that gives us only some idea about the ability of a countersilo weapon whose CEP and yield have been determined during testing. This formula, however, is not suitable for predicting reliably what would happen if we decide to attack the enemy's land-based missiles all at once, nor can it predict in any detail the actual outcome of a hypothetical attack against our missiles. If we know that the CEP of the enemy's missiles is very large, or that their yield is very small, we can conclude with certainty that an enemy attack against our silos would be relatively ineffectual. But if we think that the enemy has very precise missiles with very large warheads, we *cannot* know what the outcome of an attack would be against our land-based missile force. We can make a *worst case assumption:* that all the enemy missiles will work very well *and* that they will have zero bias, *and* that the entire operation will proceed flawlessly. But, because it is the product of the individual probabilities, the combined probability that all these assumptions will prove correct is extremely small.

It is important to know the limits of usefulness of any mathematical formula, to remember what we have left out, or assumed in order to arrive at it, and to realize how important these assumptions are to the result. Only then can we decide whether we can base national defense policy or predicate political and diplomatic actions on the outcome of such analytical calculation. What these facts really tell us is how poorly we can actually predict the outcome of an attack against the missile silos of a country.

7

BOMBERS
AND CRUISE MISSILES

ORLD WAR II introduced a new type of warfare which, until then, had not been technically feasible: strategic bombing. In World War I, airplanes were used in support of tactical operations—that is, in the fighting on the battlefield and for reconnaissance. They were used to lob hand grenades into trenches or to strafe troops in the field, but not to drop bombs. The planes were not big enough or powerful enough for that. But in the following years, several nations—Germany, Italy, France, Great Britain, Japan, and the United States—developed bigger aircraft capable of carrying bombs. By the time of the Spanish Civil War the military were ready to try their new airborne weapon. The Falangists, who were supplied by Germany and Italy, used airplanes not only to bomb positions held by the Loyalists, but, for the first time in history, to launch attacks against noncombatants in order to terrorize them. *Guernica*, Picasso's epic painting of war, suffering, and horror, was inspired by such an air raid on the village of Guernica in northern Spain.

During the early years of World War II, the Germans raided London and the rest of England with hundreds of bombers every day in order to disrupt the war effort and demoralize the British. Later on in the war, the Allies launched a massive strategic bombing campaign against German and Japanese cities involving thousands of planes, each carrying a few tons of explosive or incendiary bombs. These raids caused casualties and suffering among the civilian population, but, in fact, it has been determined since then that they actually resulted in very little disruption of the war effort of Germany or Japan. The development of the nuclear bomb has, of course, significantly improved the effectiveness of strategic bombing, since a relatively small object weighing some hundreds of kilograms can now deliver more destructive energy in an instant than 2,000 bombers attacking all at once.

Strategic bombing transformed the nature of war, in the sense that the armies of an enemy could now be bypassed to inflict damage directly upon its population and productive capacity. Nuclear strategic bombing has made possible the complete annihilation of a country, given enough nuclear weapons and vehicles to carry them. And although the land-based or sea-launched ballistic missile has superseded the bomber in military importance because of the missile's speed and certainty of reaching the target, the bomber is still an important carrier of nuclear bombs. For the fact remains that the bomber can deliver a larger weight of explosives than a ballistic missile.

Unlike the ballistic missile, which travels mostly outside the atmosphere and is powered only for a small portion of its journey by a rocket that carries its own fuel and oxidizer, the bomber is a vehicle that is continuously powered by an engine that carries only its fuel, using the oxygen of the atmosphere to burn it. In addition, the bomber is designed to use the air to provide it with the lift that enables it to fly. The long-range bomber must therefore travel in the atmosphere at all times.

The bomber and, as we shall see shortly, the cruise missile are thus "endoatmospheric" vehicles (that is, they fly inside the atmosphere) that "breathe" the air and use it to fly. They do this in the same way that an ordinary passenger airplane does. An airplane has two essential parts that make it fly: an engine and wings.

The working principle of a jet engine is quite simple (see Figure 17). Imagine a box with some holes on its side to let air in and a large hole in the back. Fuel, in this case kerosene, is sprayed inside the box and burned with the help of the air that comes in. This combustion creates a lot of hot gases, which raise the pressure inside the box much higher than atmospheric pressure. As a result, these gases rush out with much higher speed than the air that came in. There is

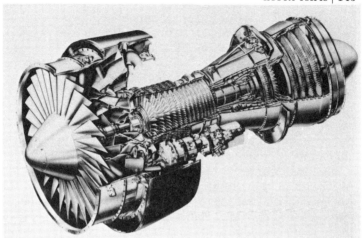

FIGURE 17. Picture of a large commercial turbofan engine. Note the very large fan at the front of the engine (*courtesy of General Electric*).

also much more gas going out than there was air coming in. So the engine does two things: It increases the amount of gas that comes out of it compared to the amount that came in; and it increases the speed with which these gases leave the engine compared to the speed with which the air comes in. (The speed with which the air comes in is equal to the speed of the airplane when it flies). Since the engine is firmly attached to the plane, the force that it develops as a result of these two processes pushes the entire airplane forward. Since the efficiency with which the engine propels the plane decreases as the speed of the exhaust gases increases, it is better to increase the mass of gases that flow through the engine in order to increase the thrust the engine imparts to the plane. That's why more thrust means bigger engines, like the ones we see on the wide-body commercial jet aircraft.

The jet engine, in order to burn the necessary amount of fuel, needs a lot of air, so a compressor is installed at the inlet of the engine to push the necessary amount of air into the box where the fuel burns. Since the pressure inside that box is very high, the compressor must do a lot of work to push the necessary air into the combustion chamber. So the designers of jet engines have put a turbine at the exit hole of the box to turn the compressor blades. As the hot gases rush out, they rotate the blades of the turbine, which in turn rotates the blades of the compressor. Some ingenious engineers thought that the whole performance of the engine would improve, namely more forward thrust would result from burning the same amount of fuel, if they also added a large fan, called a turbofan, in front of the compressor just to push some air around the outside of the combustion chamber and out the back. Some of the energy of the hot gases is spent turning the turbofan, but the resulting increased mass flow helps push the engine. This efficient engine with the fan in front is called a turbofan, and is used in all modern commercial and military aircraft. The basic engine without the turbofan arrangement is called a turbojet. It is not as efficient, but because it needs a simpler and smaller turbine, it is much cheaper. So if you need an engine to push the plane a long way for a given amount of fuel, you use a turbofan, and pay higher fabrication costs. If you need a cheap engine and you are willing to have your vehicle go a shorter distance for the same amount of fuel, you use a turbojet. We will see how these distinctions become important when we consider cruise missiles.

Consider now the wing of the airplane. As the engines push the airplane forward through the atmosphere, the shape of the wing forms two airstreams: one that flows next to the bottom of the wing and one that goes over the top. Since the top of the wing is curved and the bottom is flat, and since a straight line between two points is always shorter than a curved line joining the same two points, the airstream over the top has to travel farther than the airstream at the bottom.

Both airstreams have the same time to complete their passage next to the wing. Therefore, the airstream on top moves faster (has a greater speed) than the one at the bottom.

Back in the seventeenth century, Jacob Bernoulli, a Swiss physicist, discovered that the pressure that the passage of air exerts on a surface decreases as the velocity of the air increases. So the pressure downward against the top of the wing of an airplane is *less* than the pressure upward against the bottom, and the airplane experiences a net force that pushes it up. When this force becomes larger than the force that pulls the airplane to the ground (that is, its weight), the airplane lifts off and flies. The engines give the airplane speed, and the shape of the wings generates a net lifting force that makes the airplane fly. It is an ingenious trick.

The similarity between commercial aircraft and bombers, however, stops with these general operating principles. Bombers must find their way in an uncooperative and even hostile environment, locate their targets at any time of night or day in any weather, release their bombs or rockets to land as close as possible to these targets, and communicate securely with their command center while in the air. In addition, they must be able to take off rapidly to avoid being caught on the ground, protect themselves against enemy fighters and antiaircraft missiles and cannon, and if necessary refuel in midair and fly very low. Consequently, both their construction and their equipment are very different from those of an ordinary jet liner.

The United States has two types of long-range (intercontinental) bombers, the B-52 and the FB-111. The B-52 first flew in April 1952, but since then eight consecutive new models of this aircraft have been developed. Some varied little from the earlier model; some, like the latest (the B-52H), are drastically different in performance and equipment. This latest model weighs almost 490,000 pounds (229 metric tons) when taking off fully loaded. It carries four bombs and six guided missiles together weighing about 20,000 pounds, and has electronics that allows it to fly very low over the ground and find its targets night or day and under all weather conditions. It has eight turbofan engines, each of which develops a thrust of 17,000 pounds, and can fly unrefueled for 10,000 miles at a cruising speed of 650 mph at altitudes of up to 55,000 feet. Its wings have a span of 185 feet, and it is 160 feet long, and it has a crew of six. In all, 744 B-52s were built, but only about 255 of them are now in active service as strategic bombers carrying nuclear weapons.

The other strategic bomber of the United States is the

FB-111, a swing-wing supersonic aircraft that is a derivative version of the F-111 tactical attack plane. The United States has sixty-six of these bombers. The FB-111 can fly more than twice as fast as the speed of sound and maintain supersonic speed even while flying low. It weighs about 22 tons empty and more than twice that when loaded with fuel and bombs. Its terrain-following radar and very sophisticated electronics permit flight in all weather. It can fly unrefueled for about 4,700 miles and has the ability to refuel in the air. Carrying six nuclear bombs or six short-range attack air-to-surface missiles, the plane can attack a target with considerable accuracy from a distance of about 50 kilometers, thus avoiding air defenses close to the target. The two pilots that operate the plane sit in very cramped quarters, and their endurance may be the limiting factor in the performance of the plane.

Bombers are usually sent to drop their bombs on specific targets: a city, a fortification, or an installation of some sort. How do they know where they are, how do they find their way, and how do they recognize their target? One way is simply to steer by features on the ground, using a topographical map. But that is not terribly reliable, especially in bad weather or at night. The next best option is to use radio beacons, much as a ship navigates by lighthouses and lightships that have fixed and known locations. Radio beacons are good for civilian aircraft flying in a cooperative environment, where all the necessary beacons are working. In time of war, however, when a bomber may fly over enemy territory for several hours, the enemy is unlikely to oblige by maintaining a reliable set of radio beacons.

Thus it is essential to have other means of navigation for bombers. Inertial guidance is one possibility, using exactly the same principle as the ballistic missile. But the airplane, like the submarine, travels for long periods of time. Since the gyroscopes of an inertial measuring unit drift constantly, the longer the plane flies, the larger will be the errors in position and true velocity. So the airplane would have to update its guidance system by fixing on a star or by a visual fix on a recognizable feature on the ground. This is not always possible, however, and after long periods of flight in bad weather or at night, a bomber could lose its way. One remedy is to have a series of radio-wave beams that crisscross each other and form an invisible lattice of beams over the surface of the earth. By receiving the signals from two such crossing beams simultaneously, the pilot can know exactly where he is. An even better method will become available when the satellite Global Positioning System (GPS) becomes operational. Then the GPS receiver on the plane will be able to tell the pilot where he is at any time with an accuracy of a few meters. Finally, modern bombers have special radars that can scan the ground and produce recognizable images of terrain features or of the target itself, regardless of the weather.

With a combination of some of these systems, a bomber can navigate over hostile territory, find its target, and deliver its bombs with an accuracy of a few hundred feet. This explains why bombing was not terribly effective during World War II—a chemical-explosive bomb, even a large one, that detonates a few hundred feet from a target does not cause significant damage even if the target is quite "soft." Thus in that war bombers were used primarily against extended targets like cities, because that's all the bombers could really hit. With nuclear weapons the situation is, of course, very different. A nuclear bomb will devastate an entire city, even if it detonates a few hundred feet away from its intended point of explosion. The most common hard target, however, the silo of an ICBM, is not a suitable target for a bomber for several reasons. For one thing, even with nuclear bombs, airplanes may not have the accuracy to attack a silo successfully. Also, by the time the bomber got there, the missile would most likely have been launched. In the age of nuclear weapons, bombers are effective primarily for missions against targets like cities, which are always there, easy to hit, and quite "soft." Why bombers are considered at all for use against cities when we have ballistic missiles that can get there in a tenth of the time and cause at least as much devastation is a question we will deal with toward the end of the chapter.

A cruise missile is a dispensable, pilotless, self-guided, continuously powered, endoatmospheric vehicle that is supported by wings and powered by the same kind of jet engine as an airplane. Unlike a ballistic missile, which is powered and usually guided for only the brief initial part of its flight, a cruise missile requires continuous power and guidance, since both the velocity and the direction of its flight can be unpredictably altered by local weather conditions or changes in the performance of the propulsion system.

A ballistic missile is guided for the first five of the twenty minutes it takes to travel 5,000 kilometers; a cruise missile, which usually flies at subsonic speed, would require close to six hours of continuously guided flight to cover the same distance. Hence guidance errors that accumulate with time would be almost a hundred times larger for a cruise missile than for a ballistic missile with a comparable range, and its cumulative deviation from a preassigned trajectory of thousands of kilometers would be very large. Accurate arrival at a target could therefore be achieved with continuous inertial guidance only by correcting it from time to time with fresh information about the missile's position.

Cruise missiles have served as warhead-delivery systems in the past, beginning with the German V-1 "buzz bomb" of World War II and continuing with such weapons as the U.S. Matador, Regulus, and Snark missiles and the Russian Shaddock missile, which is still deployed aboard some Russian submarines and surface warships. None of these earlier versions were capable of updating their guidance systems with fresh positional information, and as a result they were not very accurate. Furthermore, they were powered by inefficient jet engines that in general did not allow ranges in excess of a few hundred kilometers.

The main difference between these older versions of the cruise missile and the modern U.S. cruise missiles is that recent advances in technology have made available two important new components: (1) microelectronic devices that can update the location information of a cruise missile while it is in flight and therefore improve its accuracy a thousandfold; and (2) small, efficient jet engines that for every hour of flight consume only about a pound of fuel for every pound of thrust they generate. Both of these technological advances primarily affect the performance of strategic cruise missiles,* since at shorter ranges the flight time is measured in minutes and therefore even an only moderately accurate guidance system needs no midflight correction. Moreover, a tactical missile such as an antiship or antiaircraft missile can be fitted with a homing device, such as radar, that detects the target and guides the missile to it.

Inertial guidance alone might allow a long-range, strategic cruise missile to drift as much as a kilometer or so off course for every hour of flight. The effects of weather and the imperfections of the jet engine that powers the missile usually increase this drift. After several hours of flight the missile may be 10 or more kilometers off target. If, however, the missile can from time to time "recognize" where it is and compare its actual position with where it should be according to its preassigned trajectory, the on-board computer can instruct the automatic pilot to make the appropriate maneuvers and bring the missile back to the correct trajectory.

The cruise missiles now entering the U.S. arsenal determine their actual location while in flight with the help of a terrain-contour matching system called Tercom. The operating principle of the terrain-matching technique, patented in 1958, makes use of the simple fact that the altitude of the ground above sea level varies from place to place. If one were to make a map of a rectangular area 2 kilometers wide and 10 kilometers long, divide the map into squares perhaps 100 meters on a side, and record for each square the average elevation of the ground within it, one would obtain a digital map consisting of 2,000 numbers, each number corresponding to the elevation of a small region of known position on the ground (see Figure 18 on page 156). In a Tercom system, a set of such maps, which can have squares with smaller sides if required, is stored in the memory of the computer aboard the missile.

The missile is also provided with a down-looking radar altimeter capable of distinguishing objects smaller than the map squares from a height of several kilometers. As the

---

* Strategic weapons are used against targets in the interior of an opponent's country. Tactical, or theater, weapons, on the other hand, are used in battle.

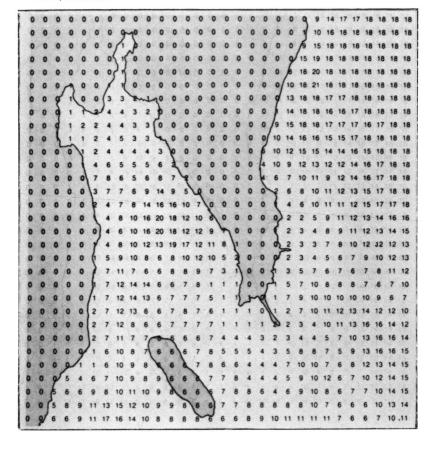

FIGURE 18. Tercom map of the area around Rockport, Maine, is an example of how the elevation of the terrain can be given by a matrix of numbers.

missile approaches the region for which the computer memory has a map, the altimeter starts providing a stream of ground-elevation data. The computer, by comparing these data with the elevation data it has in its memory, determines the actual position of the missile at that moment with an accuracy comparable to the size of the map cell. It then instructs the autopilot to take any corrective steps necessary to return the missile to its intended trajectory. As many as twenty such maps can be stored in the computer to enable a modern missile to update its locational information and correct its trajectory frequently during its overland flight. If the missile is expected to fly initially over water, where it is not possible to use the Tercom to update the locational information, the first land map is made very wide (perhaps as wide as 10 kilometers), so as not to miss the intended landfall.

The accuracy with which the missile can be guided to its target is supposed to be about equal to the size of a map square; in practice it is probably about half that good. Since map squares can be made quite small, say 10 meters on a side, it is possible in principle for the missile to have comparable accuracy. A number of factors contribute to the degradation of this level of accuracy, however, and so it is expected that the strategic cruise missile now being deployed will have an operational accuracy of some 100 meters. The biggest errors are expected to come from human inaccuracies in mapping, from the injudicious choice of terrain to map, and from the absence of suitable terrain for terrain-matching guidance near some targets.

Advances in the technology of small jet engines have also been important in the development of strategic cruise missiles, and of tactical missiles as well. Small turbofan engines weighing less than 130 pounds and yet capable of generating as much as 600 pounds of thrust are now available. Engines of this type consume less fuel than turbojets of equivalent size; they are more complex systems, however, and hence they cost much more. Accordingly, the efficient turbofan engines are considered suitable for cruise missiles with a range of more than 500 kilometers carrying expensive payloads such as nuclear warheads. The cheaper turbojets are cost-effective for cruise missiles with a range of less than 500 kilometers carrying conventional high-explosive warheads.

The modern strategic cruise missile is 53 centimeters in diameter and 6.24 meters long and has a volume of 1.37 cubic meters. Without the protective capsule in which it is carried and launched, the missile weighs about 1.5 tons.

The radar altimeter of the terrain-matching system enables the missile to fly as low as 20 meters over water, 50 meters over moderately hilly terrain, and 100 meters over mountains. (This capability makes the missile difficult to detect with ground-based radar.) At sea level it has a cruising speed of about seven-tenths the speed of sound.* The exact range of a cruise missile depends on a number of factors, but the aerodynamic properties of the missile indicate that the strategic cruise missile is capable of a range of 2,000 kilometers at low altitude and perhaps 50% more if the first 1,500 kilometers are flown at higher altitude and the rest at treetop level.

The cruise missiles now being deployed are the first models of an entirely new type of weapon system. One can expect improved versions and new generations of these weapons. Engines that can burn fuels richer in energy content, position-updating systems more sophisticated than Tercom, improved nuclear warheads, target-recognition devices—all are being actively researched and developed in the United States. Other countries are also attempting to develop a similar weapon system. France has announced the beginning of a program to do so; the Soviet Union no doubt is trying hard to catch up with the United States, as it has done successfully in the past. In the future, cruise missiles of all types will be in the possession of several countries.

Strategic cruise missiles that deliver nuclear warheads can be carried and launched toward their targets either by aircraft or by ships. Submarines can fire them from their torpedo tubes while submerged, and surface ships can serve as launching platforms. Airplanes can launch them while in flight before they actually reach enemy territory. This way the bomber would not have to penetrate the air defenses of the enemy and its vulnerability would be minimized. For that reason it is argued that we do not need bombers at all. Commercial-type aircraft like the Boeing 747 or the McDonnel Douglas DC-10 can be used as cruise-

---

* The speed of sound is 1,000 kilometers per hour. An often used unit of speed for airplanes is the Mach. One Mach is equal to the speed of sound. So when we say that a plane flies at Mach 2, we mean that it is flying at twice the speed of sound.

missile carriers. Each of them could carry as many as sixty cruise missiles and launch them toward targets in the Soviet Union while flying 500 kilometers or more from Soviet territory. The cruise missiles could then penetrate into the Soviet Union and, guided by their inertial and Tercom systems, find their ways to the preassigned targets. At the present time, the first operational nuclear-tipped long-range cruise missiles are being deployed on intercontinental bombers. There are plans to deploy them on land and on surface ships and attack submarines, but such deployment is still in the future.

While bombers and cruise missiles are reliable weapon delivery systems, capable of accommodating extensive refinements, the rationale behind their existence may sensibly be called into question. With land-based ballistic missiles each carrying up to ten individual nuclear weapons that reach their targets in thirty minutes, and submarine-launched ballistic missiles carrying numerous nuclear weapons that reach their targets in anywhere from six to twenty minutes, why do we need bombers or cruise missiles that take many hours and can be shot down on the way there? The answer is a combination of circumstance, expediency, and strategic doctrine.

To begin with, intercontinental bombers predated ballistic missiles by almost ten years. Since the first deployment of ballistic missiles, the Air Force has resisted any effort to eliminate the strategic bomber force; even without such resistance it is very difficult to eliminate a whole segment of the armed forces once it is well established. The United States, since the inception of ballistic missiles, has not shown great interest in modernizing its bomber force by designing a new, faster, better-protected plane. The B-52s have been altered, improved, and upgraded all the time; the latest model, the B-52H, is an entirely different and more capable weapon than the first models, the B-52A and B-52B. Even the B-52H has undergone continuous modernization and improvement. But the Air Force had never succeeded, until recently, in starting the production of a new bomber. Only recently did the Reagan Administration finally approve the production of the B-1; however, it is so expensive (the price tag varies between $200 million and

$300 million per plane) that there is some question as to how many the United States can afford.

Beyond reasons of tradition, however, there is a pragmatic basis for wanting to have a strategic bomber force. The pre-launch and post-launch vulnerability of bombers is different from that of ballistic missiles. Bombers can be launched, ordered to fly in holding patterns, and eventually recalled. But once a ballistic missile is launched it cannot be recalled. If you change your mind about attacking your enemy, you can only destroy a missile during the first few minutes of its flight, and only if provisions have been made for such an eventuality. Bombers therefore offer a measure of stability in a crisis situation, and provide operational flexibility as well. You can either preassign several alternative targets to them, or you can, at least in principle, communicate with them while they are far away from their bases and change their target lists. In principle, a command post on the ground can always communicate with a bomber in the air, but in practice, radio communications that depend on ground transmitting stations, especially over the polar regions, may become tenuous. In time of war these stations may be destroyed altogether. Communications that depend on satellites to relay messages to the bomber are much more secure, even though they may be affected by EMP. When such a system is installed in the near future, the U.S. command will have rather good control of bombers flying anywhere.

Finally, bombers are reusable. This option will probably not prove very helpful in the case of nuclear war, but if the United States gets involved in a nonnuclear conflict and wants to use conventional bombs against an opponent, bombers that can be sent to bomb repeatedly are quite useful.

The rationale behind the development of cruise missiles is somewhat different. Cruise missiles are an example of what are often called "sweet technologies": technological developments, in this case microelectronics, small turbofan engines, and miniature nuclear warheads, that make a new weapon possible. The cruise missile is a weapon that is not necessarily crucial to our ability to fight a nuclear war, but since the weapon promises to be relatively cheap, very accurate, and very difficult to detect and shoot down, there is great temptation to develop it and deploy it and then find ways to use it—that is, to invent missions for it. The cruise missile was a "sweet technology" that military strategists couldn't resist.

If properly exploited, cruise missile technology could indeed be very cost-effective and advantageous. Cruise missiles make bombers much less vulnerable to air defenses, and they can be launched from small aircraft as well as from ground launchers, complicating immensely the opponent's problems in trying to defend against them. A submarine, however, is not particularly suitable for launching a cruise missile. The reason is that it takes a half hour to align the gyroscopes of the inertial guidance system when a long-range cruise missile is loaded into a torpedo tube. If the submarine launches two or at most four such cruise missiles and then has to wait at least half an hour to launch some more, an alert enemy can locate the submarine from the noise of those first launches, and sink it. But it doesn't make sense to expose to attack a $500 million submarine with its highly trained crew just to launch two or four long-range cruise missiles.

Surface ships used as launch platforms for these new strategic weapons have the same disadvantage. An adversary can detect a ship off its coast and destroy it quickly with a ballistic missile carrying a nuclear weapon. Except in the case of a conventional war against an opponent with no countership capabilities a military planner will not expose a precious asset such as a large combat ship to enemy attack by placing it near the enemy coast, just for launching cruise missiles from it. So strategic cruise missiles that can carry nuclear weapons make sense only if they are carried partway to their targets by airplanes, or if they are used as intermediate-range nuclear weapons from the ground.

A very important property of strategic nuclear weapons is their pre-launch survivability. A weapon that can be preempted by a surprise enemy attack and destroyed before it is launched toward its target is undesirable. Not only won't its owner have it when he needs it, it also tempts the opponent to strike first, and by surprise, since he knows that if he does so he has a good chance of destroying the weapons on the other side. A dangerous instability would be created during an international crisis if one country with vulnerable weapons feared that the other might strike first. Such a "use them or lose them" situation puts a premium on attacking first and increases the probability of nuclear war. Such an instability can be diminished by having more than one type of strategic weapon, each with a different pre-launch vulnerability. For example, even if the U.S. bomber force were vulnerable to a sudden Soviet attack, that would not lead to a crisis instability because the United States would still have thousands of nuclear weapons in its ballistic missiles with which it could retaliate and destroy the Soviet Union. So in this case it wouldn't pay for the Soviets to attack, even if the bombers and the cruise missiles are vulnerable. But are they really?

Bombers are quite vulnerable to the effects of a nuclear detonation. A 1-psi overpressure will damage an unprotected aircraft, usually by breaking off its vertical tail fin, which is not built to take lateral forces. A 1-megaton weapon will generate 1 psi overpressure 20 kilometers away. A bomber will be destroyed by such a weapon exploded over an air base, whether it is on the ground or in the air, as long as it has not escaped beyond a distance of 20 kilometers from the airfield. Three things can be done to protect bombers on the ground from a surprise attack: (1) make them sturdier, able to withstand higher overpressures (for example, the danger radius if the bomber could withstand 2 psi would be reduced from 20 to 10 kilometers); (2) provide them with the capability of quick takeoff and escape; (3) keep them on alert at the ends of runways and make sure that they have enough warning time to take off before the enemy missiles arrive.

How much warning time can possibly be available? A land-based ICBM launched from the Soviet Union takes about thirty minutes to get to the United States. If a U.S. satellite detects the launch immediately and transmits the message at once to the bomber bases, the aircraft will have very nearly the full thirty minutes to escape, if special arrangements have been made. That is enough warning. But a missile launched from a submarine in the middle of the Atlantic takes only six to ten minutes to get to most bomber bases in the United States, and that is not enough time to allow all the bombers to escape. In times of international crisis, a fraction of the bombers can be kept airborne at all times, but an enormous amount of fuel is consumed, a dreadful expense at present prices. The next best thing is to keep the planes on the ground, fully armed and fueled, and with the crews inside them. During normal (non-crisis) times the crews are on alert, living in motel-like facilities very near the aircraft and always ready to board them and take off within ten to fifteen minutes.

The probability that the bombers will be surprised on the ground by submarine-launched ballistic missiles (SLBMs) is actually quite small. Submarine missiles do not have the accuracy to attack silo-based ballistic missiles. These must be attacked by the more accurate land-based ballistic missiles of the opponent. But if an enemy tries to destroy U.S. bombers with submarine missiles that take ten minutes to reach their targets, and at the same time eliminate U.S. ICBMs by launching his land-based ballistic missiles that take thirty minutes, the ICBMs will have twenty minutes of warning time, after the arrival of the SLBMs, and can be launched (at least in principle). If the enemy times his attack so that his ICBMs and his submarine-launched missiles arrive at the same time on the United States, he has to launch his ICBMs twenty minutes before his SLBMs. Such an attack will be detected immediately and give enough time to the bombers to escape.

The pre-launch survivability of cruise missiles carried by bombers or other aircraft is much the same as for bombers in general. Those launched from the ground, say from Western European countries toward the Soviet Union, would have equally high survivability if they could be made mobile and therefore very difficult to find and target. On the other hand, during peacetime, the trucks that carry these missiles won't be routinely traveling the highways of Europe. They will be parked in a military base. Therefore, a total surprise attack could indeed destroy them. But few if any military people believe that such an attack can ever come "out of the blue" without being preceded by days or even weeks of deepening political crisis. Thus it is fairly certain that given the "strategic" warning of a serious crisis, cruise missiles carried either by aircraft or by trucks, as well as most bombers, can escape a hypothetical surprise attack.

Assuming that the U.S. bomber force, carrying short-range air-to-ground missiles and bombs, is not seriously threatened by a surprise attack, what can we expect of its ability to penetrate Soviet air defenses and deliver its nuclear weapons to their targets? Soviet antiaircraft defenses are the best in the world. They consist of thousands of surface-to-air missiles controlled and guided to their targets by series of radars (see Appendix I) that can detect and track airplanes and help the missile find its target. In addition, they have thousands of fighter aircraft that can find the bombers and shoot them down either with air-to-air missiles or with cannon fire. The Russians spend $10 billion or more every year for this system, which, however, turns out to be of dubious value for a number of reasons. First of all, the entire system was developed and geared to intercept high-flying aircraft, while the U.S. penetrating bombers have the capability and use the tactics of flying very low over enemy territory. Second, even when flying high—as in the instance of B-52s bombing Hanoi and Haiphong in North Vietnam, which were defended by densely deployed, modern Soviet antiaircraft systems—U.S. bombers suffered at most 5% losses in each raid. In an ordinary conventional war when bombers are expected to be used again and again, such an attrition rate would be unacceptably high. But in a nuclear war when the bombers have to penetrate only once, 5% losses are trivial and can be easily compensated for by adding a few more bombers to the attacking force. Furthermore, Soviet air defenses could be easily crippled by destroying the main radar systems and command posts (which are all in fixed locations and are quite "soft") with a few submarine-launched ballistic missiles. After that, bombers could fly in with no difficulty, since there would be no radar to guide fighter aircraft and the ground-to-air missiles. As long as the submarines are invulnerable—and as we'll see in another chapter they will remain so into the indefinite future—bombers will be able to reach their targets with little if any attrition.

U.S. bombers have an alternative way of defeating the

Soviet air defenses: electronic countermeasures (ECM). Electronic circuits mounted on the bomber can drown radar signals in electronic noise, can create false targets for the radars, or can interfere with the operations of the radar in other ways that confuse the guidance of ground-to-air and air-to-air missiles. Depending on their technological sophistication and intelligence-gathering capability the enemy can, of course, design electronic counter-counter-measures that nullify some of the protection ECMs afford the bombers. This game of countermeasures and counter-countermeasures depends mainly on being able to ferret out the performance characteristics of the other side's radar systems *before* the actual confrontation. The United States, for example, has special electronic spy satellites and monitoring stations around the Soviet Union that determine the characteristics of Soviet radar whenever it is turned on. Besides these vulnerabilities, local air defenses that protect specific installations usually have short ranges. They can be defeated by air-to-surface missiles fired by the bomber from a distance greater than the range of the antiaircraft defense.

We can conclude then that low-flying U.S. bombers such as the B-52 and FB-111 would be relatively successful in penetrating Soviet air defenses. Even if the Soviets develop the ability to defend against low-flying aircraft, a few submarine-launched nuclear weapons would open broad gaps in the radar network of the Soviet defense system. What is true for the large bombers is, of course, true for small cruise missiles that are a thousand times harder to detect by radar than a B-52. Cruise missiles do not have enough electrical power or even space to carry ECM systems, but since they are very difficult to detect they do not need such protection.

New technological developments, collectively referred to as "stealth technology," will make the next generation of cruise missiles (and bombers) even more difficult to detect by radar. The only generally applicable countermeasure against a cruise missile would be to jam the radar altimeter which permits it to navigate and fly so close to the ground. In addition, to protect small hardened targets against a cruise missile, local antiaircraft defenses can be used, since cruise missiles must fly at relatively low speed. Such anti-cruise-missile defenses, however, are not suitable for protecting large vulnerable targets such as cities, large radar systems, industrial complexes, and refineries. Thus cruise missiles are even more effective than bombers for penetrating Soviet air defenses. At any rate these defenses could be weakened by attacking their radars with submarine-launched ballistic missiles before the arrival of the bombers or cruise missiles.

8

ANTIBALLISTIC
MISSILE SYSTEMS

O FTEN IN PHYSICS one learns more by understanding why something does not work than by discovering why or how something works. The basic working principle of an antiballistic missile (ABM) system, the reasons why it doesn't work, and the fierce technical debate that accompanied the decision to deploy it in this country are instructive, fascinating, and full of ironic paradoxes.

The mission of an ABM system is to defend a country, an area, or a specific target or group of targets against nuclear-armed reentry vehicles from enemy ballistic missiles. Since these reentry vehicles measure about a meter long and travel at speeds of several miles a second as they approach their target at the end of their ballistic trajectory, an ABM system has often been described as "a weapon designed to hit a bullet with a bullet." Actually, the task of an ABM is even harder than that. Exactly how hard depends both on the specific mission and on the number and sophistication of the enemy reentry vehicles. But in general an ABM system protecting a city, for example, would have to detect and trace potentially many hundreds of reentry vehicles after they have been released from the ballistic missiles that carried them into space. It would have to predict the trajectory of each of these reentry vehicles, decide whether these trajectories end at targets that need protection, launch antimissile missiles, and guide them toward the attacking reentry vehicles. Then, after these missiles have exploded, the system must observe each reentry vehicle that has been attacked and see whether it has been damaged or de-

167

stroyed. If not, it must guide additional fast antimissile missiles against each intact vehicle. All this would have to be accomplished in less than ten minutes in an environment in which radar (the eyes of the ABM system) would be blinded by the effects of nuclear detonations (see Chapter 3) and while the reentry vehicles would be concealed among thousands of decoys which, at least to radar, would look like reentry vehicles.

To do all this an ABM system must have the following components:

1. An early warning system that signals the launch of enemy ballistic missiles either from silos or from submarines.

2. Long-range, long-wavelength radar that can spot the reentry vehicles as they rise above the horizon (while they are still about 4,000 kilometers or ten minutes away).

3. Short-wavelength, short-range radar that can determine the position of each attacking reentry vehicle with precision and guide a missile with a nuclear warhead to intercept it (conventional explosives would have too small a kill radius against reentry vehicles for this purpose; see Chapter 6).

4. Many long-range (about 300 kilometers) and very fast short-range (about 50 kilometers) antimissile missiles with which to attack the incoming reentry vehicles.

5. Very large, very complex electronic computers with extremely sophisticated programs that coordinate and conduct the actual operations.

All this sounds complicated and hardly feasible, and indeed so far it has proved to be. During several tests, an antiballistic missile launched and guided against a single reentry vehicle has indeed passed close enough to destroy it with a nuclear detonation while still 100 kilometers above the earth. The trouble is, such tests have very little in common with the real situation in which an ABM system would be operating during an actual attack. Although the precise circumstances would certainly vary with the severity and sophistication of the attack, and with the kind of targets the ABM system is defending, it is possible to group the tasks of an ABM system into three broad categories:

1. The ABM system is supposed to defend the urban and

industrial centers of the United States against an all-out attack (thousands of reentry vehicles) from an enemy with many nuclear weapons and sophisticated technology, such as the Soviet Union.

2. The ABM system is responsible for defending the urban and industrial centers of the United States against only a light nuclear attack (a few tens of reentry vehicles) from an opponent of limited technical capabilities.

3. The ABM system is given the task of defending U.S. ICBMs in their hardened silos against a Soviet countersilo attack (of more than 2,000 reentry vehicles).

The number of reentry vehicles the ABM system has to counter depends on whether the attack is heavy (situations 1 and 3) or light (situation 2). The number of reentry vehicles it can afford to allow to "leak through" its defenses depends on the type of target. While in situation 3 the system can allow a fair number of reentry vehicles to reach their targets, or it can defend only a fraction of all the possible targets and still accomplish its mission, any leakage in the defense of cities is unacceptable because even a single nuclear weapon can devastate an entire city.

Thus the fundamental problem of an ABM system intended for the defense of cities is that if it does not work perfectly it is of no use at all. Suppose, for example, that an ABM system is constructed to defend the one hundred most populous cities in the United States, and it is 90% effective, that is, it misses only one of every ten warheads aimed against these cities. Without the ABM, an opponent would have to use a hundred weapons to destroy them. With the ABM, he could achieve similar destruction by increasing the number of his weapons to 1,000, and targeting ten on each city. The hypothetical ABM could destroy nine out of these ten, but the tenth could destroy the city all the same. The protection an ABM system affords to a city is not proportional to its efficacy; the slightest departure from perfection provides the occasion for complete destruction. Only if the enemy did not have many warheads and could not make many more would an ABM system be able to destroy a considerable fraction of the enemy's reentry vehicles and limit the damage such an enemy could inflict.

If an ABM is used to protect missiles in silos, it has a

better chance of being effective. Unlike a city, a silo is a small, hard target which is not nearly as valuable as a city. If, for example, a silo protected by an ABM contains a missile that carries three warheads, it does not pay for the enemy to spend more than three of his warheads to try to destroy it unless he is certain that the extra expenditure would save his cities from annihilation. If the ABM that protects it is 90% effective and capable of multiple kills, an enemy would probably be dissuaded from attacking the silo because, even if he used many warheads against it, he would still not be sure of destroying the missile inside. So the usefulness of an ABM system depends not only on its effectiveness, but also on the type of target it is defending and on the size of the enemy's nuclear arsenal.

The operating principle of an ABM is based on two physical phenomena. First, the trajectory of a reentry vehicle after it is released by the missile is entirely predetermined and therefore, if one can observe an early portion of it, the rest of the trajectory can be calculated. In this way the position of the reentry vehicle in the latter part of its journey can be predicted very accurately. Second, a nuclear detonation in outer space can destroy a reentry vehicle at a distance of more than 2 kilometers, and a nuclear detonation inside the atmosphere can damage or deflect a reentry vehicle from a distance of a few hundred meters. In space, what damages the reentry vehicle is the burst of x-rays that come from the detonation of a fission-fusion-fission weapon, while the "kill mechanism" for endoatmospheric interception is the intense flux of energetic neutrons generated by a fission-fusion weapon (a neutron bomb).

Even though the tactics of engagement might vary and the performance requirements would be different in each of the three major situations described above, the basic operations of an ABM system would remain the same. In order to examine these operations, let us consider again an attack against the hundred most populous urban centers of the United States involving as many as ten warheads per city. The ABM system would then have to deal with up to 1,000 reentry vehicles. The *detection* of these reentry vehicles will take place as long as ten minutes before they reach their targets. But if the launches are timed so that all of the reentry vehicles arrive simultaneously, the range of the ABM system is such that it will have only a few hundred seconds to shoot down those hundreds of reentry vehicles.

In order to protect the entire country from such an attack, this hypothetical ABM system must be spread out over the North American continent. The long-range radars, known as PAR (perimeter acquisition radars), will be strung out along the northern border of the United States in order to detect reentry vehicles coming over the North Pole from the Soviet Union. Only half a dozen of these huge devices are needed, and since their beams are steered electronically (see Appendix J), they have fixed flat faces pointed northward. Each of these radars must follow simultaneously about 200 reentry vehicles and provide continuous information about their locations to a computer, which calculates their trajectories and plans where and by what antimissile missile they will be attacked.

An electronically steerable radar can, indeed, if properly designed, follow 200 targets simultaneously. Detecting and tracking 1,000 objects following ballistic trajectories in space does not pose any serious technical problems. Furthermore, such ABM radar equipment would have considerable reliability. Radar beams are generated by a number of identical but independent elements. Even if a few elements fail, the radar will continue functioning very well. Only a large-scale failure of the elements of a "phased-array" radar (see Appendix J, which discusses phased-array hydrophones) will cause the quality of the beam to deteriorate to a level that renders it inoperative. Thus radar systems themselves can be considered to be about 95% reliable.

Whether the computer can handle the job of plotting 1,000 trajectories, predicting where each is going to end, and assigning antimissile missiles to intercept them while still outside the atmosphere is another reasonable question. Given a very large computer capable of 100 million calculations per second, it would be possible to perform both the tracking calculations and all the other operations needed by the ABM system, provided the computer has been appropriately programmed.

A frequently used method of establishing the reliability of a computer is to consider not *whether* it will fail but how long it will operate between failures. The "mean time between failures" (MTBF) for an ABM computer with redundant components and self-monitoring capabilities could be as long as eight days. If, on the average, it takes one day to fix whatever goes wrong with the computer each time it malfunctions, it can be said to be operational seven-eighths of the time, or to be 87% reliable.

It is the computer program (or "software") that presents by far the greatest difficulty in the computer operation. Programs would have to be so long and so extremely complex that there has always been doubt whether they would perform correctly in every one of the millions of different combinations of circumstances in which the computer must make a decision. Anyone who has ever attempted to program a computer to perform a specific set of operations or a given calculation knows that a program almost never works on the first try, and usually it takes repeated trial and error before all the errors (or "bugs") have been eliminated from a program. The difficulty with programming the operations of an ABM system is that the program could never be tested under realistic circumstances. It would, in effect, have to work flawlessly the first time it was called on to perform, without the benefit of previous "debugging." Even the most enthusiastic and confident programmer would not claim that such a performance is likely. A fraction of the computer's capacity could be devoted to checking itself for errors, but even that cannot eliminate the possibility of malfunction or, even worse (but quite common), the complete collapse of the computational process, in which the computer simply stops calculating, or "crashes." So even though technology can provide a computer fast enough and powerful enough to control the operations of an ABM system, it is by no means certain that a program adequate for the task can be written and made to operate flawlessly under all anticipated and unanticipated circumstances that may arise during an enemy ballistic missile attack.

Existing examples of other less complex systems functioning in much less demanding environments lead to very pessimistic expectations about an ABM system that is similarly designed and engineered. Complex interceptor aircraft like the F-14 or F-15 are in working order about 50% of the time. The early air defense system of the United States, code-named SAGE, never quite worked properly. The ballistic missile early warning system did not function reliably for quite a while, and even now, after many years of operating experience and improvement, it still generates numerous false alarms of incoming Soviet missiles. Numerous other large-scale systems have failed to perform as expected when first installed. It is unreasonable, then, to expect that an ABM system, by far the most complex electromechanical system ever built, should function as expected the first, and presumably the only, time that it is called upon to perform.

Let us assume for the sake of our examination of an ABM system that the PAR radars and the computer function as desired. The next major operation of the ABM defense would be to launch antimissile missiles and guide them to intercept the reentry vehicles. The designers of the ABM system that the United States decided to deploy in the late 1960s thought that the task of interception could be made easier if they provided for a two-tier defense, one outside the atmosphere and one inside. They did that both because this allows more time to attack the incoming reentry vehicles and because they realized that the atmosphere would help the system separate the real reentry vehicles from possible decoys that an enemy might have used. The reason is that in space, where there is no atmospheric friction, a feather and a bullet released at the same point with the same speed and in the same direction would continue to travel together indefinitely, but once they encountered the slightest resistance to their motion from the presence of air, the bullet would go on speeding almost unaffected, while the feather would be slowed down. The atmosphere acts as a filter that separates heavy objects from light ones that enter it with the same speed. That physical fact can be of great value to an ABM system that is designed to defeat a missile attack from a determined and sophisticated opponent.

Knowing that the computer and the radars of an ABM system can be saturated by the presence of a very large number of objects coming toward them in outer space, such an opponent might choose to load his ballistic missiles not only with reentry vehicles carrying nuclear warheads but also with very light decoys—balloons, for example, that have a thin, metallic coating on the outside that reflects radar waves, or little pieces of wire, or other decoys. In addition, he could make provisions to blow up the last stage of the missile that lofted the reentry vehicles and decoys into their trajectory, and have its fragments travel with the reentry vehicles and decoys toward their targets. As long as all these traveled in space, they would all look alike to the PAR radars and the computer would have to calculate the trajectory of each one of them and assign antiballistic missiles to intercept them. In this way the enemy could possibly overload the capacity of the radar or the computer and certainly exhaust the supply of antimissile missiles. So the use of decoys is a very attractive, cheap way to confuse, saturate, and exhaust an ABM system.

However, as soon as the group of reentry vehicles and decoys and accompanying pieces of junk enter the atmosphere, the decoys and all other "penetration aids" would slow down and quickly burn up as they were heated by the friction with the air, while the actual reentry vehicles would continue toward their targets. At that point the ABM system could recognize the real reentry vehicles and concentrate its attack against these. The trouble is that by now the attacking reentry vehicles would be only thirty to sixty seconds away from their targets, so this "terminal" or second line of defense of the ABM system must be able to respond in less than thirty seconds.

The two-tier defense developed for the U.S. ABM system envisioned two kinds of missiles, the Spartan and the Sprint, both guided to their targets by short-range but very precise radars located near the launchers of these missiles and therefore known as "missile site radars" (MSRs). The Spartan is a large missile about 20 meters long with three solid-fuel stages that can carry a rather large (about 1-megaton) fission-fusion-fission warhead several hundred kilometers into outer space. The lethal range for x-rays produced by a Spartan warhead detonating above the atmosphere is a few kilometers, and MSR radars can be made precise enough to place a Spartan about a kilometer from its target object. The Sprint is a smaller, two-stage, solid-fuel missile. Capable of accelerating very fast, it can reach its maximum range of 35 kilometers in a few seconds. It carries a smaller warhead (some tens of kilotons) that produces a very intense burst of neutrons. An MSR radar can guide a Sprint to within a few hundred meters of its target, close enough for the neutrons from, say, a 10-kiloton explosion to destroy a warhead of the types commonly used by the Soviet Union or the United States. The missiles used in the ABM systems are, however, said to be only 50% to 75% reliable.

The trouble is that there can be thousands of objects streaking toward the United States in outer space which to the PAR and MSR radars look like valid targets, while only a fraction of them are real reentry vehicles. The problem becomes one of economics if we assume that the ABM radar and computer are not overwhelmed. A Spartan missile is very expensive, and plans called for no more than fifty of them in each of ten or twelve sites in the United States. Even if they worked perfectly and each one reliably destroyed one reentry vehicle, there would be many hundred intact reentry vehicles remaining from the 1,000 that we hypothesized, continuing on their way toward their targets. In a perfectly functioning ABM system, these weapons must now be destroyed by Sprints during the last thirty seconds of travel to their targets. We can calculate how good the MSRs must be and how fast the computer must calculate trajectories, launch Sprints, and guide them to each of the several hundred remaining reentry vehicles. Suppose that together with the 1,000 original reentry vehicles there were 3,000 decoys, and the Spartans took out 500 of them indiscriminately, leaving 3,500 objects of which 875 are real reentry vehicles. As soon as these 3,500 objects entered the atmosphere, the real reentry vehicles would become apparent. The terminal ABM defense must now destroy 875 targets in thirty seconds at most (and probably in a third of that time).

Since there are supposed to be about thirty-five MSR radars, each would have to track about twenty-five reentry vehicles, giving each radar about one second of the thirty remaining to determine the trajectory of each reentry vehicle and guide one or more Sprints against it. This is quite sufficient, since on the average, the computer must spend only five hundredths of a second per reentry vehicle. Now, an MSR radar* can search a sixth of the sky above it each second. Since most of the reentry vehicles viewed by each MSR radar would be coming from more or less the same direction and would occupy roughly the same small portion of the sky as seen from an MSR, it is not unreasonable to expect that, if unimpeded, the MSR could indeed track them all long enough and fast enough to provide the computer with the needed detailed information about their trajectories. But the view of the MSRs, and, as a matter of fact, the PARs, would not be unimpeded; indeed, quite the opposite would be the case.

As mentioned in Chapter 3, a nuclear weapon detonated above the atmosphere produces copious amounts of electrons by one physical process or another. Their motion generates the electromagnetic pulse and also ionizes the top of the atmosphere. For waves of frequencies commonly used in long-range radars such as PAR, a density of 10^9 electrons per square centimeter will totally reflect radar waves, and densities even a hundred times less will weaken radar waves to the point that they cannot detect small objects like reentry vehicles or decoys.

A single large nuclear explosion is enough to blind the long-range radar over an area of 10,000 square miles. Such an explosion would come from an enemy missile, a precursor of the main wave of reentry vehicles, that is fused to detonate high above the atmosphere, out of the reach of Spartan missiles, for the express purpose of blinding the ABM radars. But radar blinding would also come from the detonations of the first Spartans that reached their targets. An ABM system that uses nuclear weapons to intercept incoming reentry vehicles would therefore be self-blinding. Blinding from a single explosion is not long-lasting—a few minutes in the case of the PAR, and a few tens of seconds in the case of the MSR, which uses shorter wave-

* An MSR radar has a 300-kilometer range with a resolution of 10 kilometers and a cross-range accuracy of 300 meters.

lengths. But radar blinding is nevertheless a persistent problem, since consecutive detonations of Spartans combined with the fireballs from Sprint explosions would produce continuous blinding. And although a fireball blinds radar over only a small patch of the sky, Sprint detonations will be numerous, and therefore cover a considerable area. Furthermore, even when a fireball cools down and once again permits radar waves to pass, it distorts and bends them. The radar's view would be much like that of a human eye looking at the world through a glass jar full of swirling water. The eye can see and recognize objects, but their apparent position is distorted and changes continuously as the water moves in the jar.

The self-blinding of the radars is the most intrinsically serious but by no means the only flaw of an ABM system of the type described. The radars, in addition, are themselves vulnerable to a nuclear attack. An opponent might well choose only the radars as the first targets. By concentrating numerous reentry vehicles on each of the fifty or so radars of a countrywide system, he could exhaust their local terminal defenses and finally destroy them. After that, the enemy could attack the targets of his choice at will.

Finally, a sophisticated opponent determined to maintain his ability to attack U.S. cities could do so by equipping his missiles with multiple reentry vehicles capable of maneuvering after they enter the atmosphere, departing from their ballistic trajectory in ways that are unpredictable to the defending ABM. Evasive* reentry vehicle technology is at hand in the United States, and is probably accessible to the Soviet Union. Even if everything else that is wrong with the ABM system could somehow be miraculously eliminated, the system would still be helpless in the face of reentry vehicles that did not follow ballistic trajectories and whose positions during reentry could not be accurately predicted.

The cumulative reliability of each of an ABM system's components—radar, computer, and missiles—is only about 40% to 60%. Such odds, together with all the difficulties

---

* An evading reentry vehicle is preprogrammed to perform maneuvers to confuse the ABM radars but cannot maneuver to hit a target.

arising from the adverse environment—self-blinding, vulnerability to enemy attack on its radars, saturation of its sensors and computer, exhaustion of its antimissile missiles, and the possibility of unpredictable reentry-vehicle trajectories—make it amply obvious that even under ideal performance conditions, an ABM system could not credibly defend the urban centers of the country, either against a heavy attack or even a light one. The weight of these arguments against the practicality of an antimissile system, further supported by the formidable obstacle of untested computer programs, convinced the U.S. and the Soviet governments that an ABM system to protect their cities would be unworkable. So in 1972 they signed a treaty banning further development and deployment of an ABM system.

While cities can never be adequately protected, an ABM system defending silo-based ballistic missiles is another matter. In the case of city defense, even if one in a hundred enemy warheads escaped the ABM, the city would be destroyed, which means the ABM would have failed utterly in its mission. If, on the other hand, the ABM system is deployed to defend a silo and allows only one of even a few enemy warheads aimed against it to escape, the chance is great that the small, hard target would survive, necessitating many more warheads for another opportunity to destroy the silo. The problem of exhaustion of the supply of antimissile missiles of an ABM system could be at least partly solved by "preferential defense," that is, choosing to defend not all of the silos, but only, say, 20% of them. If there are a 1,000 silos altogether, then there would be five times as many interceptor antimissile missiles available to defend just these 200, and the enemy would have to expend a much larger number of his warheads in order to destroy them. Such a defense would be even more effective if the enemy did not know beforehand which 200 of the 1,000 silos were defended by the ABM. In principle, at least, the defense of silos with an ABM system does not appear to be a futile enterprise.

But ABM systems for silo defense are plagued by many of the same problems discussed in connection with city defense. Decoys are still an effective countermeasure and the radar systems are still vulnerable to direct attack. The most serious obstacle, for this or any other viable ABM system, is the self-blinding effect of its own weapons. To counter this problem, some non-Pentagon scientists have proposed protecting silos with an ABM system that simply substitutes barrels of nails for nuclear-armed Sprints—a seemingly crude idea that would nevertheless be quite effective. The system would employ two small upward-looking radars 5 miles apart from each other installed 10 miles north of a silo. These would detect and determine the trajectory of a reentry vehicle as it came in at high speed toward the silo. A small computer would rapidly and easily calculate the subsequent trajectory of the reentry vehicle and would launch a barrel-like object full of small steel rods which could be easily guided into the path of the reentry vehicle. The barrel would release the steel rods in a conical pattern in front of the incoming reentry vehicle; a high-speed collision with one or more of the rods would shatter the warhead before it reached the silo. This kind of defense is possible because, in order to destroy the silo, the reentry vehicle must detonate very close by. If the reentry vehicle was intercepted by the steel rods even only 1,000 meters away from the silo, it would be destroyed before it exploded.

The weakness of this otherwise sensible and effective system is its radars. These small, upward-looking radars cannot be destroyed as easily as the MSRs of the ABM system described earlier, but they can be destroyed all the same, by exploding one warhead over them. It has been proposed that a system of small, inexpensive, upward-looking radars *that can be rapidly replaced* if destroyed by an enemy be installed to guard the silo. Thus, if a pair of radars is damaged by the explosion of a warhead above them, a second set could "pop up" into place to maintain surveillance. And if a second warhead were exploded, a third set of radars would replace the no-longer-functional second pair. And so on. So long as the radars are cheaper than warheads, the system is cost-effective. Although it could ultimately be overwhelmed by aiming numerous reentry vehicles against each single silo, it would certainly make the enemy's attack more expensive—perhaps prohibitively so.

Even more recently, another ABM system was proposed by military engineers. Mindful of the blinding effect the large Spartan warheads have on the radars of the older ABM system, they are proposing a nonnuclear method to destroy reentry vehicles while they travel in the void of space. According to this proposal, an early warning system, presumably a satellite, would alert the system that a large-scale attack is underway. Immediately, special sensors would be launched by rocket into space and remain there for about twenty minutes in a ballistic orbit. Each such sensor would consist of a sensitive infrared telescope, a data-processing and information-storing computer, and communications equipment that would transmit information to a command center on earth. The telescope would scan the horizon toward the anticipated enemy missiles and detect the reentry vehicles, the last stage of the missile that put them into orbit, and any and all decoys that the enemy might have decided to deploy. In all, the telescope would be expected to detect, track, determine trajectories, and identify up to 25,000 objects all speeding toward it.

The special technology behind this proposal utilizes the detection of infrared radiation. Infrared is the part of the electromagnetic spectrum that is less energetic—that is, has longer wavelengths—than visible light. Infrared radiation is emitted by hot objects; the higher the temperature the shorter its wavelength. Both reentry vehicles and decoys are warm when they leave the missile, but in the frigid temperatures of space the decoys cool down faster because they have less mass. By observing the rate of cooling of these 25,000 objects over several minutes, the telescope and associated discrimination electronics could presumably tell which is a decoy. At that point the sensor would transmit all these data to a ground command post, and there a large computer programmed to manage the entire engagement would launch interceptor missiles against only those objects that had been identified as reentry vehicles. The interceptors themselves would carry an infrared telescope and be equipped with several small, very agile rockets. Once the interceptor was in space, it would use its telescope to find the warhead or warheads it was assigned to destroy. With the aid of an on-board computer, the missile could plot the warhead trajectories and launch its rockets, one against each reentry vehicle. Each of these rockets would have an infrared seeker permitting it to home onto the reentry vehicle and destroy it by physically hitting it or by detonating a chemical explosive nearby.

This scheme does not rely on the use of long-range radar (which is susceptible to blinding) and at the same time avoids detonating nuclear weapons in space (which would interfere with ground radar and communications). It places, however, undue confidence on infrared detection, tracking, and homing. While in principle infrared detectors could do all these things, current technology is far from providing sensors with the required performance characteristics. In addition, it is very doubtful whether discrimination between reentry vehicles and decoys would be possible if the opponent decided to make decoys appear as warm as a reentry vehicle, a task rather easily accomplished by using a small electrical heater on the decoy to mimic the slower cooling process of a reentry vehicle. Numerous other countermeasures could be applied as well to blind, saturate, or spoof the infrared telescope of the sensor rocket. Finally, this system again would require such extensive programming of its computers that it is questionable whether it would perform reliably against a massive attack. Unlike the earlier ABM system, it has the advantage that many of its operations can be simulated and tested in detail. It is almost certain that in a real attack the system would have to face unexpected complications arising from the efforts of an enemy determined to defeat it.

This newly proposed ABM system has a second layer of defenses which is, in effect, an improved version of the old combination of MSR radar and Sprint. The new system has faster computers, faster and relatively cheaper interceptor missiles, and small radars that are more resistant to the electromagnetic effects of a nuclear detonation. Yet it suffers all the same from the basic weaknesses of the earlier system: It is easily blinded by nuclear detonations, can be saturated by numerous reentry vehicles arriving in quick succession hidden behind the remains of fireballs from earlier nuclear bursts, and is desperately short of time to detect, track, and attack an onrushing reentry vehicle during the last 10 to 20 kilometers of its trajectory. The use of many small computers and many small radars may lessen the probability that the central computer will grind to a perplexed halt as was the fear in the earlier ABM system, but this does not guarantee a significantly better overall performance.

The central point of the preceding discussion is that once reentry vehicles left the missiles that propelled them to their trajectories, there is no ABM system that could effectively prevent them from destroying either the cities or many of the silos toward which they were directed. As a result, the military has begun to explore opportunities to destroy ballistic missiles before they reach the booster shutoff point of their flight. From this basic notion arose the possibility, which we will discuss in the next chapter, of directing beams of laser light or elementary particles from satellites orbiting the earth in order to destroy the missiles as they ascend above the atmosphere.

9

DIRECTED-ENERGY WEAPONS

A S WE SAW in the previous chapter, one of the problems of all existing or proposed ABM systems is that hitting a missile with another missile is a difficult proposition, since they travel at about the same speed. If the first or second defensive missile misses the incoming warhead, there is no time to try again. But directed-energy weapons, which derive their destructive power from electromagnetic energy or subatomic particle beams aimed against the incoming warhead, would travel close to or at the speed of light. Thus a directed-energy ABM would be able to fire at each incoming warhead hundreds of times in the few minutes that it would be visible before it reached its target. Some scientists have suggested further that it might be possible to put these weapons on satellites that orbit the earth. Thus they would not fire at warheads as they neared the end of their trajectory, but at their launchers (the ICBMs and submarine-launched ballistic missiles) as they rose slowly from the surface of the earth. Such a weapon might seem the key to development of an ideal ABM system, since it would not use nuclear detonations to destroy the incoming warheads, and it would have much more time to do its job. Since, in principle at least, this sounds like an attractive idea, the notion of directed-energy ABM systems has been part of the ongoing debate on how to avoid destruction from a nuclear attack, even though testing or deployment or such systems is forbidden by treaty.

The process involved when using these new weapons against ICBMs is similar to destroying an airplane with a machine gun (a common occurrence during World Wars I and II). The machine gun imparts a lot of kinetic energy to a bullet. On its way to the target, the bullet continuously loses some of this energy in overcoming the friction of the air. In order to damage the airplane, the bullet must hit while it still has some energy left. If it does so, some of its energy is expended in friction between the bullet and the skin of the airplane, and some is transformed into deformation energy that bends and eventually punches a hole in the body of the plane. If the bullet has kinetic energy left after that, it keeps going, heating and deforming and shattering everything in its path. One bullet will usually not bring down a plane, but if the machine gunner has a sharp eye and keeps the machine gun trained on the plane as it fires, enough bullets will hit the plane to make the body break apart, damage one of the plane's vital components, or cause a fire or even an explosion.

Translating this scenario into abstract terms, we have an object, the bullet, that takes some energy and carries it to a target, using a portion of that energy to get there. The remaining energy is transformed, through the interaction of the bullet with the target, into heat and deformation energy that weaken or break the target. Note that the bullet must physically hit the target, and that, almost always, many bullets must hit the target if they are to cause significant damage. That in turn mandates that the machine gunner must know the position of the target, that he must be able to follow the target persistently and accurately, and that most, if not all, of the bullets must hit the target. Finally, we should recall that the farther the target is from the machine gun, the more energy the bullets expend in getting there, so beyond a given distance, the remaining energy they carry may not be enough to penetrate and heat and deform the body of the plane.

Instead of bullets made of metal that weigh 10 grams, directed-energy weapons use as bullets electrons, which weigh 10^{29} times less, or protons, which weigh about 10^{26} times less. Instead of the 10 or 100 bullets shot at the plane by a machine gun, 10^{20} or so electrons or protons are fired at it. While machine-gun bullets travel 1,000 or 2,000 meters per second, electrons and protons propelled by an accelerator travel at almost the speed of light, $3 \cdot 10^8$ meters per second, toward their target.

Such a particle-beam weapon is the kind of simple and elegant idea that would appeal to a physicist. But for every hundred elegant ideas only one may actually work in practice. A good physicist or engineer must always ask what technical difficulties must be overcome to develop the idea into a system that works. How much would it cost? How long would it take to build? If the system is a weapon, it is important to know whether it will work in a hostile environment in which the enemy will try to use various countermeasures against it. Will this new weapon perform a militarily useful mission that cannot be performed by another system more cheaply or more reliably? How much will it cost in money and manpower to maintain and operate the weapon? In a word, will it be cost-effective? When one asks these practical questions, particle-beam weapons appear less alluring and elegant. Let us examine such weapons more closely in order to see where this fascinating science-fiction-like idea meets with difficulties in applying it.

Particle-beam weapons would differ fundamentally from the more usual instruments of war. Ordinarily, destructive energy is transported to a target in the form of an explosive (chemical or nuclear) warhead, carried inside a ponderous vehicle such as a missile or an artillery shell. A particle-beam weapon, however, works by first increasing the kinetic energy of a large number of atomic or subatomic particles and then directing them collectively against a target. Every particle that strikes the target transfers some of its energy to the material that it hits.

Electrons, one possible choice for a particle beam, interact electromagnetically with other charged particles making up the target object. An electron coming into the lattice of atoms and molecules of the target will knock many other electrons along its path out of their atomic orbits, changing and disrupting the structure of the lattice that gives the target material its form. If numerous electrons enter the material all at once and within a small area, they will unravel the entire lattice of atoms and molecules, breaking the bonds between then. From a macroscopic perspective we would say the material has melted. The entering electrons cause this melting process as follows: As they enter the material and encounter all the negative charges of the atomic electrons, they are repelled and slowed down. The kinetic energy lost by the electrons in this way is transformed into heat, which contributes to the melting of the target material.

When protons enter a material at a high velocity, they have approximately the same electromagnetic effects as electrons, with the same structurally disruptive results. Instead of pushing the electrons, however, protons pull them away from their atoms (protons are positively charged and they attract the negative electrons). In addition, protons interact by means of the nuclear force with the protons and neutrons of the nuclei inside the material, dislodging the nuclei from their atomic positions, shattering them, knocking neutrons and protons out of them, and generating heat inside the target material. A beam of neutrons has the same effect. Although the neutrons don't interact directly with the electrons of the material's atoms, they will knock protons out of the nuclei they encounter, and the protons in turn will do damage. A large enough number of any of these particles, hitting a target in a short enough time within a small area, could in theory burn a hole in the "skin" of an offensive missile or shell and detonate the chemical-explosive "trigger" of a nuclear warhead, or disrupt the guidance electronics inside the target vehicle.

How is such an intense and energetic beam of charged particles produced? A charged particle, when subjected to the correct drop in electric potential, can be given a push that increases its kinetic energy by an amount equal to the potential. It is the same mechanism that makes a stone acquire kinetic energy when it falls from an upper-story window to the street below. At the beginning of its fall the stone has no speed at all, but when it reaches the street its speed depends on how high the window was above the street. In the case of the stone the operative force is gravitational, while in the case of the charged particle the potential difference—and therefore the force involved—is electromagnetic. For example, a proton that is subjected to a potential drop of 1 million volts acquires an additional kinetic energy of 1 million electron volts (1-Mev). (Neutral particles cannot be accelerated in this way, because they have no electric charge. High-energy neutral beams can be obtained, however, by first accelerating a beam of charged particles and then converting them into neutral particles.)

The beam-producing part of such a weapon system is called an accelerator, and would work as follows. First of all, the accelerator must produce enormous numbers of electrons or ions (electrically charged atoms), and it can do so in one of several ways. Then with the help of electron and ion injectors, these particles can be delivered as a compact, intense pulse to the entrance of the accelerating section of a particle-beam weapon. Over the years, elementary-particle physicists have invented several different ways of accelerating charged particles traveling in a straight line in order to probe the properties of matter. An electron beam used for this purpose must have very high energy but comparatively few electrons, say 10^{14} per second. The preferred technique to create such a beam is to generate a moving electromagnetic wave, which bunches up electrons in front of it, and pushes them forward, much as an ocean wave pushes a surfboard. When a million times more electrons are needed per second (10^{20}), as in a weapons system, the preferred approach is to expose the particles to a series of pushes supplied by an electric field. This electric field is induced by rapidly changing the magnetic field in a doughnut-shaped ring while the particles pass through the hole in the center.

Let us now consider in some detail what a particle-beam weapon would have to do to be a useful land-based or space-borne ABM system. As we have seen, a particle beam must strike the target in order to damage it, something that is not necessarily a requirement for conventional or nuclear explosives, which have a "kill radius." In addition, it would have to detect the target and identify it among decoys and the background clutter. Then it would have to point the beam at the target, and, if necessary, follow the target with the beam; fire the beam through the intervening medium to the target; determine whether or not the target was hit; assess the damage if the target was hit; determine by how much and in what direction the beam missed the target if the target was not hit; correct the aiming of the beam by the miss distance; fire the beam once again at the target; determine the damage or miss distance depending on the results of the shot; repeat the cycle until the target is destroyed; if necessary engage a new target; and communicate the results of each beam burst to some command center that is managing the entire antiballistic defense operation.

To perform all these functions the weapons system would need in addition to the accelerator some other kinds of equipment. It would need a power supply to provide the necessary energy to the accelerator and to run the rest of the equipment. It would need an energy-storage and staging system to feed energy to the accelerator during the short periods when the particle-beam burst was being generated, accelerated, and fired. It would need a complement of sensors (some combination of radar, optical, and infrared devices) capable of locating and identifying the target, of detecting whether or not the target was hit, and of assessing the damage it suffered if it was hit. Finally it would need control devices to aim the beam and to couple the sensors to the aiming mechanism so that the beam could follow the target.

Next we need to consider the operational requirements of a space-borne particle-beam weapon designed to attack enemy missiles that carry nuclear warheads. Typically, the boosting phase of an ICBM's trajectory lasts for about three minutes, but since, as will be shown further on, the missile would have to rise above the atmosphere before it could be attacked by the particle-beam weapon, the time available for the weapon to attack and destroy the 1,000 targets would be only about 100 seconds. During this time, their rocket motors are burning and therefore the missiles are easy to see; they are also moving relatively slowly compared to their final speed.

In order to be an effective defense system against an enemy ICBM attack on cities in the United States, the weapon would have to cover all possible launching sites an enemy might use, not only in his own territory, but anywhere in the oceans from which submarines might launch missiles against the United States. Thus, the particle-beam weapons would have to be deployed on large satellites orbiting the earth. Satellites placed in a geosynchronous orbit (an orbit about 40,000 kilometers above the earth's surface that would keep a satellite stationary above one point on the surface) can look down on roughly a hemisphere of the earth, and two or three of them are sufficient to monitor the entire globe. In fact, however, it would be impractical to fire at ICBM boosters with a particle-beam weapon from a distance of 40,000 kilometers or more. As we will see, the distance is simply too large.

Therefore the weapons would have to be placed in orbit much closer to the earth, perhaps no more than 1,000 kilometers above the surface. But a satellite in such a low orbit rotates with respect to the surface of the earth; it may not be in the right place when it is needed. Many such satellites carefully spaced around the earth must be deployed to ensure complete coverage. Furthermore, a satellite in a close earth orbit can detect and attack rising ballistic missiles over only a fraction of the earth's surface—the closer in to the earth, the smaller the area it can survey at any one time. As a result, as many as one hundred satellites with particle-beam weapons would be required to achieve complete coverage of the earth from an altitude of 1,000 kilometers. Even then only one or two of them would be in position to attack ballistic missiles rising from their silos or launched from submarines (which could converge to fire from the same vicinity, thus saturating the capability of the satellite). The other ninety-eight satellites will be somewhere else around the earth, too far away from the rising missiles to shoot at them.

Yet even at these ranges, the aiming of the weapon would be problematic. Since an ICBM booster is about 10 meters long and the distance to it from the satellite would be around 1,000 kilometers, the detector would have to determine the position of the missile with an angular accuracy of one part in 100,000, a feat that is currently difficult.

The operation of such a particle-beam weapon would also be severely limited by a number of unavoidable physical phenomena relating to the beam itself. For one thing, a beam of electrons fired from a satellite in space would cause the satellite to acquire a net positive charge. Since electrons are negative, they would be attracted back to the satellite. Detailed calculations predict that most of the particles in an electron beam with a diameter of 1 centimeter and a steady current of 1,000 amperes would not propagate more than a meter or so beyond the exit port of the accelerator (this is called the "virtual cathode effect"). Just as serious a limitation is the fact that each particle in a beam of similarly charged particles is subject to repulsion by all the other particles of the beam. In a uniform beam the net force on each particle is radially outward, and as a result, the beam tends to diverge and disperse soon after it leaves the exit port of the accelerator. When a beam propagates in a gas such as the earth's atmosphere, it produces by ionization enough charges of the opposite sign in its immediate vicinity to counter the outward repulsive force. In the vacuum of outer space, however, no such effect obtains, and a charged particle beam would diverge drastically because of its self-generated repulsive force. A 1-billion-electron-volt (1-Gev) electron beam 1 centimeter across as it emerged from the accelerator would spread to a diameter of 5 meters 1,000 kilometers away, while a 1-Gev proton beam would spread to a diameter of 3 kilometers at the same distance. A beam that spreads out to cover a circle 5 meters in diameter could conceivably be used as a weapon, but there is another physical phenomenon that makes it impossible to aim such a beam reliably at a target.

The earth is surrounded by a magnetic field that is subject to significant and unpredictable fluctuations in strength as a function of both location and time. A magnetic field makes charged particles follow circular orbits with a radius proportional to the speed and mass of the particles and inversely proportional to the strength of the magnetic field. More precisely, the deflection of a charged particle beam in space from its original direction is dependent upon the strength of the geomagnetic field *at each point* along the beam's path. In order to be able to predict the amount of deflection the beam would undergo, it is necessary to know the exact strength of the geomagnetic field at every point. The uncertainty in the position of the beam is directly proportional to the uncertainty in the strength of the geomagnetic field. If the geomagnetic field could be known with an accuracy of, say, one part in 1,000, then the uncertainty in the position of a 1-Gev electron beam at the end of a 1,000-kilometer range would be 1 kilometer. But we do not know the value of the geomagnetic field at any one point and time even with an accuracy of one part in ten. That precludes aiming the beam with the accuracy required to hit a target a few meters long. So immutable physical laws make the use of charged-particle beams as long-range weapons impossible.

What about the possibility of using a beam of neutral particles? Particles without charge, such as neutrons or gamma rays, do not have any difficulty propagating in a vacuum along a straight line, but precisely because they lack an electric charge, they cannot themselves be accelerated or focused into a beam. High-energy neutrons can be produced by bombarding a target with an intense beam of protons from an accelerator. A proton that has entered a nucleus exchanges its charge with one of the neutrons in the nucleus and emerges as a neutron. The neutrons that come from such a reaction tend to move in the same general direction that the proton had as it entered the nucleus. The average angle a neutron would make with the original proton beam, however, would be such that at a distance of 1,000 kilometers the neutrons would be spread over an area of several hundred square kilometers, and their density per unit area would not be high enough to do any damage to a target.

It has been suggested that by using hydrogen atoms it would be possible to accelerate charged atoms and, after forming them into a beam, neutralize them before they passed into the vacuum of space. Since a hydrogen atom consists of a positively charged nucleus (a single proton) and an orbiting electron, the atom as a whole is neutral. It is possible, however, to add a second electron to the atom and thereby make it negatively charged. Such atoms can be accelerated to high energies and focused into a beam, and then immediately neutralized by stripping that second electron from the atoms. It would therefore be possible (at least in principle) to generate an intense high-energy neutral-hydrogen beam suitable for use as a weapon.

There are several ways in which the stripping of the extra

electron from each negative hydrogen ion can be achieved with reasonable efficiency, but, as with the conversion of a proton beam, they all contribute to the spreading of the beam. For example, if the stripping is achieved by passing the charged hydrogen atoms through a very thin sheet of material, or through some rarefied gas, a beam that starts out having a 1-centimeter diameter at the accelerator exit will spread to about 10 meters in diameter 1,000 kilometers away. With this degree of spreading in the beam, it may in principle still be possible to do damage to a target.

To see whether it would be practical to use such a beam to damage missiles, let's estimate how energetic and intense such a beam would have to be in order to cause detectable damage to a target 1,000 kilometers away. The damage must be detectable, because otherwise the operator of the beam weapon would not know if he had succeeded and could now shift to another target. Detectable damage would result either from the burning of a hole through the walls of the missile's fuel container or from the detonation of the chemical-explosive triggers of its nuclear warheads. To burn a hole in the walls of the missile, the beam would have to deposit about 1,000 joules per cubic centimeter of material; to detonate the explosive, about 200 joules per cubic centimeter.

In a neutral hydrogen beam it is advantageous for a number of practical reasons not to generate a very energetic beam. A 200-Mev particle beam that illuminates an area totaling about 1 million square centimeters at the target would have to carry $6 \cdot 10^{10}$ joules of energy in order to cause detectable damage to its target.* How fast the necessary destructive energy must be deposited on the target determines the power that the beam must have. The power of an accelerator beam is equal to the product of the total poten-

* Here is how the figure of $6 \cdot 10^{10}$ joules of energy is arrived at: Each 200-Mev proton would deposit $3.2 \cdot 10^{-11}$ joule of energy for each centimeter it travels in a lightweight material. So in order to deposit 2,000 joules of energy per cubic centimeter of target, $2,000/10^{-12} = 2 \cdot 10^{15}$ particles would have to hit each square centimeter that the beam illuminates at the target. Since we saw that the total area of the beam would be a million square centimeters, the total number of particles in the beam must be $2 \cdot 10^{15} \cdot 10^6 = 2 \cdot 10^{21}$ particles. Each carries 200 Mev, so the total is $2 \cdot 10^{21} \cdot 2 \cdot 10^2 \cdot 1.6 \cdot 10^{-13} = 6 \cdot 10^{10}$ joules.

tial drop to which the particles are subjected (while they are inside the machine) multiplied by the current in the beam. (A current of 1 ampere is equal to the flow of about $6 \cdot 10^{18}$ singly charged particles per second.) Therefore an accelerator that imparts 1 Gev (1 billion electron volts) of kinetic energy to each particle and has a beam current of 1 ampere has a power of 1 gigawatt (1 billion watts). The total energy in a pulsed beam from such an accelerator is equal to the power in the beam multiplied by the duration of the pulse. Now, since 1 watt is equal to 1 joule per second, a pulse of particles that carries 1 billion watts of power but lasts only one millionth of a second contains 1,000 joules of energy. It is energy that ultimately destroys the target, so this is the measure of a beam's utility as a weapon. Thus a $6 \cdot 10^{10}$-watt beam would deposit the necessary $6 \cdot 10^{10}$ joules in one second of continuous deposition. A beam ten times as powerful ($6 \cdot 10^{11}$ watts), which could be achieved in practice by increasing the number of particles in the beam tenfold, would be needed, however, if the damage had to be completed in a tenth of a second. But current technology is a long way from achieving any beam capable of such a large power output that it could damage a distant target in any reasonable length of time.

The use of any particle-beam weapon in space has still another technical problem. An accelerator needs a power supply capable of providing enormous spurts of energy in very short periods of time. Ordinary gasoline-powered generators won't do. Neither will solar panels. As for the possibility of using nuclear explosives for powering a particle-beam weapon, problems of energy and radiation containment would make nuclear explosive unsuitable. A good way to produce the necessary energy would be to detonate some chemical explosives inside a magnet. This would generate a very brief but very intense pulse of electric current, which is exactly what the accelerator needs. The technology for this is well known. Assuming an overall conversion efficiency of 40%, the energy input to the magnetic generator in order to produce $6 \cdot 10^{10}$ watts would be $1.5 \cdot 10^{11}$ joules. The energy stored in high explosives is 1,000 calories or about 4,000 joules per gram. Therefore 37.5 tons of high explosives would have to be set off in the magnetic generators to provide the necessary energy for one beam pulse that lasted a second.

It is possible that a beam a hundred times weaker could damage the electronic computer inside an ICBM, and such a beam would take only hundreds of kilograms of explosives detonated per second to provide the necessary energy. The resulting damage, however, might not cause any readily detectable damage to the missile. Under these circumstances the operator of the particle-beam weapon would not know whether the ICBM he had been shooting at was incapacitated and whether he could engage another target. That would be a serious operational flaw of the entire weapon system, since no time can be wasted.

A particle-beam weapon based on neutral particles suffers from an additional serious shortcoming. It would be impossible to determine by how much and in what direction a neutral beam had missed a target. Therefore, it would be necessary to fire the weapon "blindly."

But assume for a moment that technology has overcome the formidable difficulties of generating a very intense neutral beam in space. Consider then the operational demands on a space-borne particle-beam ABM system: Remember, it would have to consist of about a hundred orbiting weapons, deployed at 1,000 kilometers above the earth. Each of these would need an accelerator, a power supply, an energy-staging system, and subsystems for target detection and tracking, beam aiming, and damage assessment. Each particle-beam weapon would also have to be able to detect, identify, and track simultaneously at least 1,000 boosters while they were still in their boost phase above the atmosphere, which lasts for about 200 seconds. Since a 10-meter object would have to be hit 1,000 kilometers away, the tracking and aiming mechanism would have to locate each booster with an accuracy of one part in 100,000. Since all these one hundred stations would have to be unmanned, they would have to have a communications link with some command post on the earth. Since they would be over hostile territory when they would be shooting at their targets, we can't expect their command posts to be within sight. So a relay satellite is needed.

If we were to build such a system, the aiming mechanism

of the neutral beam would consist of precalibrated magnetic lenses and focusing magnets, which would be mechanically steered for accurate aiming with the aid of an optical telescope. This mechanism would be supplemented with a feedback system so that as the target was being tracked the beam's sights would remain on it. Since it would not be possible to ascertain by how much and in what direction the beam missed the target, it would be necessary to fire repeatedly and blindly at the target until there was observable damage. Such a procedure is time-consuming, since the total time needed for a single shot would be approximately 0.4 second: the time it would take the beam to reach the target 1,000 kilometers away, the time it would take the optical signal to return to the platform indicating a kill, the time it would take the signal to reach the controlling station on the ground by way of a geosynchronous relay station, and the time needed for the return command from the ground instructing the weapon what to do next. But, as we have seen, the time available per missile in a large-scale attack is less than the time it takes to complete a single shot.

But the practical difficulties do not end here. It is by no means certain that radars or other sensors could determine the position of the target with the required accuracy of one part in 100,000 or even of one part in 10,000. Furthermore, to fire accurately and rapidly at an ICBM booster with a neutral hydrogen beam from a range of 1,000 kilometers is a very difficult technical problem. Accordingly, even if a suitable accelerator could be built, it would still be technically unfeasible to deploy a particle-beam weapon that could be operationally effective against a massive ICBM attack on the United States.

One must also assume that a weapon system for boost-phase ballistic missile defense would operate mostly within the line of sight of enemy territory. Consider then the countermeasures a military planner, faced with the threat of a particle-beam satellite-based ABM system, could direct against it. The most obvious method would be to destroy the particle-beam weapons. But a simpler method would be to jam the link between the weapon and its ground control and thereby incapacitate the system.

Other countermeasures an enemy might resort to are jamming the satellite's radar system or deploying decoys to confuse the system's many sensors. The enemy could deploy a cloud of "chaff" (thin strips of aluminum, say) above the ICBMs so that even if the particle-beam system could detect the general location of the target, it could not see through the cloud and aim the beam with the needed precision. Chaff could be carried by missile boosters of sea-launched as well as land-based ICBMs.

Another effective countermeasure against a neutral-hydrogen-beam weapon based in space would be to interpose a thin layer of air between it and the ICBMs it is designed to attack during their boost phase. A 200-Mev neutral hydrogen beam would be stripped of electrons if it passed through even a thin layer of air and would turn into a charged proton beam, which would disperse rapidly and never reach the target. A 700-kiloton nuclear warhead exploded at the upper edge of the atmosphere could provide the energy necessary to lift enough air into the vacuum of outer space for this purpose. All these countermeasures would be fairly inexpensive, easy to deploy, and probably, impossible to overcome.

The worst difficulty, however, has not been mentioned yet: If each pulse of the beam requires 37.5 tons of fuel to energize it and several pulses, let us say ten, are needed to destroy the target, the system would need 375 tons of high explosives for each target it destroys. The Soviet Union has about 1,500 ICBMs, and all of them would probably be engaged by the one beam weapon that happened to be overhead during their launch. This means that each satellite with a neutral-beam weapon must carry 562,000 (375·1,500) tons of explosives. And since one hundred such satellites would be needed for a completely effective space-borne ABM system, the total amount of high explosives we would have to lift into space would be over 50 million tons. Since the Space Shuttle can carry about 30 tons of cargo into space, it would take 1.8 million shuttle trips. Even if the United States had ten shuttles and each one made three trips a year, it would still take 600,000 years to move the necessary amount of high explosives into space.

All these difficulties point to the conclusion that even though it might be possible to construct an accelerator that would produce a beam of hydrogen atoms intense and energetic enough to cause some damage to an ICBM, a satellite-based neutral-particle-beam ABM system would not be practical. If particle-beam weapons deployed in space are not effective ABM systems, could they defend missile silos if they were deployed on land? To do this, charged-particle-beam weapons must be built near the silos they are intended to protect, and would be designed to attack enemy warheads during reentry, not during the booster stage. Thus the situation would now be quite different from the one we just discussed. First of all, the beam must travel through the atmosphere to reach its target, rather than through the vacuum of outer space. Second, the beam would not have to travel long distances, because it could engage the target at close range. And third, the reentry warhead is a smaller, faster, and much less fragile target than an ICBM in its boosting stage.

The first question then we must take up is: Can a charged-particle beam travel in the atmosphere and remain focused and powerful enough to destroy a target a few kilometers away? The answer is a conditional yes. Imagine a 5,000-ampere beam of 500-Mev electrons streaming from the exit port of the accelerator toward the target. As the particles travel through the atmosphere they collide frequently with air molecules, losing some of their kinetic energy in each collision. These collisions have three noteworthy effects: (1) They create by ionization a large number of positively charged atoms around the beam (the resulting free electrons fly away). (2) The positive charges around the beam reduce the repulsion of the electrons within the beam. (3) The magnetic field generated by the streaming of the beam's electrons through the surrounding positive charges nullifies the now weakened repulsive forces among the electrons and keeps the beam together. (In a vacuum, the beam would disperse because of these repulsive forces.) The net effect is an electron beam confined to a stable channel.

As might be expected, however, the collisions themselves scatter and disperse the beam particles away from their original direction of motion. Since this scattering would be cumulative, a 500-Mev electron beam with a diameter of 4 centimeters at the exit port of the accelerator would have a diameter of about 14 meters 400 meters away from the accelerator and about 130 meters 1 kilometer away. In addition, the collisions would remove energy from the beam by slowing the electrons down. As a result, at a distance of 400 meters from the accelerator, the electrons in the beam would have only about 30% of their original kinetic energy, and at a distance of 1 kilometer they would retain only about 6%. Hence even though an energetic electron beam could propagate in the atmosphere to a distance of 1 kilometer from the accelerator, it would be so dispersed and weakened that it would not be able to inflict any damage on a missile at that distance.

If we could somehow thin out the air where the electrons had to pass, the number of collisions an electron would undergo as it traveled would be reduced, and they would disperse less and lose less energy. In order to achieve that goal the number of air molecules in the space occupied by the beam would have to be reduced. In short, an evacuated hole must be bored in the atmosphere through which the beam could propagate with little scattering of the particles and minimal energy losses.

Let's see how this could be done, if at all. Consider a pulsed 5,000-ampere, 1-Gev electron beam with a diameter of 2 centimeters and a pulse duration of a tenth of a microsecond. Since the electrons would travel essentially at the speed of light, a pulse that lasted for a tenth of a millionth of a second would be about 30 meters long. The total energy carried by all the electrons in such a pulse would be 500,000 joules. The electrons in such a pulse would lose energy in collisions with air molecules in two ways: by transferring energy to the air molecules and by radiating energy away, that is, by emitting electromagnetic radiation in the form of light. The loss of energy to the air molecules (ionization) is approximately 2,000 electron volts per centimeter for such an electron beam, and the rate of radiation loss would be about ten times higher.

As a pulsed beam of this type traveled through the air, it would deposit energy at the rate of 3 million watts per cubic centimeter through ionization and about ten times as much energy through radiation emitted mostly in the forward direction. The radiated energy would be deposited in the air molecules in and around the beam, giving them even more kinetic energy. Collectively this would manifest itself as an increase in heat and consequently as an increase in pressure of the air in the vicinity of the beam. The end effect of the rise in pressure would be to cause most of the air molecules to move radially away from the path of the beam pulse. The hot low-density air left behind would form a channel through which subsequent pulses could propagate with lower energy losses and less dispersion. So what would happen in effect would be that the 30-meter-long pulse of electrons would open a "hole" in the air.

Assume now that it is necessary to generate a channel in which the pressure would be only a tenth of atmospheric pressure. To do this, the air inside a channel measuring 1 kilometer in length and at least a centimeter in radius would have to be heated to a temperature of 3,000 degrees centigrade, a task that would call for 1.5 million joules of energy. If one assumes that all the energy carried by each beam pulse is deposited within the channel, only a few pulses would suffice. But this actually would not be the case. For a target a few kilometers away, it would take as many as several dozen pulses. In any case, once the channel is created, the 1-Gev electrons propagating in it would lose no more than 20% of their original energy, and the radius of the beam would increase only by a factor of three after a kilometer of travel. The beam then would probably have enough energy left over to destroy the target.

· The rudimentary analysis of the propagation of a pulsed electron beam given here indicates that the electrons might propagate stably, but the analysis is still incomplete. We have not dealt with the effects of chopping the beam into several thousand pulses per second. We have ignored the fact that each pulse would be followed by an electromagnetic wake, much like the wake generated in water by a speeding motorboat, and that the wake of each pulse would disturb the propagation of the next one. Nor have we accounted for the physical behavior of the heated channel: How long would the channel remain open? By how much could its radius shrink and still accommodate a beam with a diameter of 2 centimeters? Which effects or conditions would prove to be predictable and reproducible and which not?

Indeed, it is not even certain that such a beam could propagate at all. Experiments with charged-particle beams have shown that long beams suffer from what physicists call "magnetohydrodynamic instabilities": They kink and coil like a garden hose or pinch like a string of sausages. Once these instabilities set in they tend to grow until they completely disrupt the beam.

What about a proton beam, then? Since protons are 2,000 times more massive than electrons, perhaps they could barrel through the atmosphere and not disperse as badly as an electron beam. Actually, things are worse with protons because not only do they interact electromagnetically with the atoms of the atmosphere, but they do so strongly. So they are stopped much more readily once they get out of an accelerator. In fact, they don't go anywhere; they would spread out and become an amorphous charged cloud right outside the accelerator port. And a neutral hydrogen beam inside the atmosphere would be immediately stripped of its electrons and thus become a proton beam with the same kind of problems.

Once again, let us now assume that an electron-beam weapon intense enough to destroy reentry vehicles can be built. Hard targets such as missile silos are vulnerable to nuclear explosions in their immediate vicinity; therefore a reentry vehicle attacking a silo must penetrate the atmosphere and explode near the silo. In principle a particle-beam weapon defending the silo could wait until the attacking warhead had approached to within a kilometer before attacking it. A modern reentry vehicle would have a velocity of no less than five times the speed of sound, and so it would take about six-tenths of a second to cover the last kilometer to its target, during which time the particle-beam weapon would have to either destroy it or cause it to veer off course.

The particle-beam weapon would have to be able to defend its own aiming radar, which could be physically destroyed by a 1-megaton nuclear weapon exploding as far away as 2 kilometers or even more. Therefore the beam must be able to propagate for several kilometers in the atmosphere in order to destroy an incoming reentry vehicle a few kilometers away. The beam, however, would be bent by the earth's magnetic field. The uncertainty in the position of the beam that would result from this effect would be several dozen meters over a range of a few kilometers. A nuclear reentry vehicle would be typically about a meter long and some fraction of a meter wide. So the magnitude of the aiming uncertainty of a particle-beam ABM system would be larger than the size of the target, with the result that the beam could not find it and hit it. Moreover, when one considers the operational requirements of such a system, it becomes clear that an attacker could complicate the operations of such a particle-beam ABM further by perturbing the geomagnetic field in an arbitrary and random fashion, and by blinding the system's radar by exploding nuclear weapons above the atmosphere. A determined enemy could explode a nuclear warhead high above the silos to blind the radars and disturb the geomagnetic field, then explode another warhead close enough to the radars to destroy them and lift some dust into the atmosphere, and (since by now the particle-beam weapon would be blinded) proceed to attack the silos themselves unhindered.

Particle-beam radars could be blinded for extended periods of time by a nuclear explosion in the stratosphere over the silos. These are the same vulnerabilities that plagued earlier ABM schemes that were supposed to rely on missiles rather than particle beams. Using a particle beam would not change the vulnerability of the radars; on the contrary, it would increase the required accuracy of the radar manyfold, since a direct hit on the target would be mandatory.

If not particle beams, what about lasers as directed-energy weapons? Lasers are devices that produce light; it is well known that light can be used to burn things. Focused sunlight can ignite paper or wood. Archimedes used mirrors to concentrate sunlight and burn the Peloponnesian fleet that was besieging Syracuse. In principle, then, lasers, which produce extremely intense and uniform beams of light, could be made into weapons.

Laser light is in some ways quite different from light

waves produced by incandescent sources like the sun or the filament inside a light bulb. These more familiar sources of light produce waves with many different frequencies and phases, and so they interfere and often cancel each other's effects as they strike a surface. A laser, on the other hand, produces a very intense stream of electromagnetic waves, all with the same frequency and direction of motion, and exactly in phase with one another. Since laser light waves arrive at a surface exactly in step with each other, their effects are greater. Furthermore, while the maximum intensity of light from an incandescent source is fixed by the temperature of the radiating body (the sun, the lamp filament), the intensity of laser light is in principle unlimited, depending only on the size of the laser and the properties of the material in which the laser light is generated. In order to have a clearer picture of the difference between light from an incandescent source and light from a laser, let's begin by looking at light production at the atomic level.

In an ordinary incandescent lamp, external energy in the form of heat is supplied to the filament of the lamp. The filament consists of atoms which, although they are bound to each other, vibrate more or less vigorously depending on how much energy they have absorbed. Some absorb a lot of energy and thus vibrate quite vigorously. It is a property of matter, however, that an atom in a highly "excited" vibrational state will shed some of its energy in the form of a radiation wave and return to a more quiescent vibrational mode. The frequency of that wave is proportional to the energy the atom has shed, and it usually corresponds to frequencies that the human eye can see. So as a very large number of atoms of the filament of an incandescent lamp keep absorbing the external energy and then shedding it in the form of visible electromagnetic waves, they create the light that we perceive leaving the filament.

A laser, on the other hand, operates on an entirely different principle and produces an entirely different kind of light. External energy in some form is provided to a collection of gas molecules enclosed in some kind of box. A fraction of this energy increases the kinetic energy of the molecules, and that results in the heating of the gas that the molecules compose. But another fraction of that energy is absorbed into internal vibrational and rotational motion of the molecules. Since the molecules are not rigid, they can oscillate like jelly or rotate like a top, but can have only a limited number of states of rotation or vibration. In which of these fixed states the molecule can be is determined by how much energy it has absorbed. Normally the molecules of a gas are at a vibrational and rotational state called the "ground state." But when they absorb energy, they can occupy higher energy states.

In a laser, if many gas molecules absorb energy in this way, this results in a depopulation of the ground state, and a significant occupation of the higher energy states. This is known as a "population inversion." The gas in a laser is selected so that if one of its molecules leaves a highly excited energy state, which we can call H, it is most likely to go to still excited but lower energy state L, with the emission of a photon of frequency f, proportional to the energy difference between H and L. When such a photon interacts with another molecule still in state H, it causes the molecule to go to the lower state L and emit a new photon of the exact same frequency (f), phase, and direction as the original photon (see Figure 19 on page 204). The result is that there are now two photons with the same frequency that can stimulate additional molecules in state H to do the same thing. If this collection of molecules is enclosed in a long tube with parallel mirrored surfaces on both ends, and if energy is provided to cause a population inversion, the system will spontaneously generate a large number of photons of frequency f. As these photons travel back and forth between the two mirrors, they keep stimulating additional molecules in energy state H to emit additional photons with the same frequency. Each photon generated by this process has very little energy, about 10^{-19} joule, a fraction of an electron volt. Yet the energy output of a laser can be many thousands of joules within a few millionths of a second. This is possible because a significant fraction of the molecules in the box (say between 10^{22} and 10^{23}) can be stimulated to radiate again and again during a very short time, thereby emitting photons much more frequently than they would spontaneously.

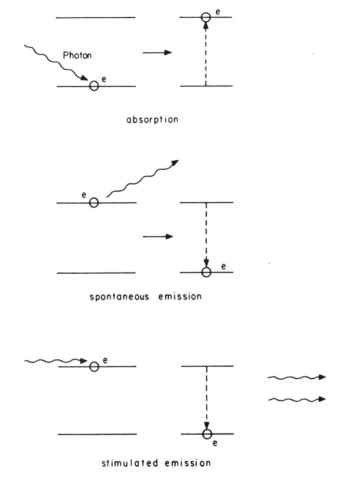

FIGURE 19. Schematic illustration of the possible interactions of a photon with a bound atomic electron. The stimulated emission is the basis of the laser.

The key requirement for the operation of a laser—population inversion—is achieved in a variety of ways. One approach, used in gas dynamic lasers, is to "trick" the molecules, so to speak. The process starts by generating hot carbon dioxide gas (CO_2) by burning kerosene. The molecules of a hot gas have a lot of kinetic energy but also a larger number of them have been raised to high, excited rotational and vibrational states of motion. Some of these excited states can depopulate faster than others when the ground state is empty. To create this condition the hot CO_2 is made to go through a nozzle and expand suddenly into a large chamber. When a gas expands it cools down rapidly. The sudden cooling of the gas creates the necessary conditions for a brief moment during which the molecules can be stimulated to produce a pulse of laser light. After that the chamber has to be evacuated and the process is repeated with a new quantity of hot CO_2 molecules.

Another way to achieve a population inversion is to bombard the molecules of the gas with a beam of electrons that impart some of their kinetic energy to the molecules upon collision. Part of that energy increases the speed with which the gas molecules move, in effect raising the temperature of the gas. But the rest of the energy is absorbed by the molecule, raising it directly to a vibrational or rotational state that is higher than normal for a gas at that temperature. This method can be used to generate and maintain a population inversion. The gas then has to be recirculated and cooled.

A third way to obtain a population inversion is to combine two gases like hydrogen (H) and fluorine (F) in a chemical interaction. The resulting hydrogen fluoride (HF) molecule is generated in a vibrationally excited state. Since all the HF molecules are produced in an energy state higher than their ground state, this method creates a complete population inversion. Under standard atmospheric pressure and roomlike temperatures, the excited HF molecules would rapidly go to their ground states without stimulated emission of light, but carefully controlling their environment can keep them excited long enough to create a pulse of laser light. These three methods are suitable for generating population inversions in large collections of molecules with good efficiencies.

Consider now how a large laser could be used as an ABM weapon: how it would work, how large it must be, and what technical and operational problems would have to be solved before such a weapon could be made effective and preferable to other weapons. Laser weapons (like beam weapons) would differ in three important ways from all weapons that have been deployed to date. First, destructive energy is transported to the target in the form of an intense beam of electromagnetic waves rather than in the form of an explosive charge carried inside a missile or shell. Second, this energy travels at the speed of light, that is, $3 \cdot 10^8$ meters per second, compared to 1,000 or 2,000 meters per second that a supersonic missile would be capable of. Third, the laser beam can damage a target only if it physically strikes it.

Consequently, a laser weapon would have to perform the same twelve operations mentioned in connection with the particle-beam weapons (detect the target; identify it among possible decoys or the background noise; point the beam at the target and follow it; fire the laser light beam through the intervening medium; determine whether the target was hit or not; assess damage if target was hit; assess by how much and in what direction the beam missed the target if the latter was not hit; correct the aiming of the beam by the miss distance; fire the beam again at the target; determine damage or miss distance depending on the results of the shot, and repeat until target is destroyed; communicate results to a central command post; engage a new target if necessary). For such a weapons system to work it would need a variety of components beyond the basic laser. It would need a large, movable, precisely controlled mirror to point the beam at the target. It would need sensors capable of detecting, identifying, and locating the target with the requisite precision and stability, and control devices to couple the sensors to the mirror. It would also need specialized sensors to determine the damage to the target or the miss distance of the beam. Energy stores, a power-generating system, and an energy storage-and-staging system would be needed to provide the laser with intense pulses of energy for its operation. So far, these are not unlike the requirements for a particle-beam weapon, but the similarities end here.

Laser light, which consists of photons, is massless and neutral; photons are not affected by the geomagnetic field, nor do they repel each other, as was the case with charged-particle beams. As a result, a laser beam in the vacuum of space is affected only by a phenomenon called diffraction: It will gradually spread out at great distances from its transmission mirror. A beam of such waves spreads as it travels in space into an angle equal to the wavelength λ of the single-frequency stream of photons emitted, divided by the diameter of the mirror D. The spreading angle is very nearly λ/D measured in radians.* The larger the wavelength, the more the beam spreads. The larger the mirror, the less the beam spreads. Since one would want to keep the spreading of the beam as small as possible, it is advantageous to use large mirrors and light of small wavelength in lasers intended as weapons. For example, light from a hydrogen fluoride chemical laser has a wavelength of $3 \cdot 10^{-4}$ centimeter. If the mirror that aims it to the target is 100 centimeters in diameter the laser beam will diverge only three parts per million due to diffraction, that is,

$$\frac{3 \cdot 10^{-4}}{100} = 3 \cdot 10^{-6}$$

So 1,000 kilometers away (1 million meters) a beam that started out as 100 centimeters (1 meter) in diameter will now be about 3 meters in diameter and will have only one-ninth its original intensity.

In the atmosphere, however, a laser beam is weakened by a number of effects. The molecules of air and the particulate matter in it (dust, water droplets, smoke particles, etc.) both scatter and absorb light. An infrared beam of a CO_2 laser would lose half its intensity after traveling 4 kilometers in clean cool air, and would lose the same amount in only 1.5 kilometers on a hot, humid day. Similarly, clouds or smoke would absorb a beam almost completely, as would dust, thick haze, or fog. The efficacy of laser weapons operating in the atmosphere would be critically dependent on weather, a serious drawback for any weapon system, but especially a defensive one, which would have to cope with an enemy attack at a time (and therefore weather) of the enemy's choosing. Long-range laser weapons are therefore limited to use in space.

A laser weapon causes damage by concentrating thermal

---

* A radian is equal to $\frac{1}{2}\pi$ of a full circle or $360°/2\pi = 57°$.

energy on its target in excess of what the target could withstand without malfunctioning. Damage to the target is caused only by that fraction of the laser beam's energy that is actually absorbed by the target's surface. Unlike both charged and neutral particles, photons do not penetrate the target to any appreciable depth. As a matter of fact, most of them are reflected from the target surface. This phenomenon is seen every day. Something is "shiny" if most photons that hit it, whether they come from the sun, a lamp, or a laser, bounce back and enter our eye. (Conversely something is "black," for example black velvet or a soot-covered object, if it absorbs most of the photons of visible light that strike it.) Metallic objects are usually shiny, and they can be polished to an even higher degree of shine. Or a thin film of reflecting material can be put on them to make them shiny. The percentage of light that is absorbed by a target depends on the wavelength of the light, the material of the target, and the condition of its surface. Only 4% of the light from an infrared laser illuminating a shiny aluminum target would be absorbed by it. The other 96% would be reflected and cause no damage to the target. On the other hand, ultraviolet radiation is largely absorbed by metallic surfaces, so more than half of the energy of an ultraviolet laser that reached a target would cause damage.

How much light energy must be absorbed by a target to cause damage? In general an absorbed energy of about 1,000 joules per square centimeter would certainly melt a metallic surface a few millimeters thick, like the walls of a missile. An infrared laser must generate twenty times more energy than this—that is, about 20,000 joules/cm^2, since 96% of it will be reflected by the target. However, if the intensity (the amount of energy that reaches the target per unit time) is very high, for example 1 million watts/cm^2, the surface of the target would rapidly lose its shine. In this way increasingly larger fractions of the beam energy would be absorbed by the target with every consecutive pulse. Thus it is possible, as indeed has been demonstrated in carefully prepared tests, to "burn a hole" in a target with a pulsed laser beam.

There is another way to damage a metallic target using a very powerful laser beam. A very intense beam of light energy can actually evaporate the surface of the target. The evaporated metal flies away from the surface at great velocity, and its momentum causes an equal and opposite momentum pushing against the target. The resulting impulse can be so large that it tears a metallic target apart.* Even if a laser is not powerful enough to tear the skin of a missile with a single pulse, it can be used as an antimissile weapon. If it fires pulses in rapid succession and is pointed so precisely that consecutive pulses hit the same spot on the target, the impulse delivered by each additional pulse dents the target surface more and more deeply, while the continual rise in temperature progressively weakens it. "Thermomechanical" destruction caused in this manner by a repetitively pulsed laser may require less total energy to damage a target than it would take to melt a hole with a continuous laser beam or to damage it with a single shot.

We now know enough about laser beams and their effects on metallic targets to make quantitative estimates of the operational requirements of a hypothetical laser weapon developed to destroy enemy ICBMs during their boost phase. The thermomechanical damage mechanism would require about 10^3 joules/cm^2 per pulse *absorbed* by the target, at beam intensities about 10^7 watts/cm^2 for impulses that last a few tens of millionths of a second. How many pulses would be needed to punch a hole in the missile under these circumstances? If we assume that the laser can be pulsed so rapidly that the target doesn't have time to cool between pulses, laboratory experiments indicate that about ten pulses would be necessary. That's rather optimistic and in all probability many more pulses would actually be required, but let's use ten pulses as a working assumption.

With this working assumption, we can now estimate how much energy we need to produce each pulse of light. Let

---

* An intense laser beam can generate a mechanical impulse of 2 dyne-seconds per joule of absorbed energy on an aluminum target in outer space. How big an impulse is a dyne-second? Physicists, who sometimes like to give things poetic names, call the impulse of 1 dyne-second per cm^2 a "tap," because it is as strong an impulse as that generated by tapping something with one's finger. An impulse of a few thousand "taps"-worth can tear a 2-millimeter aluminum or a 0.5-millimeter steel plate.

us assume that a hydrogen fluoride (HF) laser is used and that its mirror is 1 meter in diameter. A simple calculation indicates that such a laser weapon would need $3 \cdot 10^9$ joules per pulse or a total of $3 \cdot 10^{10}$ joules to destroy a target.* For an HF laser we would need a bit more than 6 tons of fuel and coolant per pulse. The same laser equipped with a 4-meter pointing mirror would require about a third of a ton per pulse. A 4-meter mirror of the perfection and ruggedness that would be required in a laser weapon system, however, is not within either the present or the foreseeable technical capabilities of this or any other country.

How much effort and expense would be necessary to establish a laser satellite ballistic missile defense system? To provide complete and continuous coverage of the earth from an altitude of 1,000 kilometers, one would have to deploy between fifty and a hundred satellites, each capable of destroying, say, 1,000 enemy missiles (the same requirements that we postulated for the particle-beam space-based ABM system). Since it would take at least ten pulses to destroy an ICBM, each weapon platform would need fuel for at least 10,000 pulses. Since each pulse requires 6 tons of fuel, if an HF laser were used with a 1-meter mirror it would require 60,000 tons of fuel stored on board; therefore, the entire complement of satellites would require 3 million to 6 million tons of fuel lifted into space, or approximately 100,000 to 200,000 Space Shuttle flights. Even if there were ten shuttles each flying three trips per year it would take 3,200 to 6,400 years to complete the transportation of just the fuel necessary for a space-borne laser defense system. Even if the laser weapons were equipped with 4-meter mirrors, it would still take more than 1,000

---

* Here is the calculation: Since only a fraction, say 10%, of the light that strikes the target is absorbed and contributes to the damage, 10^4 joules/cm² are needed at the target in order that the necessary 10^3 joules/cm² will be absorbed. The area of the beam spot of such a laser 1,000 kilometers away will be ten times the area of the laser beam at the transmission mirror, and the total area will be $8 \cdot 10^4$ cm². So the total energy that must leave the laser per pulse is $10^4 \cdot 8 \cdot 10^4 = 8 \cdot 10^8$ joules. But the laser itself is at best about 10% efficient and the energy-generating and staging system is also not perfectly efficient; optimistically we assume that it is 30% efficient. So the total amount of energy needed would be $8 \cdot 10^8$ joules/$10^{-1} \cdot 3 \cdot 10^{-1}$ or about $3 \cdot 10^{10}$ joules.

years to transport the necessary fuel into orbit.

So even without examining the numerous other technical, operational, and military problems that a space-borne laser ABM system would face (many of them similar to those we discovered analyzing the performance of the neutral-particle-beam ABM), it is apparent that once again an elegant idea has bumped against harsh reality and is not practical. There is a difference, however, between lasers and particle beams. While the basic laws of nature simply forbid the use of charged-particle beams in outer space, and make the production and aiming of a neutral-beam ABM system in outer space technically unfeasible, the same is *not* true for lasers. There seem to be fewer technical difficulties with lasers used as weapons. The entire field of laser physics is largely new and unexplored, unlike the field of particle beams, which is rather well understood and exploited. So the physics of lasers may hold surprises for us. One day in the future a discovery *may* be made that will make practical laser weapons possible.

10

ANTISUBMARINE WARFARE

A SUBMARINE is a warship that travels underwater for long periods of time and therefore remains invisible because light cannot penetrate seawater to any significant depth. There are two types of submarines: those that carry torpedoes and other weapons with which to attack other submarines and surface vessels, and those that carry intercontinental ballistic missiles with nuclear warheads. The range of the weapons of the first kind of submarines, which are called "attack," "tactical," or "hunter-killer" submarines, is not more than a few tens of kilometers at most. The range of the ballistic missiles carried by the so-called "strategic" submarines can be many thousands of kilometers, and their targets are the cities and the industrial and military installations of the adversary. Obviously, the range of the weapons of a submarine determines the distance within which it must approach its targets. So while a strategic submarine can loiter unseen in the ocean thousands of kilometers away from its inland targets, the tactical submarine must approach its target, be it a convoy or a single warship, to within a few kilometers.

Antisubmarine warfare against attack submarines is a tactical naval operation designed to protect friendly surface vessels by discovering enemy submarines and destroying them. Since these enemy submarines must approach the friendly ships within a few kilometers in order to fire their weapons, the range of tactical antisubmarine warfare is typically some tens of kilometers. Antisubmarine warfare against strategic submarines, on the other hand, aims at destroying the missile-carrying submarines of the opponent and thereby preventing the nuclear warheads that the missiles carry from being launched. Since modern strategic submarines can occupy a large fraction of the oceans of the globe (about 160 million square kilometers) and still be within range of their targets, operations against these submarines must be ocean-wide.

Antisubmarine warfare consists of detecting, localizing, and destroying (or under certain circumstances just trailing) enemy submarines. But since certain basic information about enemy submarines is necessary in order to perform these operations, intelligence-gathering is the very first step of all ASW (antisubmarine warfare) missions. For example, does the enemy have diesel-powered submarines that have to surface about every twelve hours, or nuclear-powered ones that can remain submerged indefinitely? How many subs does he have and what kinds of weapons do they carry? How able are his subs to detect other subs? Do they have good sonar equipment, good passive acoustical detectors? What is the maximum speed of the enemy subs and for how long can they maintain this speed? (For example, a nuclear submarine has speed that can exceed 30 knots and can maintain it indefinitely, but a diesel-powered submarine relies on batteries to power its electrical motors when submerged and can maintain high speed only for a few hours.) How much noise do the enemy subs generate at different speeds? How many enemy submarines are out of port at any one time and where do they usually patrol? All this information must be known before one attempts to mount ASW operations.

Detection, which is the single most important step in ASW operations, consists of ascertaining whether a submarine is or is not in a given area of an ocean. Localization, on the other hand, is the task of pinpointing the position of the submarine within that region, usually a mile or so on a side. The last task of ASW is to "kill" that is, sink, the enemy submarine; under certain circumstances, such as most peacetime operations, it is necessary to follow an enemy submarine continuously, rather than attempt to sink it as soon as it is localized. For the rest of the chapter we shall examine each one of these operations separately and explore the physics and the specialized requirements of each one. We begin with the task of detecting ballistic missile submarines.

Because ballistic missile submarines do not have to approach their target closely, or be at any specific place in order to fire their missiles (since the range of their weapons is measured in the thousands of kilometers), they can roam the oceans of the world. As a consequence, antisubmarine warfare operations designed to detect and destroy strategic submarines require the capability of searching many thousands of square kilometers of the oceans per hour. The question, then, is how does one find a submarine submerged in the ocean? Or even more generally, how does one "find" anything?

Finding something means becoming aware of its presence at a given location by using one of our sensory organs. For example, we "find" an airplane flying in the sky by seeing it. That means that we receive some electromagnetic radiation (in this instance, light enters our eyes) that was either emitted or reflected from the object. In general, when we try to find something by looking for the light—or any other form of energy—that it *emits*, this is "passive detection." If we try to detect something by intercepting some form of energy—visible light (from the sun or a searchlight), radar waves, or even sound waves—that the object *reflects*, this is "active detection."

Consider the airplane example again: Light from the sun strikes the airplane, is reflected by the surface of the plane, and enters our eyes. If the airplane were not there, this particular light would not be reflected, would not enter our eyes, and therefore we would not see anything in the sky. At night, lacking a natural light source, we cannot see the airplane and must provide our own light source, such as a powerful searchlight, to illuminate the aircraft: Light waves from the searchlight hit the airplane, some of them bounce back to earth and enter our eyes, and we can see the plane. In both instances we are dealing with active detection since we see light reflected off the airplane. We can also find the airplane if it is carrying a light of its own: Light waves from the light are emitted out into the space surrounding the airplane, and some of them enter our eyes and let us know where the airplane is. This is passive detection.

On a cloudy day we can hear an airplane passing overhead, but we cannot see it. The sun is still there providing light waves, the light waves are reflected off the plane, but they do not reach our eyes because they are absorbed by the tiny water droplets in the clouds between our eyes and the plane. So light waves are readily absorbed by water but sound is not, since we can hear the plane even though we cannot see it. We could, however, locate the plane on a cloudy day by using a radar set. Radar is an electrical device that sends out waves of electromagnetic radiation which, although they are of a different frequency than light waves, are reflected by solid objects in much the same way. Radar, in addition, contains a device that detects these reflected waves and therefore can determine the presence of the object. Radar waves have longer wavelengths than visible light, and because of that can pass more easily through clouds and fog, but they too are eventually blocked and attenuated. In torrential rain, a radar set detects objects less well than in clear weather.

Ultimately, all electromagnetic radiation (except waves with very long wavelengths measured in hundreds of kilometers) is either reflected or absorbed by water; after an electromagnetic wave has traveled a few tens of meters through this medium, hardly any energy is left to it. This is the reason we usually cannot see objects such as submarines, either by eye or by radar, regardless of their reflectivity, once they are submerged: The energy of the wave is dissipated as it travels in the water and never returns to our eye or to the radar receiver. If the submarine is very near the surface of unusually limpid waters, it is possible that, since the wave must travel a relatively short distance in the water, the part of the wave reflected off the submarine may still have enough energy left as it reemerges from the water to register in our eye or the radar receiver. But one cannot hope to find submarines that way, because they take care to be submerged at greater depths. So another energy-carrying type of wave must be used to search for submarines.

The fact that we can hear an airplane through the thickest of clouds even though we cannot see it is a hint that perhaps sound, or acoustical waves, would be suitable for locating submarines in the ocean. And indeed they are. Sound waves are periodic mechanical disturbances that carry energy within a distributed medium like air or water. They are not like the waves on the surface of the ocean, which are generated by the wind blowing on the surface of the water. Instead, they are a series of condensations and rarefactions caused by the motion of individual water molecules. These local changes in the density of the medium cause, in turn, changes in the pressure. So a sound wave is actually a change in pressure within the medium, a change that spreads out in all directions from its source.

In order to understand how underwater sound is used to detect submarines, we must first examine the way sound propagates in the ocean. Sound propagates in water, as well as in other substances, by the transmission of the motion of one molecule to its neighbors. In water, the motion of the molecules is parallel to the direction of propagation of the sound wave (Figure 20). Two things are of interest here. First, the source of sound in water is something that vibrates and in doing so puts the water molecules right next to it in motion. In this manner these molecules acquire some kinetic energy. Second, as more and more molecules share this energy, the energy that each individual molecule carries becomes less and less, so the farther away from the source, the feebler is the motion of the molecules and therefore the feebler the sound.

This is exactly what happens with a loudspeaker of an ordinary music-reproduction system in air. The loudspeaker is nothing more than a diaphragm, a thin sheet of material set into vibrational motion by a signal that originates at the needle of the record player and is amplified and strengthened before it reaches the loudspeaker. The vibrating diaphragm sets the air molecules right next to it in motion, and these molecules transmit this motion to adjacent molecules and eventually to air molecules right next to our eardrums. The vibration of these air molecules sets our eardrums in motion, at which time we hear the sound that comes out of the loudspeaker. Exactly the same thing happens underwater but with some significant quantitative differences. Because the speed of sound in water is 4.5 times larger than the speed of sound in air, and the density

compression   rarefraction   waves

ocean   waves

FIGURE 20. Sketches of the series of compressions and rarefactions of a medium that constitute an acoustical wave, and of the Raleigh waves that travel on the surface of a medium such as the ocean.

of air is one thousandth that of water, it takes more than sixty times greater pressure to transmit a given amount of energy over a fixed period of time into water than it takes to transmit it into air.* So while the diaphragm of a loud-speaker in air is a flimsy sheet of material that moves a lot as it transmits sound to air molecules, the device that would do the same in water must be sixty times stronger—it is very stiff and moves very little. Thus devices that generate and feed sound into the water are functionally like our familiar loudspeakers, but structurally, they are massive devices able to withstand large pressures. Those used for

---

* A sound wave of pressure P that travels with velocity v in a medium of density ρ has an intensity $I = P^2/\rho \cdot v$. So for two sound waves, one in air and the other in water, to have the same intensity we must have:

$$P_W^2/\rho_W \cdot v_W = P_A^2/\rho_A \cdot v_A \quad \text{or}$$

$$P_W/P_A = [\rho_W \cdot v_W/\rho_A \cdot v_A]^{1/2} = [\rho_W/\rho_A \cdot v_W/v_A]^{1/2}$$

$$= [(1/1.2 \cdot 10^{-3}) \cdot 4.5]^{1/2} = 61$$

To gain a sense of the size of underwater sound makers, recall that in order to transmit the same amount of energy in water a sound radiator (like a loudspeaker) must be twenty times—$(v_W/v_A)^2 = (4.5)^2 = 20$—the area of a radiator in air.

ASW are closer to the size of rooms and houses than to the size of ordinary loudspeakers.

We can use these underwater sound sources to find submarines in the ocean just as we use radar to find planes in the sky: A powerful sound radiator is put into motion, and it sends acoustical waves that carry energy. When a sound wave strikes a submarine, some of the energy is absorbed by the hull, and some is reflected back into the ocean. The reflected portion can be detected by a sound-receiving device, functionally similar to the human ear or to a microphone (but structurally very different). There is a great difference, however, between detecting a submarine and finding or localizing it, since the position of the submarine —that is, its distance from the sound detector and its direction with respect to it, not just its presence—must also be known. How to localize submarines with acoustical detectors is the subject of most of this chapter.

But before we consider localization, it is important to point out one more fundamental difference between the way sound travels in the air and in the ocean. The velocity of sound in the ocean changes with the density of the water, and the density of water in the oceans varies because of differences in the amount of salt the water contains and with the water's temperature and pressure. Pressure, in turn, varies with depth; salt content varies from place to place in the seas of the earth; and temperature varies with location, depth, and time (it is different at different times of the year and different times of day). So while the velocity of sound in air is more or less constant and uniform, the velocity of sound in water varies with depth, location, and in time. While sound waves in air travel in straight lines, variations of the velocity of sound in the ocean cause sound waves in it to bend in ways that depend on depth, location, the season of the year, and the time of the day.

For example, Figure 21 gives an idea of the variation of the speed of sound in the ocean, as a function of depth: In the *surface layer* of the ocean, which extends to a few tens of meters, the speed of sound changes from morning to afternoon to night, and is also affected by the local weather. In general, however, it tends to increase with depth (proportionately with increasing pressure), since wave action

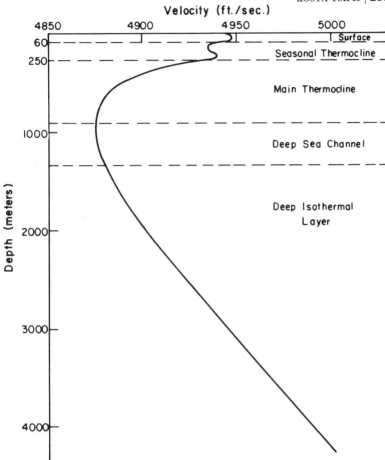

FIGURE 21. The variation of the velocity of sound in the ocean as a function of depth.

tends to mix the water in this layer and make it all have the same temperature. The next layer is called the *seasonal thermocline*, and extends to about 300 meters below the surface. The speed of sound generally decreases with depth in this layer, since the temperature drops as depth increases, but this temperature decrease is greatly affected by the seasons of the year. The *main thermocline* layer, which is not greatly affected by the time of year, extends down to 1,000 meters. In this layer, the speed of sound decreases with depth because the water keeps getting colder. Finally, below 1,000 meters the temperature of the ocean becomes a constant 4°C (40°F), and there the increase of pressure with increasing depth makes the speed of sound increase again. There is then a depth in the oceans between, say, 1,200 and 1,400 meters at which the speed of sound is more or less constant and has its smallest value. Sound either generated or arriving at that layer tends to be trapped there. Instead of spreading upward and downward, it propagates in it, as if it were in some kind of pipe or channel. For this reason, this part of the ocean is called the *deep sea channel*. Sound generated in the deep sea channel tends to stay in it and therefore, because it spreads much less, it can be transmitted over very long distances without rapidly losing intensity. Because the speed of sound generally decreases with depth above the deep sea channel, sounds generated above it tend to travel in great concave arcs that bend upward away from it, and are reflected off the surface of the water (Figures 22a and b).

The fact that sound travels in arcs of circles in the ocean has a number of important effects relevant to antisubmarine warfare. First, the source of sound such as a submarine may not be in the direction from which it appears to come. Second, the combined effects of circular paths and reflections off the surface of the water cause "convergence zones" in the oceans (Figure 22c). These are areas on the ocean surface, as much as 5 kilometers across, in which sounds from a distant source are much louder than in adjacent areas of the ocean. A third phenomenon is that there are areas in the ocean in which the sound waves do not penetrate, even though the source of the sound may be quite near.

As sound energy propagates in the ocean, it is both absorbed and reflected by the myriads of molecules of matter mixed in the water. Dirt, microorganisms, even chemical substances in solution in the ocean all take part in reflecting and absorbing sound. The absorption manifests itself as a weakening of the sound wave proportional to the distance it has traveled from its source. A second reason for the weakening of a sound wave as it travels away from its

A

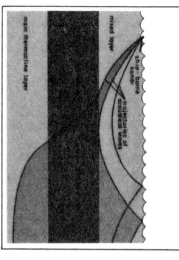

FIGURE 22A. A sonar located at the surface of the ocean is limited by the formation of a shadow zone in which a foreign submarine can remain undetectible.

FIGURE 22B. A sonar placed deep in the ocean avoids that phenomenon. Therefore a submarine-mounted or deeply submerged sonar is a more effective detector.

FIGURE 22C. The convergence zones created by the bending and reflecting of the sound waves in the ocean are concentric bands of intensified sound centered on a moving submarine.

B

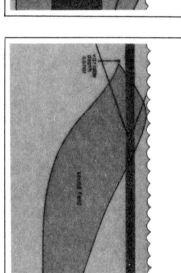

C

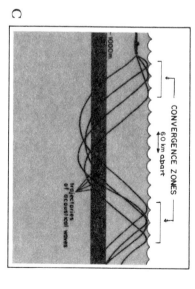

source is that as sound energy leaves its source it spreads out equally in all directions. As the original sound energy is spread over a larger and larger area, the intensity of the sound wave decreases as the square of the distance it has traveled from its source. So a sound wave with a given intensity, say 1 meter from the source, will have one hundredth that intensity 10 meters away and one millionth its original intensity a mere 1 kilometer away.

The sound from a submarine is not only quickly attenuated as it propagates in the ocean waters, but it is also masked by a lot of noise. The ocean is full of sounds generated by natural and man-made sources. The motion of ocean waters as they are pushed by winds and tides, volcanic activity under the ocean, the pelting of the ocean surface by rain, the sounds made by animals that live in the oceans, the turbulence of oceanic currents, and numerous other phenomena create sounds of different frequencies and intensities. Human activities such as drilling in the ocean bottom, surface ships that ply the oceans, and industrial activity near the water's edge also contribute to the ubiquitous ocean noise.

So far we have established the following physical facts about the ocean and the way waves travel in it that affect detection of submarines:

1. Electromagnetic radiation (such as sunlight and radar waves, which are often used to find objects in the air and in space) is rapidly absorbed by seawater and so cannot be used to detect submarines underwater.

2. Sound waves, which are mechanical waves, are absorbed less rapidly by water; in the case of the deep sound channel they are transmitted rather efficiently in it.

3. Sound waves do not travel in straight lines in the ocean but follow curved paths. The curvature of these paths varies with location on the surface of the earth, the season of the year, the time of the day, and the depth. As a result, it is difficult to figure out where a given sound is coming from in the ocean.

4. The ocean is a noisy medium; it contains innumerable sources of sounds besides submarines. These other noises tend to mask the feeble sounds generated by subs. In addition, since water reverberates when sound passes

through it, the mere passage of sound through the ocean creates noise (which increases proportionately with the intensity of the initial sound signal).

So unlike the atmosphere, the ocean is a noisy, nonuniform medium whose properties change with time, and from point to point on the surface of the earth. Given this difficult environment, how does one attempt to detect and localize a submarine?

Consider first the nonacoustical properties of a submerged submarine that can betray its presence in the ocean. There are several such properties or activities of a submarine that could indicate its presence. If the submarine attacks a surface ship, for example, one can safely surmise that it is somewhere in the vicinity. Or a submarine, especially a nuclear submarine, could leave behind it a wake of substances uniquely related to submarines, or under certain circumstances even a trail of hot water that could be detected as an elongated source of infrared radiation either from a satellite or from an appropriately equipped airplane flying overhead. Diesel submarines, traveling either on the surface or near the surface with the aid of a snorkel through which their engines breathe air and get rid of their exhausts, can be detected not only by radar but by a device that "smells," so to speak, the diesel exhaust fumes. Another sign of the presence of a submarine detectable by satellite could be a "swelling" on the surface of the ocean caused by the "bow wave" the submarine creates underneath the surface, especially if it is moving rapidly. But it turns out that none of these effects can be relied upon to detect submerged submarines.

There are other, more effective nonacoustical ways of detecting submarines, however, depending on their number, type (nuclear or not), and characteristics. With conventional (nonnuclear-powered) submarines, one can detect them by radar, either from aircraft or even from satellites (see Chapter 11 for more details), when they surface and recharge their batteries by running their diesel engines (which they must do every twelve hours or so). Radar can detect a submarine even if only its periscope or snorkel is above the surface of the water, and so can special low-light TV cameras mounted on airplanes or helicopters.

Another method would be to intercept the submarine's radio communications with its command bases on land. When a submarine merely receives messages and keeps radio silence, it is not possible to find where it is with this technique. But when the submarine sends out radio signals, these signals can be intercepted, and by determining from which direction they are coming, one can not only detect the presence of a submarine, but also localize it to within a few miles. Radio emissions from a submarine can be detected by receiving equipment on satellites overhead, ships, aircraft, and land-based receivers.

Unlike conventional diesel-electrical submarines, nuclear-powered subs can remain submerged indefinitely, and can receive messages by floating a small antenna. Once in a while, they may surface their periscopes to take a star fix and determine their exact location in the ocean. Even this is not necessary anymore, however, because submarines can now receive navigation information from special satellites by floating a special antenna to receive the signals beamed to them from the satellite. As a consequence, a nuclear-powered submarine cannot be confidently detected by any means other than listening for it underwater, either with hydrophones (underwater microphones), which pick up the sounds caused by its motion, or with sonars, which listen for the echo of a sound wave reflected off the submarine's hull.

As a submarine travels underwater, it emits characteristic sounds generated by the vibrations of its engines or by human activities on board, and by the vibrations of its hull and its propellers caused by its very motion. These vibrations set the molecules of water immediately around the submarine in motion, in effect generating sounds of different frequencies. This acoustical energy generated by the submarine propagates over considerable distances in the ocean and can be detected by sensitive hydrophones.

Passive listening devices, such as the one described in the previous paragraph, depend on the submarine's being in motion or otherwise generating sound. But a silent, motionless submarine can be detected by an active system, called sonar, that generates a powerful sound wave underwater and then listens for the return echo of the portion of that wave that bounced off the hard hull of the submarine. Sonar consists of a sound generator that emits pulses of acoustical energy into the ocean and a sensitive listening hydrophone capable of detecting the return echo of this sound wave reflected off the submarine. It is then very much like radar, but instead of sending and receiving electromagnetic waves, it sends and receives acoustical waves. The passive approach has two advantages: The submarine does not know that it is being detected and the position of the passive detectors in the ocean remain unknown. The advantage of the active approach is that a submarine can be detected even if it is lying dead-still in the water. The disadvantage is that a submarine can easily hear (with its own hydrophone) the pulses of sound emitted by a sonar, and thereby know that it has probably been detected.

Hydrophones or sonars can be deployed in the ocean in a number of ways. Hydrophones, for example, can be scattered all over the floor of an ocean, or they can all be arrayed together in a tight configuration measuring some tens of meters on a side. Sonars can either be deployed in such concentrated arrays or consist of a sound-maker at a central point in the ocean and several listening devices installed on the periphery of the ocean basin.

In order to appreciate the difficulty of the task of detecting a submarine submerged somewhere in the oceans of the earth, one must bear in mind that the areas of the major oceans (Pacific, Atlantic, and Indian) are respectively 163, 80 and 70 million square kilometers, for a total of about 330 million square kilometers, while the area of the United States is just about 7.7 million square kilometers. Trying to detect a nuclear submarine somewhere in the Atlantic Ocean by listening for the sounds it makes is comparable to trying to find a person wearing wooden clogs somewhere in the streets of Los Angeles by listening for the sound of his steps. Another factor that we must consider is the element of time. If one had weeks or months to find the sub in the Atlantic or the man in the streets of Los Angeles, the task would be much less difficult than trying to detect either of them in a few minutes or even hours, as would be necessary during a nuclear war.

How could one, by using dispersed passive acoustical

detectors, find a man walking with wooden clogs in the streets of Los Angeles? One way would be to replace every traffic light at the intersections of Los Angeles with a microphone, bring all the cables from all the microphones into a central location, connect them to a computer (which also stores information about the location of each microphone), and then tell the computer to identify the microphone that can hear the man's footsteps the loudest. Since the computer knows at which intersection that particular microphone is, it can quickly tell where the man is. By keeping track of the location of the microphones that consecutively hear the sound of his footsteps the loudest, the computer can tell in what direction the man is walking and where he turns from one street onto another. If the streets of Los Angeles were empty, such a task would be relatively easy: The listening microphone could easily hear the man's clogs, even at a distance of many blocks. So in the early hours of the day, say two or three in the morning, it would be easy to detect, track, and localize the man with the wooden clogs. But at noontime, for example, the noise from the millions of other people walking the streets, the sound of cars traveling, and all the other sounds of everyday life would make detection of the man's footsteps much more difficult, almost impossible. The sound of his clogs would be drowned out by the noise of the streets. We would have then to introduce some very clever programs into the computer in order to detect the man's footsteps.

Something analogous to this can be done to detect submarines in the ocean basins. A very large number of hydrophones can be arrayed in the ocean depths, dispersed over the entire ocean basin, each connected to some on-shore listening facility with an electric cable. Each hydrophone listens for the sound a submarine makes, and a computer, by knowing where in the ocean each hydrophone is, can determine the presence and even the approximate location and direction of motion of the submarine. But just as the footsteps of the man in Los Angeles would be drowned out by the street noise at high noon, so would the sound of a submarine get drowned out by the noises in the ocean. Thus the computer that receives all the signals from all the hydrophones dispersed in the ocean must sort out the sounds of a submarine from all the other underwater sounds the hydrophones pick up. Since this is a signal-processing problem that is common to all acoustical submarine detection methods, it will be discussed later on in this chapter, after some detection systems other than the "dispersed array" of hydrophones just described.

Another approach to the problem of detecting a submarine in an ocean basin is to concentrate all the hydrophones close together so that they cover an area, say, a few hundred meters on the side. Consider now just one row of hydrophones in this two-dimensional array, stretching for 200 to 300 meters along a horizontal line, each hydrophone spaced the same distance from the next one, for a total of one hundred hydrophones on the line (see Figure 23 on page 228). Consider next a sound wave (A) arriving at the line of hydrophones, but at some angle to it. Clearly hydrophone 1 will receive it first, then 2 and so on until the front of the sound wave reaches hydrophone 100. There is a lapse of time, say one second, between the time hydrophone 1 and hydrophone 2 receive the sound wave A, and the same delay occurs between hydrophones 2 and 3, 3 and 4, and so on down to the last hydrophone, which will receive the sound wave 99 seconds after hydrophone 1 received it. Now if the signals from all one hundred hydrophones are added together, the sum will be a series of signals, one second apart, lost in the noise that accompanies the sound wave. But if the signal from hydrophone 1 is delayed electronically by 99 seconds and added to the signal from hydrophone 2, which is delayed 98 seconds, and all the way down all the signals are added together with appropriate delays (the signal from hydrophone 100 is not delayed at all), the resulting sum is going to be a signal loud and clear, with most of the noise canceling itself out.

This is enormously advantageous for two reasons. First, the noise that accompanies the sound wave has been largely suppressed and the signal enhanced. Second, the computer can make the array of hydrophones listen to sounds that come from a particular direction only, and reject all other signals coming from all other directions merely by changing the value of the time delays added to the signal from each hydrophone. Consider, for example,

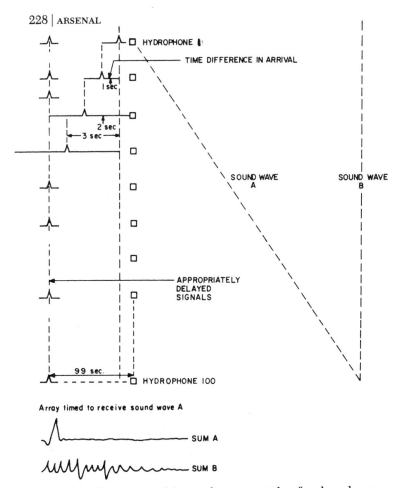

FIGURE 23. Illustration of the working principle of a phased array of hydrophones. The same principle is applicable to a phased array of radars.

another sound wave (B), coming from another direction, specifically face on to the line of hydrophones. The wave front, which at large distances from the source looks like a plane wave, will reach all the hydrophones simultaneously, so as each signal from each of the hundred hydrophones is added up without any delays introduced to any of them, the sum of the signals from wave B will be a hundred times stronger than all other signals. So in a sense the computer can form a "listening beam" that sweeps the ocean, listening for submarines.

Consider now several such "phased arrays" of hydrophones in an ocean basin placed far apart from each other and all listening for submarine sounds. The sound of a submarine in that ocean basin will reach each of the arrays from a different direction. One now can find the location of the submarine using this information: Knowing the position of each array and the direction for each from which the submarine sound was received, one can quickly locate the submarine. In this fashion, just two arrays suffice to locate a submarine, not precisely, but within an area in the ocean a few tens of miles on a side.

Large passively listening arrays of hydrophones, such as these dispersed arrays and phased arrays, are perhaps the best systems available to detect submarines hiding in very large bodies of water such as an entire ocean. They have, however, two disadvantages. First, they are extremely expensive, and second, they can be used only by a country that has access to and control of the shoreline of the ocean that must be surveyed. So while the United States can use these arrays in the Atlantic, Pacific, and Indian Oceans (because we have access to the shorelines of many of our allies, and control many islands and stretches of the continental shelf ourselves), the Soviet Union cannot use these arrays because it has insufficient access to shorelines near which it can place arrays and on which it can bring out the necessary electrical cables.

But hydrophones are not just used in conjunction with these massive arrays. For tactical antisubmarine operations, for example, a single hydrophone can be used to detect a submarine in an area of a few hundred or thousand square miles, or small arrays of hydrophones can be installed on the side of a submarine to provide information about the presence of other submarines or surface ships out to distances of a few hundred kilometers. In order to avoid the noise caused by their own motion and the problems of sound propagation in the surface layer of the ocean, surface ships can trail small arrays of passively listening hydrophones some distance behind and below them. Airplanes and helicopters can use solitary hydrophones to listen for submarine sounds. A helicopter can hover a few tens of meters above the surface of the water, lower a hydrophone into the water, and listen for sounds generated by a nearby submarine. A patrol aircraft can drop sonobuoys, each one outfitted with both a hydrophone that lowers itself into the ocean after the buoy has hit the water and a small radio transmitter that beams to the aircraft circling above the signals that the hydrophone receives.

Active sonars, which emit very powerful pulses of sound and then listen for the echo of this sound pulse reflected off the hull of a distant submarine, also range from the very massive to the very small. In addition to the hydrophones that receive the return echoes, a sonar must have a device, analogous to the loudspeaker, that generates sound pulses in the ocean. The easiest way to do that is to use a transducer, which is a mechanism that takes electrical energy and transforms it into mechanical energy in the form of vibrations of some sort of a piston. When the piston is immersed in the ocean, its vibrations set the water molecules next to it in motion, thereby generating a sound wave underwater. For sonars such as these, transducer pistons are massive metallic plaques, securely attached to special crystals of ceramics that transform pulses of electrical energy to mechanical motion. Many identical pistons can be put together in a two-dimensional array. Such an array carried by a submarine can be as large as a two-story house. Fixed arrays permanently installed on the bottom of the ocean can be much bigger. By energizing these pistons sequentially with differing time delays, one can form narrow beams of sound (see Appendix K), which is the same technique, but the reverse process, of the "listening beam" formation described earlier. These sound beams can be made to sweep the ocean. When such a sound beam hits an object in the water, such as a submarine, a whale, or even a school of fish, it is reflected and part of it returns to be detected by the hydrophones of the sonar.

The sound-emitting transducers and hydrophones of a sonar system can be installed near each other or thousands of kilometers apart. For example, the sound-pulse generator of a sonar may be located somewhere at the center of an ocean basin and the hydrophones listening for echoes dispersed around this basin. The sound generator may even be mounted on a ship that is not stationary, but travels around in the ocean. The ship may also have listening hydrophones or it may just be towing an array of pistons deep in the ocean, filling the water with sound that bounces off submarines and thereby makes their presence known to listening hydrophones that may be stationary or carried by other ships, friendly submarines, or even sonobuoys especially designed to remain active only for a period of months.

Another form of active sonar uses high explosives detonated underwater as a sound source. High explosives are convenient, since they can be dropped from aircraft and detonated at any desirable depth, creating a sharp pulse of sound in the water. An aircraft can sow a series of passive sonobuoys in the ocean, drop a small bomb that detonates deep underwater, and then listen through the string of sonobuoys for echoes of the explosion reflected off the hull of a submarine.

So far the description of detecting submarines by acoustical means has not dealt at all with the difficulties that such a task entails. The ocean is a noisy place, sound waves rapidly attenuate in it, and they do not travel in straight lines but instead follow circular, often unpredictable paths. So the sound of a submarine can be attenuated beyond detection, drowned in noise, or deflected away from the listening hydrophones. These difficulties are compounded by the fact that a very large number of underwater sound signals can be easily mistaken for those of a submarine by an undiscriminating acoustical detection system.

So detection of a submarine always involves a decision, made by either a computer or a human operator, of whether a sound signal caused by a submarine is present or absent in the jumble of sounds that a hydrophone, or array of hydrophones, receives. This implies that there is a "detection threshold," below which the submarine cannot be heard due to the background noise, and above which it can be confidently identified as coming from a submarine. Clearly if the detection threshold is set too high, sounds coming from actual submarines will be missed. If, on the other hand, it is too low, the system will be overwhelmed with signals that may appear to be coming from submarines, but actually are false.

A number of ingenious systems (see Appendix K) have been designed to improve the ability to detect a sound signal produced by a submarine in an ocean where the noise is louder than the signal. There are, for example, elaborate electronic systems programmed to perform millions of matching trials per second in an attempt to match the pre-recorded characteristic sounds of a submarine to the confusing incoherent sounds of the ocean, which may include a very weak submarine sound coming from afar.

The United States has an enormously elaborate system that begins wih a large amount of information picked up in each ocean basin by all the listening devices in it. Signals from big fixed arrays of hydrophones and smaller arrays towed by ships, signals picked up by sonobuoys sown by overflying aircraft, sounds picked up by dipping hydrophones carried by helicopters—all are collected and transmitted continuously via aircraft and satellites to a central signal-processing computer. In addition, this integrated system transmits to the central computer weather information and information about the temperature of the surface of the ocean water gathered by satellites that overfly the oceans. With all this information, the central computer of the system predicts how sound will bend in a particular location of the ocean and, together with all the myriad other bits of information, reconstructs the actual location of sound sources in that ocean basin as identified by the various acoustical detectors. Then it can decide which may be actual submarines and which are probably just noise.

Let us now examine localization of a submarine, which is the second operation of antisubmarine warfare. Acoustical submarine detection systems, be they large fixed arrays of active or passive detectors or fixed-winged aircraft that patrol the ocean sowing sonobuoys and listening for submarines, give some broad indication of the location of a submarine when they detect it. It is not uncommon for detection systems to be able to determine that a submarine is in an area of the ocean about 50 kilometers in diameter. This information is not sufficient to attack and destroy the submarine, because the effective radius of most antisubmarine weapons is somewhere between 1 and a few kilometers. Even if one intended to destroy a submarine with a nuclear weapon, he would still have to know the position of the submarine within 5 or so kilometers, since the distance at which a large nuclear weapon could damage or destroy a submerged submarine is not much greater than that: a 1-megaton weapon has on the average a lethal radius against a submarine of about 6 kilometers. Homing torpedoes also have effective ranges of only a few kilometers. So to destroy a submarine, one must know its position with an uncertainty of no more than a few kilometers.

There are several methods used in pinpointing a submerged submarine. One is for a plane or helicopter to fly over the area within which the submarine has been detected, carrying a magnetic anomaly device (MAD), a sensitive instrument that measures the local strength of the geomagnetic field. Since most submarine hulls are made out of ferromagnetic material, like iron or steel, they tend to gather together and concentrate the local magnetic field. So a sudden intensification of the earth's magnetic field detected by the MAD means that there is a submarine somewhere within a kilometer.

Another approach is to use a series of sonobuoys with a detection range of about 10 kilometers that are able to indicate from what direction the sound of a submarine is coming. By correlating the readings from at least two such directional sonobuoys, one can determine the exact location of the submarine. Still a third way is to have several (at least two) helicopters search an area where a submarine is suspected to be with dipping sonars that can tell the direction from which the reflected echo is coming. Other techniques, using hunter-killer submarines with sonar arrays or surface ships with towed arrays, can determine both the direction from which the sound is coming and the distance of its source from the detector. But none of these methods for localizing a submarine is overly successful. In fact, more frequently than not, experienced submariners with information of the local ocean conditions can slip away and disappear. The newspapers are full of accounts of submarines detected but not localized, which eventually manage to slip away from the area in which they were detected.

Once localized, there are a number of methods of killing a submarine, be it in a tactical encounter or as part of an operation aimed at destroying preemptively the opponent's fleet of ballistic-missile–carrying submarines. During tactical operations, a localized submarine can be destroyed by a depth charge, by a homing torpedo that listens for submarine sounds and eventually homes onto them, or by a mine. Torpedoes can be carried to the submarine location by ballistic or cruise missiles launched from ships tens or more kilometers away, or they can be launched by fixed-wing aircraft, helicopters, surface ships, or submarines. The latter two platforms can use wire-guided torpedoes which receive guidance instructions through the wires from the launch ship.

During peacetime, the purpose of strategic ASW is to detect, localize, and then trail as many enemy submarines as possible, all simultaneously. Unlike tactical ASW, however, once it becomes necessary to attack, the goal is not to destroy one or even a few of the enemy ballistic missile submarines, but *all of them all at once,* within a period of time measured in minutes. Anything else would not make much sense, because even if only a few of the enemy's ballistic missile submarines, each with sixteen or twenty-four missiles carrying multiple nuclear weapons, survive, and communicate with their command center, they can completely destroy the urban and industrial centers of one's country. For example, the United States has thirty-one ballistic missile submarines, each with sixteen missiles onboard, for a total of 160 nuclear weapons per submarine (on average, each missile carries ten warheads), and two with twenty-four missiles each. Of the thirty-one, between fifteen and twenty are always on station, submerged somewhere in the oceans of the earth within range of Soviet cities and towns. It makes no difference to the final fate of the Soviet Union if its ASW forces find and destroy one or five of these U.S. submarines within a short time, because the remaining ten will have over 1,600 nuclear weapons, each several times as powerful as the Hiroshima bomb, with which they can level every major city and town of the Soviet Union, several times over. Furthermore, it will do the Soviet Union no good to sink one U.S. ballistic missile submarine today, one a week later, and perhaps two the day after, because as soon as one or at most a few U.S. ballistic missile submarines are sunk, the rest would be ordered to launch their missiles. So in the case of strategic ASW, *all* of the enemy's ballistic missile submarines must be sunk at once before they have time to launch their missiles; it is not worth trying to sink them over an extended period of time.

This kind of antisubmarine warfare could be thought of as the most efficient antiballistic missile defense, since it doesn't wait for the missiles to be launched. And it destroys large numbers of missiles in one strike. Sinking a typical U.S. ballistic missile submarine destroys 160 warheads at once; a rather efficient defense, if it were possible. It is important to point out, however, that antisubmarine warfare against missile-carrying submarines differs in one fundamental respect from the other ABM systems we have considered so far: It is preemptive. ABM systems and directed-energy weapons are designed to attack enemy missiles after they have been launched—that is, after the enemy has committed the ultimate hostile act of launching nuclear weapons. But antisubmarine warfare against ballistic-missile submarines would have to be a preemptive operation. This would be an aggressive rather than a defensive operation, as provocative and destabilizing as an attempt to destroy preemptively the enemy's silo-based ballistic missiles. But as it turns out, technical problems and the physical properties of water make this approach even less effective than the ABM systems discussed in Chapter 8.

Are there ways in which such a sudden and total destruction of an entire fleet of ballistic missile submarines would be possible? In principle there are two: trailing, and attack by nuclear ballistic missiles. Using the first method, the Soviet Union could build a very large number of hunter-killer submarines and position them outside the home ports of the U.S. ballistic missile submarines. Every time a U.S. submarine left port, several Soviet submarines would begin to trail it, using active sonar to determine its position. Thus, all the U.S. ballistic missile submarines would either be in port, where they could be destroyed by nuclear ballistic missiles, or be trailed closely, and thus vulnerable to sudden and simultaneous torpedo attacks from the Soviet hunter-killer submarines.

There are numerous difficulties that make such an approach practically impossible. For example, U.S. submarines, upon leaving their ports, could confuse the Soviet trailers by dispensing noisemakers that simulate the sonar signal of a submarine; they could jam or drown out the underwater sound of the Soviet sonar detectors; U.S. hunter-killer submarines or surface vessels or aircraft could attack and destroy the Soviet submarines lurking outside the U.S. ports. Thus, even though theoretically possible, continuous overt trailing is not practical.

The second possible method of attacking simultaneously a country's ballistic-missile–carrying submarines requires two capabilities: first, the ability to track all the submarines as they patrol, and to localize each one within an area of a few hundred square kilometers; and second, the ability to target quickly ballistic missiles or other nuclear weapons against each one of them. Suppose, for example, that the U.S. ocean surveillance system with its large fixed arrays, the increasingly efficient communications network, and the extremely sophisticated computers and electronics that process the sound signals received could detect and keep track of the movements of all Soviet ballistic missile submarines. Even though the Soviets have about sixty such submarines, fewer than ten are out of port at any one time. It is then conceivable that the U.S. ocean surveillance systems could detect and localize all that are out of port. If in addition the United States had the capacity of targeting some of its land-based intercontinental ballistic missiles on these moving submarines and could barrage the general area where they were detected with, say, ten nuclear warheads per submarine while attacking the remaining fifty in their ports, it is conceivable that it could succeed in destroying completely *all* the Soviet ballistic missile submarines at once. A variant of this approach is to dispatch aircraft to drop nuclear weapons against the Soviet submarines at sea, and use ballistic missiles only against those Soviet submarines that remained in port.

This method of strategic ASW requires the ability to survey all the large bodies of water on earth at all times and detect all submarines in them. The Soviet Union is geographically and technologically constrained from achieving such capability in the foreseeable future. The United States is, in principle, able to achieve such assured surveillance, but is actually far from doing so with any confidence, primarily because the nonuniform, varying, and variable character of the water of the oceans makes the probability of detecting simultaneously a large number of submarines rather small. The examination of the techniques and the difficulties of detecting and localizing submerged submarines permits us now to draw some conclusions about the efficacy of ASW against a sophisticated and determined opponent.

Tactical ASW can bring to bear an entire armada of ASW platforms (ships, submarines, helicopters, fixed-wing aircraft) against a lurking enemy sub intent on attacking a convoy or a carrier task force. One would think that the ability of the submarine to survive, let alone attack its targets, would be questionable. Yet submarines have repeatedly displayed their ability to elude ASW forces and approach their target. There are even stories of military exercises during which submarines, through their periscopes, have photographed the propellers of aircraft carriers protected by an entire retinue of ASW forces!

Of course, the situation is much worse for strategic ASW. Because of the intrinsic properties of the ocean and the difficulty of separating and recognizing true submarine sounds from ocean noise, submarine detection is never a certainty. Depending on the weather, the time of year, the properties of the submarine, and its location in the ocean, one can have a better or worse chance of detecting it. But one can never be sure. The entire effort in ASW detection is to improve the chances for detection under an ever-broader set of conditions. Yet there is no system, either at the present time or within the predictable technological horizon, that can assuredly detect all submarines in an ocean. Some systems may be able to detect 90% of the submarines in an ocean, but under sea conditions that prevail only 10% of the time; the same system may be able to detect only 10% of the submarines in sea conditions that prevail the other 90% of the time. A system that detects all submarines all the time would probably detect a hundred more signals that are false for every real submarine sound, and thus would be hopelessly overwhelmed with false signals.

The one prediction that can be safely drawn from a careful examination of existing and conceivable acoustical underwater submarine detection systems is that they could be expected, with a given confidence, to detect most submarines some of the time, and with a higher confidence, some submarines most of the time, but not all the submarines all the time. Consequently we can conclude with some confidence that the bulk of the ballistic missiles aboard strategic submarines are immune to surprise attack.

Submarines can be made smaller and coated with sound-absorbing material to make active sonar less effective. Small torpedo-sized vehicles with sound-makers that simulate the sounds of submarines can confuse acoustical detection systems. Large sound-makers can jam the hydrophones and overwhelm the ability of sophisticated processors to extract the sound of a submarine from the overwhelming noise that such jammers generate. All these countermeasures can make the probability of detection of a submarine and its subsequent localization even smaller than it already is. Even if a technical or scientific discovery eventually made the detection of submarines more certain, technological advancements in anti-detection, as suggested above, will no doubt keep pace.

The probability of detecting ten submarines simultaneously is the product of the probabilities of detecting each one of them individually. So even if the probability of detecting one of these submarines were 50%, the combined probability of detecting all ten of them all at the same time would be $(1/2) \cdot (1/2) \ldots (1/2)$ ten times, or $(1/2)^{10}$, which is to say less than one chance in 1,000. One then must conclude that even though technological advances keep improving the ability of ASW systems to detect and localize submarines in the oceans of the world, the ballistic missile submarine forces of the United States and the Soviet Union are quite secure when out of port and submerged. The chance of a successful preemptive attack against either of these forces that would destroy all or even most of the submarines is at the present time and for the foreseeable future small. This statement applies with greater confidence in the case of the United States, first because the U.S. fleet is more suitable for protecting strategic submarines, and second because given the U.S. superiority in strategic ASW and the small number of Soviet ballistic missile submarines deployed at any one time, the probability of detecting all of them at one time is larger than the probability of detecting all the U.S. strategic submarines all at one time.

11

TELEMONITORING

T HE EARLIEST ACCOUNTS of warfare, such as we find in Homer's *Iliad*, suggest that gathering information about the activities of a military adversary has a long history indeed. In the modern world, information about an opponent's military enterprises is an essential element of national security, and the need for it has increased dramatically since World War II. The memory of Pearl Harbor is still quite vivid in the minds of U.S. military leaders. That surprise attack cost the country not only a large fraction of its standing fleet, but a protracted war in the Pacific. Nevertheless, in the pre-nuclear era, a country could be surprised by an enemy attack and still be able to recover and eventually win a war. Now, in the era of intercontinental ballistic missiles and megaton-size nuclear weapons, a surprise nuclear attack can mean the end of a nation as a viable society, within thirty minutes from the moment the enemy decides to attack. There is no time to react and no chance of recovery. Avoiding nuclear surprise therefore entails constant and routine monitoring of an enemy's activities.

A new element in intelligence gathering is the recognition by the United States and the Soviet Union that it is in a nation's *own interest* to allow the other country to have some knowledge of its nuclear might and activities. By the early 1960s it became clear to both the United States and the Soviet Union that ignorance about each other's nuclear arsenals could trigger a nuclear exchange by miscalculation or mistaken assumptions based on lack of information. As a result, both countries tacitly, and after SALT I explicitly, agreed that nonintrusive means of collection of information regarding the size and capabilities of their strategic nuclear forces was a stabilizing and mutually beneficial activity. It is now accepted practice not to interfere, by camouflage or other means, with satellite-borne monitoring systems that collect information about strategic forces. This represents a marked change in the national attitudes of only a few decades ago.

There is yet another reason for the tacit, and sometimes explicit, understanding between the United States and the Soviet Union to permit each other to monitor military activities. Both countries have recognized the need to constrain, if not actually reduce, the nuclear arms race between them by negotiated arms-control agreements. To do so, however, it is necessary that compliance with the terms of these agreements be unilaterally verifiable by each country. Such verification requires that each country have a reliable and objective means of monitoring the activities of the other. As a result both countries have over the years developed an entirely new family of systems intended for gathering information unobtrusively, and from a distance. Hence the relatively new field of telemonitoring, which means monitoring from a distance.

What can telemonitoring reveal? Not the other country's intentions, to be sure. But it can provide information about the other country's capabilities (from which intentions may be inferred, though perhaps somewhat questionably), single events, ongoing activities, or any military or other preparations a country may be undertaking. Telemonitoring systems can also warn of the beginning of a nuclear attack, or some other hostile act.

In general, telemonitoring systems can be grouped into two categories independently of the specific technology they incorporate. One kind of system gathers information about activities, events, and developments in the other country, stores it, and eventually transmits it to some collection center that processes, collates, and interprets the information. The other kind provides information in "real time," that is, while the event it monitors takes place. For example, a storage-type monitoring system may be called on to count how many land-based missiles, missile-carrying submarines, and bombers a country has, how big its missile silos are, or the yield of nuclear explosives tested deep underground. Information may also be stored which results from careful observation of the opponent's weapons tests, interception of his communications, or determination of the frequencies of his radars. A real-time system, on the other hand, is a warning system, designed to report instantly such things as the launching of several missiles simultaneously or detect the mobilization of troops or the preparations and takeoff of a large number of bombers.

Essential for all these functions is the ability of the tele-monitoring system to detect and recognize whatever the object or activity it is designed to monitor. A system intended for counting enemy submarines must be able to "resolve," that is, be able to distinguish, at the necessary distance, the difference between a submarine and a ship; a system designed to count the opponent's tanks should be able to resolve tanks from cars or trucks. Its power of resolution is a key characteristic of any monitoring system, regardless of whether the system transmits the information as it collects it (a real-time system) or stores information for later transmission.

The telemonitoring systems most people are familiar with are the satellites which, from their orbits high above the surface of the earth, survey the ground below. However, monitoring and warning systems can also be ground-based, such as the seismic arrays which monitor underground nuclear explosives tests or over-the-horizon radars, and electronic communications interception systems which monitor the testing of ballistic missiles. Other ground-based systems include cameras and powerful ordinary radars which can monitor the traffic of satellites and other objects (at last count about 4,700 of them) in orbit around the earth.

Satellites, as mentioned earlier, can be put into geosynchronous orbit or asynchronous orbit. Synchronous satellites are launched into orbits 36,000 to 44,000 kilometers above the earth, where they take twenty-four hours to complete one orbit, and so appear to remain immobile over the same point on the surface of the earth. These usually carry real-time sensors that perform a warning function by gathering information about such activities as missile launchings. The United States has for a number of years used scanning infrared detectors mounted on slowly rolling and pitching satellites in geosynchronous orbits, as an early warning system for Soviet missile launches. These sensors can easily detect the intense infrared radiation* of a missile plume as soon as the launcher clears any cloud cover. Visible-light sensors can also be used in conjunction with the infrared sensors.

More advanced U.S. early-warning satellites do not have to roll or pitch, because the detector can "stare" at the scene underneath, rather than scan it. This improvement has been made possible by the development of large arrays of infrared detectors that can, in effect, take wide-angle pictures with high resolution in the infrared part of the spectrum. With the information from these large arrays and the help of on-board computers, current satellites can detect the movement of infrared sources and, given the proper optics and resolution, monitor not only ballistic missiles in their boost phase, but also jet aircraft traffic.

Lower-orbiting satellites that move with respect to the terrain beneath them use the storage method and for this reason are given routine monitoring missions—to detect and identify objects such as the opponent's aircraft and missiles, structures such as silos, command posts, or shipyards, and military maneuvers. The ability to distinguish the size and shape of an object through high-resolution image-forming is a key element in such monitoring. A camera suitable for this purpose may use film to record the picture of the object, or it may use an array of minute photosensitive devices that transform the image directly into electrical signals, which, like ordinary television signals, can then be transmitted over large distances and electronically reconstituted by the receiving equipment. The obvious advantage of the latter method is that its information is available almost immediately. If film is used, one must wait while a film capsule, ejected from the satellite, is recovered by airplane and the film inside developed.

---

* This radiation is several thousand watts per steradian. A steradian is an angle that subtends ¼π of the surface of a sphere.

The original satellite-borne monitoring system consisted of two types of satellites, both with film cameras. One was a close-surveillance satellite, in a low orbit, that ejected its film in special capsules. These capsules were then recovered in midair by airplanes equipped with special grappling hooks. The other was an area-surveillance satellite, in a higher orbit, that would process the exposed film itself and then transmit the picture electronically to the ground. The pictures taken by the area-surveillance satellite were processed by techniques now used in Polaroid cameras, and the developed film was then passed through a television-camera-like system that in a couple of seconds would transform the image into a long string of numbers that could be transmitted electronically back to earth.

How can this be done? If one looks at a picture with a magnifying glass, it is quickly apparent that a photograph is nothing more than a very large number of dots (called grain) of varying shades of gray. One can then describe the contents of a picture by indicating the shade of gray (on some scale that has, say, ten values where ten is absolutely black and zero totally white) of each point on the picture. A small laser beam can do this by rapidly scanning each point on the picture, determining its shade of gray, and reporting its number over the radio to a receiving station. The process is limited only by the resolution of the camera.

The resolution of a camera—that is, the size of the smallest object one can detect with it—depends on three parameters: the distance between the camera and the object, the size of the film grain or of the individual photosensitive detectors used in the camera, and the focal length of the camera lens. A larger focal length will allow detection of a smaller object (see Appendix L). As an example of how these different factors relate to one another, a camera 200 kilometers above the surface of the earth with a focal length of 40 centimeters and a film grain such that 200 grains would fit side by side in 1 millimeter could detect an object 10 meters across on the surface of the earth.

Even more sophisticated image-forming systems have been developed and orbited. A new generation of U.S. monitoring satellites uses arrays of minute electro-optical detectors. Each detector produces an electrical signal proportional to the amount of light falling on it. Put next to each other in a big array at the focal plane of a camera, these detectors record an image of the entire terrain beneath the satellite, and transmit it instantaneously to earth via a relay satellite hovering in a geosynchronous orbit always in sight of the receiving station in the United States. A human operator can monitor the transmitted images on a screen, and if desired, immediately command the satellite to take another look at a particular object of interest with better resolution by zooming in with the lens.

U.S. satellite-borne cameras can be expected to have a resolution on the ground of a few centimeters (Appendix L). Indeed, it is said that cameras on U.S. satellites can take pictures on the surface of the earth in which human faces are recognizable. Such high resolution, however, causes difficulties when transmitting the information to the ground. As the resolution improves, the number of individual points per picture increases. If, for example, the camera takes a picture of an area on the ground of 1,000 × 1,000 meters and has a resolution on the ground of 1 meter (see Appendix L), there are 1,000 × 1,000 = 1 million different dots on the picture, each with a different shade of gray requiring a number to describe it. But if the resolution on the ground is 10 centimeters, there will then be 10 × 1,000 × 10 × 1,000 = 100 million dots with different shades of gray to be "described" to the receiving station. Since satellites in low orbits move fast with respect to the earth, they are usually within sight of their receiving station for only a few hundred seconds in each revolution. During this time they must unload all the information they have gathered throughout their orbit. Thousands of pictures may need to be sent back, each requiring the transmission of 100 million numbers. But the limited power supplies aboard these satellites are not sufficient for such high-speed transmissions.

In order to alleviate this difficulty, U.S. monitoring satellites now have on-board computers that are programmed to recognize "interesting patterns" in a picture, for example missile silos, or aircraft, or submarine pens. The transmitter can be commanded by the computer to send only those pictures that have interesting information, thus lessening the burden on the transmitters and allowing the use of cameras with high resolution. But the large number of high-resolution pictures needed to cover an area also places a burden on the highly trained human photoanalysts who must examine each picture for useful data. Since what one is actually looking for is changes in the opponent's terrain, recent pictures of a given part of the opponent's country are compared by machine with earlier pictures of the same part of the country and a human operator takes over only if the machine discovers a difference—if something new appears on the most recent pictures. The technique requires that the satellite make passes over the same point on the surface of the earth at the same time of the day, otherwise the comparing machines would detect differences caused by shifting shadows rather than human activity.

Monitoring by orbiting photoreconnaissance satellites is a very sophisticated and complex task, but the technology has advanced to the point that one can have great confidence in their ability to detect activities in the interior of another country. Beginning in 1972, the United States has replaced older systems by deploying a very sophisticated photoreconnaissance satellite that uses visible, ultraviolet, and infrared cameras. These satellites can both transmit real-time pictures and record images on recoverable film. They can also zoom in on a particular area of interest, and distinguish objects on the ground no bigger than about 10 centimeters across. The satellite is maneuverable and can maintain its orbit (usually 200 to 300 kilometers in altitude) by occasional use of small rocket engines.

In addition to photoreconnaissance satellites, other types of monitoring satellites carry equipment for remote sensing of a variety of phenomena and features on the surface of the earth. For example, the NASA Seasat satellite, designed to monitor the oceans, has two passive radiometers, which measure temperature by observing the reflectivity of the ocean surface, and three radars. One of the radars is a satellite altimeter with an altitude resolution of ± 10 centimeters, another one is a synthetic-aperture imaging radar with a resolution of 25 meters* (see Appendix M), and a

* It is believed that a greatly improved synthetic-aperture radar could, in principle at least, detect the effect that the bow wave of a submerged submarine would create on the surface of the ocean.

third is a microwave scatterometer that measures radar reflection from waves to determine their speed. From an orbit of 800 kilometers, Seasat can monitor wave heights, current patterns, surface winds, and temperature of the ocean, and the location, size, and direction of icebergs. The information is transmitted when the satellite is within line of sight of any one of several ground stations. The expected orbiting lifetime of such a satellite is several years, and a number can be placed in orbit simultaneously so that the whole surface of the earth's oceans is continuously monitored. Such information about the temperature and state of agitation of the oceans is of great use in antisubmarine warfare operations, since it makes possible the prediction of the path that sound will follow in a given area of an ocean. Satellites can, of course, also carry ordinary radars which can monitor naval traffic on the surface, or (sometime in the future) can track other satellites in lower orbits.

Still a third type of monitoring satellite carries passive listening receivers that gather information about enemy communications and radar signals by "eavesdropping" on his communications. There is very little unclassified information about the technical characteristics of these "ferret satellites," as they are called, but it is certain that both the United States and the Soviet Union have deployed them regularly for many years. Finally, there are high-flying satellites equipped with detectors for radiation, both nuclear and electromagnetic, characteristic of a nuclear detonation. These detectors instantly pick up the burst of x-rays that is produced by a nuclear explosion, and can also detect the characteristic double flash of visible light that is the unmistakable signature of a nuclear explosion inside the earth's atmosphere. As well as detecting the presence of nuclear detonations, these satellites can also determine their approximate location.

Ground-based monitoring and warning systems are also relevant to nuclear weapons and nuclear war. Ground-based radars (see Appendix I) can detect ballistic missiles and bombers only when they are within the line of sight of the radar. Because radar waves do not ordinarily bend to follow the earth's curved surface, the curvature of the earth prevents them from detecting and monitoring the flight of aircraft or missiles many thousands of kilometers away. But high-frequency radar waves are reflected off both the surface of the sea, if they impinge upon it with a very shallow angle, and off the ionosphere. So these waves can be channeled around the earth, bouncing first off the sea, and then the ionosphere, to detect objects well out of sight. This high-frequency radar, called over-the-horizon (OTH) radar, requires very powerful signals (several hundreds of kilowatts) and highly directional transmitters and receivers. Their operation is very sensitive to the reflectivity of the ionosphere, which varies significantly and must be compensated for. This type of over-the-horizon radar can detect aircraft flying out of sight of the radar, and measure their speed. The speed of an aircraft can be determined, to within a few hundred meters per hour, by calculating the effect of the Doppler shift* on the radar signal. This type of radar is equally useful for detecting ballistic missiles early in their boost phase.

Another characteristic of these high-frequency radar beams, which gives them even greater flexibility, is that they can be bounced forward from an object, in the same general direction that they were originally traveling, and be picked up by a receiver many thousands of miles from the transmitter. The United States uses this "forward scattering" of OTH radar beams to monitor aircraft and missile traffic in the Soviet Union and China. The transmitters of these radars are in Europe beaming eastward, and the receivers are located in the Pacific looking westward. Very large antennas are necessary to form the narrow beam needed for this purpose and also in order to receive the signals. Such antennas are usually deployed near the sea, to take advantage of the good shallow-angle reflectivity of the high-frequency signal on seawater.

Ordinary but powerful ground-based radars are used for two important functions: to monitor Soviet ballistic missile tests and to keep track of all the objects that orbit the earth. One can learn practically everything there is to know about

---

* The Doppler shift is the change in frequency of an acoustical or electrical signal caused by the motion of the signal's course. The rising pitch of the sound of an approaching car and the deepening of its roar as it moves away is the most familiar example of the phenomenon.

a ballistic missile by observing, with high-resolution radars, both the launching of the missile during a test and the return of its reentry vehicles back into the atmosphere on their way to their test target. When a missile is tested, information about on-board conditions is radioed back to the scientists who are performing the test. How much fuel is being burned per second, the missile's instantaneous velocity and acceleration, when a stage of the booster is sloughed off and the next takes over, what the temperature inside the rocket is, and other data are all transmitted to a receiving center. By eavesdropping on these transmissions and correlating these data with radar observations, one can calculate how powerful the missile's rocket is, how big a payload it is carrying, how precise its guidance instruments are, and a host of other useful information.

At the other end of the test range, powerful radars can pick up the reentry vehicles as they descend toward the earth, and by following their precise trajectories scientists can derive additional information about the reentry vehicles' precision, how much they can be affected by meteorological conditions, and how fast they reenter the atmosphere. In all, the combination of launch and reentry data gathered by observing such tests can provide a country with a rather complete picture of the opponent's ballistic missiles, except for their accuracy (see Chapter 6). The ability to monitor the opponent's ballistic missile tests has permitted the United States and the Soviet Union to enter rather complex arms-limitation agreements specifying the size and performance of their ballistic missiles, since compliance with such agreements can be verified unilaterally.

The other use of large, powerful ground-based radars is to keep track of existing and newly launched space-borne objects. There are about 4,700 satellites (or large pieces of debris) orbiting the earth. In addition, there is a plethora of smaller pieces of space garbage—nuts, bolts, springs, and chunks of metal—that also float in space around the earth in a multiplicity of orbits. All these objects are monitored by very large and very powerful radars based on the ground around the globe. When a new satellite is launched, these radars quickly determine its trajectory and keep track of it. This is possible largely because trajectories of satellites are fixed, exactly determined by the pull of gravity, the drag of the atmosphere for the lower orbits, and the solar wind in the case of the higher orbits. If in the future many satellites become maneuverable and are able to change orbits with the help of on-board rockets, their monitoring will become much more difficult and may have to be performed by radars on other satellites parked in geosynchronous orbits above the earth, rather than by the existing land-based ones.

Information about nuclear weapons can also be gathered by land-based systems. For example, special kinds of seismographs are used to monitor underground nuclear weapons tests. Underground nuclear explosions generate elastic waves in the ground that propagate over very large distances. Such waves can be detected and amplified by seismometers rigidly attached to the ground. A variety of such instruments are used by a number of countries to monitor underground nuclear explosions many thousands of kilometers away. By detecting and recording both the waves generated by the explosion that travel inside the earth and the waves that travel on its surface, it is possible to discriminate between waves caused by earthquakes and those generated by nuclear explosions, and at the same time determine the location of the explosion within a few kilometers and its yield of energy with good accuracy.

Weak signals from distant or low-yield nuclear tests can be lost in the background noises from the constant motion of the earth's surface, the crashing of waves, the vibration of buildings and trees in the wind, and vibrations caused by traffic or machinery. In order to distinguish the signal in all that noise, scientists use arrays of seismometers in the same way hydrophones can be used underwater to detect submarines. By the introduction of appropriate time delays in the signal from each instrument before summing them all together, the signal is made stronger in relation to the background noise. Complex seismic arrays have been developed (such as the U.S. large-aperture seismic array—LASA—in Montana) that can, with the help of computers, be electronically organized into real-time search "beams" that detect underground nuclear explosions as they occur. Although the concept of the seismic array is not new, the functions that can be performed by such a setup and the accuracy of its results have been greatly improved in recent years by new and more sensitive detectors as well as by improved computational capabilities. It is now possible, for example, to differentiate underground explosions from earthquakes down to an explosion of about 10 kilotons yield or even less. More important, it is possible to determine the yield of an explosion with considerable precision by measuring the magnitude of the wave that travels on the surface of the earth. This method has yielded increasingly accurate results as the output of arrays is improved by more advanced signal processing.

A global chain of such teleseismic array clusters could monitor continuously and verify with high confidence a ban on underground nuclear testing. The sensitivity of these instruments is now such that a nuclear explosion in rock that yielded 3 kilotons of energy could probably be detected. If the explosion occurs in soft earth, the smallest explosion that could be detected and measured is about 30 kilotons.

These monitoring capabilities must be judged from the perspective of military requirements in war and peace. For example, we can know the yield of underground nuclear tests of an opponent to a few thousand tons of TNT-equivalent explosive yield. Is that adequate for our purposes? The answer, of course, depends on what our purposes are. If we are interested in making sure that the enemy is not testing nuclear explosives at all, our purpose is served only if we can tell confidently whether he is testing or not, no matter how small the yield of his test explosion. The current monitoring systems we have cannot provide us with such assurance for nuclear explosives of less than 10 kilotons yield. Would it make sense to sign a complete test-ban treaty with only this system of verification? Again, the answer depends on the circumstances. If the opponent had no nuclear weapons at all, then his testing a 10-kiloton weapon would be an event we would most certainly want to know about. So in that case our ability to detect only explosions over 10 kilotons would not be good enough. On the other hand, if an opponent has 20,000 nuclear weapons, most of them much bigger than 10 kilotons, as the Soviet

Union does, what military difference would it make if he tested a 10-kiloton weapon? None. In this instance, our ability to detect explosions only above 10 kilotons would be adequate.

This basic thinking can be generalized to all monitoring activities. For example, our satellites can count how many land-based intercontinental ballistic missiles the Soviets have. But how accurately can we count? Within 10 missiles, within 100? If the Soviets are allowed 1,500 land-based missiles under some agreement, whether they have 1,400 or 1,600 doesn't matter a great deal. But if they have agreed to have only 100 it would make a great difference whether they had zero or 200.

In general, it is hard to feel confident about verifying agreements that involve small numbers other than zero. A complete ban on a weapon is easier to verify than an agreement that allows, say, 100 such weapons. If the opponent is supposed to have none, the moment the monitoring system detects one, it becomes apparent that the opponent is cheating. But if the agreement allows 100, it is quite difficult to know whether he indeed has 100 or, say, 120. In general, therefore, arms-control agreements that completely forbid a weapon system, a practice, or an activity are much easier to monitor and verify than agreements that permit small numbers of weapons.

What about the warning function of telemonitoring systems? How confident can we be in that? Again the answer cannot be given outside a specific context. An early warning system that misses a single, solitary missile launch would be a perfectly good system so long as it does not also miss 10 or 100 missiles launched in quick succession. This is because it is a massive surprise attack we should be concerned about, and not a single missile.

It is important, then, in public discussions of the ability of the United States to monitor Soviet development, production, and deployment of nuclear weapons, to keep in mind both the size of existing nuclear arsenals and the military significance of a particular lapse of detection.

AFTERWORD

FOR ONE COUNTRY to extract major political or other concessions from another uncooperative nation, that country must threaten punishment and destruction. Before the discovery of intercontinental bombers and ballistic missiles, one first had to defeat the often well-equipped protective armies of a country before such punishment of the general population was possible. But now, with the development of nuclear weapons and the delivery systems that carry them many thousands of miles, this condition has fundamentally changed. Now entire populations can be threatened and entire armies sidestepped by delivering nuclear weapons, with planes or missiles, to the heartland of the other country. So in order to understand the present situation, it is important to understand both the weapons and their long-range carriers, the combination of which has brought about an enormous change in the way war is waged.

But the proliferation of nuclear weapons on both sides of the Iron Curtain and the increasing sophistication of long-range carriers have also brought about fundamental changes in the assumptions which for centuries have formed the basis of international relations. Since the time that people stopped being gatherers and hunters and organized themselves in the first villages and communities, it was evident that by killing an enemy who threatened one's welfare and life, one's own survival was enhanced. But now, with nuclear weapons and unstoppable delivery systems that can completely devastate a country, this fundamental assumption is no longer valid. No matter who starts a nuclear war, no matter who strikes first, if one nuclear country tries to destroy the population of a second nuclear country, the second country can assuredly destroy the population of the first. So now killing an enemy does not assure one's own survival, but rather one's own annihilation. In other words, the instinct that for millenia promoted self-preservation will now result in self-destruction.

Because we cannot advantageously resolve our conflicts by fighting, we must resolve them in other ways. Besides war, there are three ways to resolve a conflict. One way is by threat of force—through posturing, intimidation, or coercion it is possible to convince an opponent to capitulate rather than fight. Another way is to negotiate an outcome that is beneficial to both sides. A negotiated solution may leave each party with a less than perfect settlement from its point of view, but since negotiation avoids fighting, then perhaps there is a compensation for the imperfection of the solution. Finally, there is recourse to courts of law in which conflicting parties abide by impartial decisions based upon mutually agreed-upon laws.

Given their enormous nuclear arsenals, how can the United States and the Soviet Union resolve their conflicts? Obviously, not by war. Both countries have so many nuclear weapons and delivery systems that they would most certainly destroy each other in a war. Because there is no world judiciary capable of enforcing its decisions, what is left is either posturing or negotiation. And here is the essence of the debate on our defense and foreign policy that we, the public, should take part in. The United States and the Soviet Union are resorting to posturing, more commonly known as "the arms race." We build a weapon system, trying to convince the Soviet Union that our strength is so decisive that it should defer to our wishes; the Soviet Union tries to do the same by building still another better, bigger, more threatening weapon system in order to intimidate us. We, in turn, respond to their response with yet another weapon, and so in the last thirty-five years weapon system has piled upon weapon system. So far the arms race has avoided combat, but it has become terribly expensive, terribly dangerous, and virtually endless. Therefore, some people argue the arms race is not going to get us anywhere, that negotiation is the only viable solution. But there are others who say that negotiation is not possible in all circumstances. For example, they claim that we cannot or should not negotiate with the Soviet Union. Because we cannot fight, they claim, the only recourse we have is to keep on posturing and building more powerful and effective weapons.

And if we do keep on building more weapons, what kind of systems are we going to build? Are they appropriate or inappropriate for such a race? Are they too costly for their purpose? Are they too dangerous? Do they provoke combat, which we all agree would be really disastrous? These are questions that affect all of us; they affect our own survival, the survival of our children, the survival of the human race, and the survival of the earth as we know it.

Clearly, public debate is essential. But in order for public debate to be useful, it must be intelligent and based on facts. It must be an educated debate. This book contains a physicist's description of nuclear weapons, how they work, and how they affect the environment when they explode. It contains a description of the delivery systems that carry such weapons from one country to another. And it describes possible ways to verify arms agreements if we were to cease our arms race and rely instead on negotiation: After all, a negotiated agreement is not terribly valuable unless one can verify that both sides are adhering to the agreed rules of conduct.

I hope this book has fulfilled the promise made in the Foreword: to provide information about nuclear weapons and their delivery systems and to explain the physics governing the performance of strategic weapons. The motivating ambition in writing this book has been to enable the reader to intelligently address the issues of nuclear weapons and nuclear war in order to restore open, informed debate on defense matters. National defense policy is best served when it is formulated according to the democratic tradition of this country.

APPENDICES

APPENDIX A
CALCULATION OF THE TEMPERATURE
OF EXPLOSION VAPORS

CONSIDER THE FISSION of a plutonium or uranium nucleus by a neutron that strikes it, during which two neutrons are created. Each one of these neutrons ideally proceeds to fission another nucleus, creating the chain reaction that releases the explosive energy of a nuclear weapon. Since each doubling step or "generation" doubles the number of neutrons available to fission the heavy nuclei, after n generations the number of neutrons N will be 2^n. Now we can ask how many generations will produce enough neutrons to fission, for example, 10 kg of plutonium. Since each gram mole contains $6 \cdot 10^{23}$ nuclei, we shall need

$$\frac{10,000 \text{ g}}{240 \text{ g}} \cdot 6 \cdot 10^{23} = 2.5 \cdot 10^{25}$$

neutrons. So solving the equation for n we have

$$2^n = 2.5 \cdot 10^{25}$$
$$n ln2 = ln(2.5 \cdot 10^{25})$$
$$n = 84 \text{ generations}$$

Each generation takes time τ to complete itself. This time represents both the actual fission process and the neutron's travel time from its originating nucleus to the one it fissions. Since, however, it takes only 10^{-22} seconds for the neutron to fission a nucleus, τ is essentially the neutron's travel time between nuclei. On the average a neutron travels 3 cm in the fissionable material at a speed about one tenth that of the speed of light. So $\tau = 3 \text{ cm}/3 \cdot 10^9 \text{ cm} = 10^{-9}$ sec or 1 nanosecond.

Thus the entire process of fissioning 10 kg of plutonium will last 84 nanoseconds! Note that the number of neutrons at 80 generations into the chain reaction is

$$N = 2^{80} = 1.2 \cdot 10^{24}$$

which is 5% of the $2.5 \cdot 10^{25}$ fissions that need be completed. So 95% of the energy released by the 10 kg of fissioned plutonium is generated in the last 4 nanoseconds of the reaction. How much energy is this? Since each fissioned plutonium nucleus gives out 240 Mev of energy, the 10 kg will generate

$$[10,000/240] \cdot 6 \cdot 10^{23} \cdot 240 \text{ Mev}$$

So the total energy is $6 \cdot 10^{27}$ Mev or $6 \cdot 10^{27} \cdot 1.6 \cdot 10^{-6} \simeq 10^{22}$ ergs. At the end of the fission process all this energy is contained in 10 kg of fission debris that occupies a volume $V = 10,000/15 \simeq 660$ cm^3 (since the density of plutonium is 15), so the energy density of the ball of fission debris at the end of the process is 10^{22} ergs/660 cm^3 = $1.5 \cdot 10^{19}$ erg/cm^3. This energy E is divided between the material of the debris and the radiation field, so

$$E = C_V T + C_R T^4$$

where $C_V = 6.2 \cdot 10^7$ and $C_R = 7.6 \cdot 10^{-15}$ so

$$1.5 \cdot 10^{19} = 6.2 \cdot 10^7 \cdot T + 7.6 \cdot 10^{-15} \cdot T^4$$

For such high-energy densities the radiation term dominates, so $1.5 \cdot 10^{19} \simeq 7.6 \cdot 10^{-15} \cdot T^4$ or $T \simeq 10^8$ K°. At such temperatures an object would give out photons with energies from a tenth of a Mev to a few kev. The wavelength of these photons is given by the simple expression $\lambda = h \cdot c/E$ where λ is in centimeters, c is the speed of light, and h is Planck's constant. Putting the values of c and h in the formula, we have

$$\lambda(\text{cm}) = 1.2 \cdot 10^{-10}/E(\text{Mev})$$

So for E = .1 Mev, $\lambda \simeq 10^{-9}$ cm, and for 10 kev (i.e. 10^{-2} Mev), $\lambda \simeq 10^{-7}$ cm, which are characteristic wavelengths of γ-rays and x-rays respectively. Consequently very energetic photons such as these can be emitted only by very hot objects. By comparison, the detonation of chemical explosives generates temperatures of a few thousand degrees. The photons emitted by a body at these temperatures predominantly have energies of a few ev. So their wavelengths are $\lambda = 1.2 \cdot 10^{-10}/10^{-6}$ or 10^{-4} cm, which is the characteristic wavelength for the visible light. Therefore the fundamental differences between nuclear and conventional explosives derive in large part from the very different temperatures that the two types of explosion generate.

APPENDIX B
INGREDIENTS OF A
FISSION-FUSION-FISSION WEAPON

IT IS INTERESTING to attempt an order-of-magnitude estimate of the amounts of fissionable and fusion materials needed for a 1-megaton nuclear explosive. We assume here that half the explosive yield comes from the fusion of D + T atoms and the other half (500 ktons) from the fissioning of U^{238} nuclei of the mantle around the weapon.

Since 1 kiloton of energy comes from $1.45 \cdot 10^{23}$ fissions, we need $500 \cdot 1.45 \cdot 10^{23} = 7.25 \cdot 10^{25}$ neutrons from the fusion process to fission enough U^{238} nuclei. The other 500 ktons must come from fusion. Since 500 ktons TNT equivalent is $1.3 \cdot 10^{28}$ Mev and since each D + T fusion releases energy of about 17 Mev, we need $1.3 \cdot 10^{28}/17 = 7.5 \cdot 10^{26}$ fusions to produce that energy. That is ten times the number of fusions needed to produce enough neutrons to fission the U^{238} blanket. So even if only one in ten neutrons from the D + T reaction is captured by the U^{238} blanket the U^{238} nuclei will be fissioned completely. Now $7.5 \cdot 10^{26}$ fusions is $1.2 \cdot 10^3$ gram moles worth of deuterium and tritium. So the weapon needs about 2 kg of deuterium and 4 kg of tritium to generate 500 ktons by fusion. This is an enormous amount of tritium to assemble considering how difficult it is to produce this isotope. So the "fuel" mixture of a fusion weapon must contain the amount of Li_3^6 that will produce (by absorption of a neutron) a comparable quantity of tritium. To generate 500 ktons of fission energy one needs about 60 kg of U^{238} nuclei that would be completely fissioned.

As we saw earlier, only a fraction of the fissionable material is expected to undergo fission before the kinetic energy of the fission fragments blows the weapons apart. So the actual weight of the U^{238} needed in a 1-megaton weapon may be 2–3 times the amount calculated here.

If about .5 Mev is needed to push D and T nuclei over the Coulomb barrier so they can fuse and produce $7.5 \cdot 10^{26}$ fusions, how much energy must be provided to the thermonuclear fuel by the plutonium trigger? Since $.5 \cdot 7.5 \cdot 10^{26} \simeq 3.7 \cdot 10^{26}$, this is the number of Mev needed, and since a quarter of a gram mole of plutonium releases $2 \cdot 10^{25}$ Mev we need about 4.5 gram moles—about 1 kg—of completely fissioned plutonium as a trigger. Actually, with a judiciously designed weapon, the fusion process can be self-sustaining; that is, the energy released from the initial fusion of D and T nuclei can be channeled into fusing the rest of the thermonuclear fuel.

When LiD is used as the source of T for the D + T reaction a neutron is needed to break up the Li into a T and a He atom. This is a slow neutron originally produced by a D + T reaction and then slowed down in lithium or beryllium to make it suitable for interacting with the Li^6. In effect, then, a small amount of pure microencapsulated T and D must be included in the fusion package of a weapon to act as "kindling" for the LiD + n reaction.

APPENDIX C
FIREBALL TRANSPARENCY
TO ELECTROMAGNETIC RADIATION

AT THE END of the explosion process the fission fragments and the atoms of the weapon itself are almost completely ionized. Without electrons they cannot absorb any photons, since absorption involves the interaction of a photon with an electron attached to an atom in which the photon disappears outright while the electron either jumps to a higher energy level within the atom or is knocked out of the atom altogether. So the vaporized weapon debris is transparent to photons, which escape out into the surrounding air. The average distance an x-ray would travel in the air before it would be absorbed (that is, "the mean free path") is given by the formula

$$L \simeq \frac{E^3}{5} \text{ cm}$$

where the energy is in kev. So for x-rays generated by the nuclear detonation the mean free path ranges from a few centimeters to a few tens of centimeters. But as they get absorbed in this layer around the point of detonation they knock electrons out of the atoms of the air, making the layer transparent to additional x-rays that are coming from the vaporized weapon fragments. These new x-rays are absorbed in, and heat up, a layer of air farther out, in turn ionizing it. This way the sphere of superheated air around the point of detonation expands very rapidly. For the first millisecond or so after the detonation of a megaton weapon the fireball is still several hundred thousand degrees hot but has expanded to only about 100 meters radius. The

growth of the fireball by means of this "radiative" mechanism continues until its temperature decreases to the point
that the mean free paths of the photons emitted by the
superheated gas inside the fireball are small compared to
the radius of the fireball. At that point the expansion of the
fireball slows down to the speed of sound. A shock wave is
then formed and the growth of the fireball continues by
means of a complicated hydrodynamic mechanism.

APPENDIX D
DESTRUCTIVE EFFECTS OF
A NUCLEAR EXPLOSION
UPON STRUCTURES

THE VERY LARGE AMOUNT of energy ($4.2 \cdot 10^{15}$ joules per megaton) released by a nuclear explosion is variously partitioned as a function of time into thermal, electromagnetic, and nuclear radiation, and into mechanical motion in the form of airblast, ground shock, and crater formation.

Initially, the energy is largely in the form of kinetic energy, which then becomes radiation energy, gets converted into blast and thermal energy, and eventually—except for the small portion that escapes as nuclear radiation—is reconverted back to heat. Except for the prompt electromagnetic and nuclear radiation, most of the yield of the weapon goes into the blast in the form of kinetic and heat energy. Much of the energy that goes into the ground in a surface burst quickly returns to the blast wave. Eventually, only about 10% remains in the long-term persistent radioactivity of the fallout [1].*

Chapter 3 described the destructive effects of nuclear (neutrons, γ-rays), thermal (mostly visible and infrared), and electromagnetic (EMP) radiation, as well as the effects of airblast, ground shock, and cratering caused by a nuclear explosion on the surface of the ground or at an advantageous height of burst above it. This appendix offers a somewhat more technical treatment of the same material for the readers who would like to have the means to do some simple calculations of their own.

* Bracketed numbers refer to the reference list at the end of this appendix.

1. NUCLEAR RADIATION

Nuclear radiation from fission or fusion weapons consists of α- and β-particles, protons, neutrons, neutrinos, and photons of a wide frequency spectrum, from γ-rays and x-rays to infrared and radio waves. The protons, α-particles, and β-particles quickly lose their energy by interacting with matter and, therefore, do not travel far from the point of detonation. Neutrons are strongly interacting particles without electric charge and therefore are scattered and captured by nuclei of matter rather than slowed down gradually because of loss of energy by ionization. Thus one can hope to reduce the flux of neutrons but never to eliminate them complete from the interior of a house or a silo. The same principle is true in the case of γ-rays.

The average number of neutrons per cm² at a distance R from a nuclear explosion is [2]

$$N(n) \simeq 2 \cdot 10^{22} \cdot \frac{Y}{R^2} \cdot \exp\{-R \cdot \rho/780\} \qquad (1)$$

$$\simeq 5 \cdot 10^{13} \cdot \frac{Y}{R^2} \cdot \exp\{-R \cdot \rho/780\} \qquad \text{rads}$$

where Y is the yield of the weapon in megatons, R the distance from the point of detonation in feet, and ρ the density of air (= 1.1 g/liter).

The respective expression for γ-rays is [2]

$$N(\gamma) \simeq 3.5 \cdot 10^{13} \cdot \frac{Y}{R^2} \cdot f \cdot \exp\{-\frac{R \cdot \rho}{\lambda}\} \qquad \text{roentgens} \qquad (2)$$

where R and Y are as in equation (1), $\lambda = 1070 + 1.5 \cdot Y^2$, the mean free path of γ-rays in feet, and an amplification factor,

$$f = (1 + 6Y^2)/(1 + 3 \cdot 10^{-2} \cdot Y^2 + 5 \cdot 10^{-3} \cdot Y^3)$$

To reduce the neutron flux by a factor of 10, one has to provide a shielding of concrete or damp earth of 25 or 40 cm, respectively. Each additional such thickness will further reduce the neutron flux by another factor of 10. Specially loaded concrete, used in shielding accelerators, for example, will achieve the same reduction factor with 15 cm of shielding.

Nuclear radiation causes both functional disruption and permanent damage to electronic equipment. Gamma rays, and to a much smaller degree neutrons, can cause ionization in solid-state electronic components which manifests itself as voltage and current pulses in the circuitry. These random pulses can overload circuitry or erase information in memory and logic circuits. The severity of these effects is dependent on the intensity of the radiation pulse; it is possible, then, that a circuit could "recover" after such a pulse.

Neutrons, on the other hand, can cause damage to a solid-state circuit by displacing atoms from the crystal lattice of a semiconductor. Some of this damage is permanent, and its extent depends on the total number of neutrons that impinge on the component. Various semiconductors are known to remain undamaged after exposure to $10^{11} - 10^{16}$ n/cm^2 [3]. Therefore, careful selection of semiconductor components and redundant circuitry on a missile can minimize its vulnerability to nuclear radiation. Proper circuit design can result in electronic components that will tolerate 10^{15} n/cm^2 without damage. These considerations are hardly relevant for civilian equipment but must be taken into account in the case of military electronic equipment and the electronics of a missile in its silo.

2. THERMAL RADIATION

A portion of the energy generated by a nuclear detonation is emitted in the form of x-rays. In an atmospheric detonation the "soft," or lower-energy, x-rays are rapidly absorbed by the ambient atmosphere, which heats up rapidly and forms the fireball that emits thermal radiation—mainly photons in the visible and infrared portion of the spectrum. The x-ray flux from a weapon of Y megatons a distance of R kilometers away is

$$N(x) = 7.9 \cdot 10^3 \cdot \frac{Y}{R^2} \cdot \exp\{-\delta \cdot R \cdot \rho \cdot 10^5\} \qquad \text{cal/cm}^2 \quad (3)$$

where Y = yield in megatons
R = range in km
δ = air mass absorption coefficient
ρ = density of air
= $1.2 \cdot 10^{-3}$ g/cm³ typically

The value of δ depends critically on the photon energy; for a 10-kev photon, δ is about 4 cm²/g and rapidly drops to .15 cm²/g for 100 kev.

The heated gases inside the fireball of a nuclear explosion can reach temperatures of 10^6 C°; at these temperatures the air inside it becomes transparent to x-rays, which consequently escape and cause the fireball to grow by heating the surrounding layers of cold air. The fireball growth involves two pulses of thermal radiation: a prompt one that contains less than 1% of the total thermal energy, and a second one that peaks about a second after the detonation and lasts, in the case of a 1-megaton weapon, for about 10 seconds. This duration is proportional to the 0.33 power of the yield. Eventually, about one-third of the total yield of the weapon is radiated in thermal energy.

The amount of thermal radiation from an explosion in the air of yield Y a distance R (in km) away is

$$Q = 1.8 \cdot 10^3 \cdot \frac{Y}{R^2} \cdot t \qquad \text{cal/cm}^2$$

where t is a transmission factor dependent on weather conditions. Where visibility is 15 kilometers, t is equal to about .9 at a distance of 300 meters from the detonation and is equal to about .8 at a distance of 1 kilometer. The corresponding formula for a surface burst is

$$Q = 1.15 \cdot 10^3 \cdot \frac{Y}{R^2} \cdot t \qquad \text{cal/cm}^2$$

3. ELECTROMAGNETIC PULSE

Gamma rays with energies from a fraction of an Mev to about 10 Mev emitted by a nuclear explosion undergo

Compton scattering in the atmosphere. The recoil electrons ionize the air molecules and release a large number of additional electrons and positively charged ions. For a surface or near-surface burst, the earth's surface confines this phenomenon to a hemisphere around the point of detonation, thereby creating an asymmetrical distribution of electrical charges in the space around the detonation. The Compton electrons move rapidly away from the center of a detonation, ionizing in an avalanche fashion more air molecules as they go, while leaving the much heavier positive ions behind. From a distance, this moving shell of electrons looks like a current pulse that radiates electromagnetic waves over a large frequency range. Eventually, the positive charges left behind attract the electrons back toward the point of explosion, creating a second current pulse. These plasma oscillations gradually die out because of the recombination of electrons and ions, but while they persist they create intense electromagnetic fields that induce currents to flow in nongrounded conductors in a very large area. This effect, known as the electromagnetic pulse (EMP), can damage electronic equipment over very large areas. In the case of silos the reinforcing steel structure of the silo can reduce the EMP amplitude by an order of magnitude. Attenuation, however, is a sensitive function of frequency; consequently it is very difficult to isolate all equipment completely. Attenuation by factors of 10^3 to 10^4 for high-frequency components of EMP may be necessary to safeguard the operational readiness of such circuit elements as transistors or semiconductor diodes.

A different type of EMP produced by exoatmospheric bursts has similar effects, except that its signal can travel over very large distances. It is not discussed here in detail since the high-altitude EMP effect and its implications are discussed elsewhere in this book. It is conceivable, however, that the attacker could attempt to damage sensitive electronic devices in the command and control system of an opponent with the powerful EMP pulse exoatmospheric detonations generate.

4. AIRBLAST EFFECTS

A nuclear explosion in the atmosphere is essentially a point source of large amounts of energy ($4.2 \cdot 10^{12}$ joules per kiloton equivalent) released in a very short time interval (3–10 nanoseconds). A very large fraction of this energy goes into the formation and propagation of a shock wave generated by the rapid expansion of heated gases in the immediate vicinity of the explosion. Like a wall of air expanding at supersonic speed, the shock wave compresses and therefore heats new layers of the atmosphere, losing some of its energy and slowing down as a result (see Figure D.1). The transient increased pressure in the shock wave, defined as the "side-on overpressure," is the overpressure above atmospheric pressure that will be recorded by a gauge flush with the ground as the shock wave passes over it (see Figure D.2). The highest value of this pressure is referred to as "peak overpressure." The peak overpressure as a function of weapon yield is given by [5]

$$P_O = 3300 \cdot \frac{Y}{R^3} + 192 \cdot \left[\frac{Y}{R^3} \right]^{1/2} \tag{4}$$

where Y is in megatons, R the distance from the point of explosion in kilofeet, and P_O the peak overpressure in pounds per square inch (psi) or

$$P_O = 14.7 \cdot \frac{Y}{R^3} + 12.8 \cdot \left[\frac{Y}{R^3} \right]^{1/2} \tag{5}$$

where R is in nautical miles. For values of P_O larger than 100 psi this formula can be simplified to [6]

$$P_O = \frac{16.4Y}{R^3} \tag{6}$$

All three formulas are valid for *surface* bursts. In general, the blast effects of surface bursts are assumed to be twice as strong as the effects from an air burst of equivalent magnitude. Peak overpressures versus range are plotted in Figure D.3 (page 274) as a function of yield.

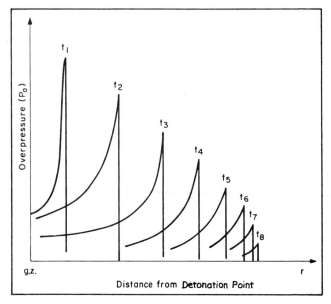

FIGURE D.1. Motion of an idealized shock front. The shock front is depicted at equally spaced time intervals ($t_{i+1} - t_i$ = constant, where i = 1, 2 ... n), and, therefore, the "bunching up" in r indicates the slowing down of the front.

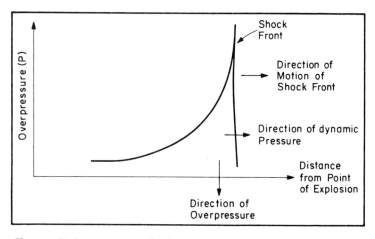

FIGURE D.2. Direction of relevant vector parameters of a propagating shock front.

As the blast wave moves away from the point of detonation, it generates behind it violent winds that blow away from this point. These winds generate a pressure on surfaces they encounter, known as *dynamic* pressure. The drag forces that develop as a result depend on the shape, size, and orientation of the surface or structure subjected to them, as well as the peak value of the dynamic pressure. The peak value of dynamic pressure, Q_O, is related to the value of the peak overpressure P_O by the formula

$$Q_O = \frac{5}{2} \cdot \frac{P_O^{\;2}}{7P_A + P_O} \tag{7}$$

where P_A is atmospheric pressure (14.7 psi). This formula assumes ideal gas conditions and agrees rather well with experimental data for values of P_O to 1000 psi. Since few essential parts of a silo extend vertically above ground, where they would be exposed to the drag forces of the winds accompanying the shock, the survivability of these structures is not directly affected by the magnitude of the dynamic pressure. However, dynamic pressure is an important destructive mechanism for civilian structures such as houses, factories, power lines, etc.

The presence of nonideal conditions in a nuclear explosion makes the predictive value of the formulae for peak overpressure and dynamic pressure somewhat uncertain. In general, Q_O for a given range can be reliably predicted within a factor of two, while the range for a given Q_O can be predicted to ± 25 percent. Peak overpressure at a given range is uncertain to ± 20 percent [7]. The uncertainties are caused by the variable nature of the ground surface and the formation of a precursor wave ahead of the main blast wave. These effects, particularly that of the precursor wave, are significant at overpressures much lower than those relevant to the survivability of silos, and are quite important for the case of "soft" structures like houses and factories.

The velocity of the shock front as it moves outward from the point of explosion is given by

$$U = C_O \cdot \left[1 + \frac{6P_O}{7P_A} \right]^{1/2} \tag{8}$$

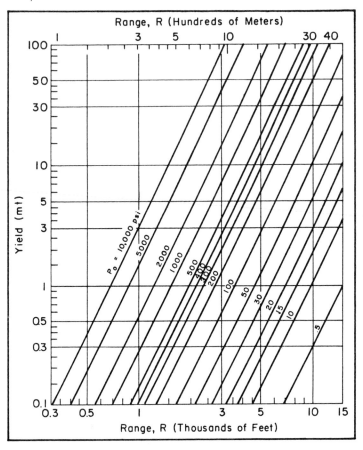

FIGURE D.3. Peak overpressure isobars as a function of yield and range. (Ref. 4)

where C_O is the speed of sound in the unshocked atmosphere ahead of the blast wave equal to 340 m/sec (1120 ft per sec) and P_A is the atmospheric pressure (14.17 psi). This relation is illustrated in Figure D.4.

When a nuclear weapon explodes at some height above the ground, the blast wave is reflected when it hits the

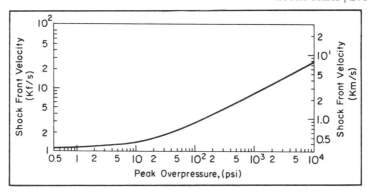

FIGURE D.4. Variation of shock front velocity with peak overpressure. (Ref. 4)

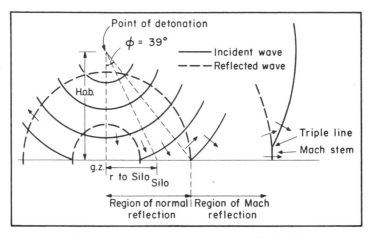

FIGURE D.5. Diagrammatic representation of the formation of Mach stem due to the fusion of reflected and incident waves beyond the normal reflection region.

ground. The reflected wave now travels in a volume of air that has been heated and is highly compressed; since the velocity of sound is higher in that environment than in undisturbed air, the reflected wave travels faster than the incident shock front, and at some distance from ground zero —the point on the ground directly beneath the point of detonation—it catches up with the incident wave, fuses with it, and forms a front perpendicular to the ground known as Mach stem (see Figure D.5). Figures D.6 and D.7 show the peak overpressure on the ground resulting from bursts at various heights above the ground in the high-pressure and low-pressure regions respectively. It is seen that in the Mach region there is considerable enhancement of the area covered by a given minimum overpressure for an optimal height of burst. For example, the 10 psi isobar would be found 1,100 feet from the point of explosion for a surface burst, but extends to almost 1,450 feet for a burst at 700 feet above ground. This effect is caused by the Mach stem formation, since, as is seen in Figure D.7, for the region of regular reflection the 10 psi isobar extends at best to 1,100 feet. There is little if any enhancement of the range for a given overpressure in the high-overpressure region (Figure D.6). Very recent studies [8], based to a great extent on small-high-explosive-charge experiments, indicate that the "high overpressure Mach reflection region is now understood to be characterized by a double-shock system." In the regular reflection region, this double peak does not materialize. The main effect, relevant to calculations of the damage to silos, that this discovery has introduced is that the initial decay of the first pulse, which causes the initial response of the silo, is much faster than older studies indicated, and that its duration may be substantially shorter than the free air positive phase. Since these studies also tend to suggest lower initial overpressures than those now in use [9], one may expect that the total impulse as a function of range from the point of explosion will be considerably smaller in the Mach reflection region. Thus a silo located in that region will be subjected to smaller overpressure than given by formula (4) above.

When a nuclear weapon explodes above a nonreflective surface, such as dry soil, the thermal radiation that outruns the shock front heats up the absorbent surface of the ground and thus creates a layer of hot air immediately above it. The shock wave propagates faster in this layer, and this causes an auxiliary shock wave to run ahead of the main blast wave. This auxiliary wave is known as the "precursor front" and its formation removes some of the energy from

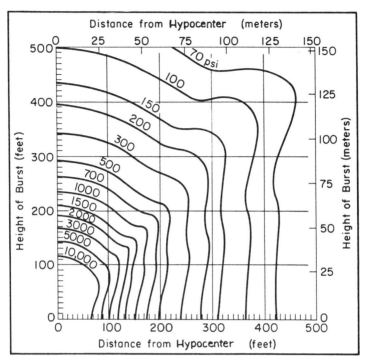

FIGURE D.6. Variation of peak overpressure on the ground with height of burst and range from the hypocenter (a point on the ground underneath the detonation point), in the high-pressure region. (1-kton explosion) (Ref. 4)

the main shock wave. As a result, the peak overpressure is less than anticipated by the formulae, but the dynamic pressure may increase. Thus, formation of a precursor tends to enhance dynamic pressures and certainly makes prediction of the effects of a given nuclear explosion on a civilian structure more uncertain, but does not influence appreciably the effects on a silo.

The overpressure in the shock wave rises instantaneously to what is essentially the peak overpressure value and then decays in a complex manner.

The exact pulse duration is defined as the time it takes the atmosphere over a given point to return to ambient pressure. The importance of the duration of the pulse varies

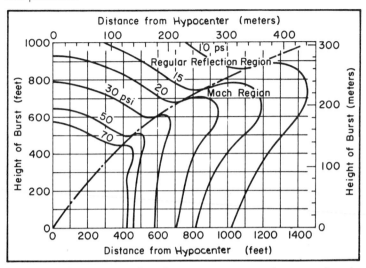

FIGURE D.7. Variation of peak overpressure on the ground with height of burst and range from the hypocenter, in the low-pressure region. (1-kton explosion) (Ref. 4)

with the type of target under attack. For targets vulnerable to dynamic pressure, for example, the duration of the entire pulse may be quite important, while for targets such as silo covers that experience only the overpressure of the shock wave, duration may be less important. Whether the silo cover survives or not depends on the characteristic time constant of the cover. This is because the response of a silo cover to an impulsive load, that is, the time integral of overpressure over the pulse duration of the blast wave, depends strongly on its own structural characteristics.

The laws of physics that determine the development and growth in space and time of a spherical blast wave caused by a nuclear explosion in the atmosphere produce two very useful, related corollaries:

1. The effects from two explosions of nuclear warheads of different yields Y_1 and Y_2 under similar initial and boundary conditions (that is, both air bursts or both ground bursts) are related to each other as the cube root of the ratio of the yields.

2. The same values of dynamic variables, such as peak

overpressure, impulse, etc., occur at a range that scales as the cube root of the yield of the weapon for all nuclear explosions (with initial and boundary conditions that follow the same scaling).

Then, since a given peak overpressure will occur at a distance from an explosion R which is proportional to the cube root of the yield—see equation (6) above—at a time t after the explosion, we have

$$\frac{R_1}{Y_1^{1/3}} = \frac{R_2}{Y_2^{1/3}} = \dots \frac{R_n}{Y_n^{1/3}} \tag{9}$$

where $Y_1 \dots Y_n$ are different weapons' yields and $R_1 \dots R_n$ the range at which the same overpressure will be felt for each yield and

$$\frac{t_1}{Y_1^{1/3}} = \frac{t_2}{Y_2^{1/3}} = \dots \frac{t_n}{Y_n^{1/3}} \tag{10}$$

where $t_1 \dots t_n$ are times at which a given overpressure will be at a specific point for the various yields. Or

$$R_1 = R_2 \left[\frac{Y_1}{Y_2} \right]^{1/3} \tag{11}$$

$$t_1 = t_2 \left[\frac{Y_1}{Y_2} \right]^{1/3} \tag{12}$$

So if a 1-kiloton explosion causes 10 psi overpressure .117 nautical miles from the point of detonation, a 1-megaton explosion causes the same 10 psi overpressure 1.17 nautical miles away.

These relationships, which hold for explosive yields from a few grams to many megatons of TNT equivalent [4], permit the prediction of the blast effects of a weapon of any yield from the effects of a test blast of, say, 1-kton yield. Thus, in many instances in this appendix, graphs relating dynamic variables to space-time variables are plotted for 1-kton-yield explosions. From these one can derive the respective relationships for any yield. Note that in graphs such as Figure D.6 *both* the height of burst *and* the range must be scaled.

In a nonidealized environment not all damaging effects scale. For example, the time and intensity of exposure to thermal radiation, the depth of debris, and the frequency and intensity of EMP are higher than expected at scaled ranges [1]. Also, such variables as duration of positive pulse and amplitude of ground motion may cause greater response, and therefore greater damage at corresponding overpressures.

5. GROUND-SHOCK EFFECTS

The detonation of a nuclear weapon, either at the surface of the earth or in the air, causes violent motion of the ground in its immediate vicinity. In a surface burst, a portion of the released energy (mainly in the form of highly kinetic weapon debris) couples directly to the ground and excites a ground shock wave. This released energy also excavates a crater that, because of conservation of momentum, gives rise to a secondary ground shock which becomes part of the overall *directly induced* ground shock. As the airblast shock wave starts propagating outward from the point of detonation it excites a ground shock immediately beneath itself. In the case of an aboveground explosion, only the *airblast-induced* ground shock is created, since there is little or no cratering, and practically no energy couples to the ground directly. The motion experienced by the ground at a given point is a combination of airblast-induced and directly coupled effects and depends on the range from ground zero, the depth of the point, the geology of the ground, the height of burst, and the yield of the weapon.

It is important to note, however, that the separation of the ground motion caused by a nuclear explosion into air-blast-induced, directly induced and crater-induced ground shock is theoretically incorrect, since any point in the ground experiences a composite motion resulting from all three ground shocks. The separation is artificial and is done in order to facilitate the analysis that permits the formulation of predictive relationships between the variables that characterize the explosion (yield, h.o.b., range from the point of explosion) and the values of kinetic variables such as acceleration, velocity, and displacement at that point. These relationships describe the *free-field* ground shock, that is, the value of the kinetic variables in the absence of any structures. The interaction of the free-field ground shock with a silo is quite complex.

Airblast-induced ground shock is the most important source of ground acceleration beyond the crater region. While the direct ground shock or the crater-induced shock are rapidly attenuated to harmless levels by the damping, inertial, and nonlinear properties of the soil, the airblast-induced shock travels for great distances from the point of detonation as its driving mechanism, the air shock front, propagates in the atmosphere (see Figure D.8). In layered media, however, large displacement amplitudes caused by direct-induced motion can be experienced even at large distances from the point of detonation [1]. The expanding shock front applies instantaneous loads of an intensity continuously decreasing in time, at an infinite number of points on the ground. Thus, the resulting ground shock is a time-dependent superposition of all these loads. Near the point of detonation the airblast wave travels at supersonic velocities that are generally greater than the velocity of the ground wave in the soil. In that region, the ground shock front is immediately under the airblast (Figure D.8a). But as the air shock front expands, it slows down (see Figure D.1) to a point where the wave propagation velocity in the ground is larger than its speed in the air. From that point on, the ground shock wave outruns the airblast (see Figure D.8b) and points in the ground experience ground motion before they experience the direct airblast effects. The high-frequency components of the shock wave are not attenuated rapidly (as is the case in the directly induced ground shock). Therefore the stress wave in the ground caused by the traveling shock front has a short rise-time, which in turn causes high accelerations. In order to conserve momentum, the rise-time becomes longer with distance from the point of detonation, as does the duration of the pulse. The peak magnitude of the stress, which can never be more than the peak overpressure that caused it, varies at least as rapidly

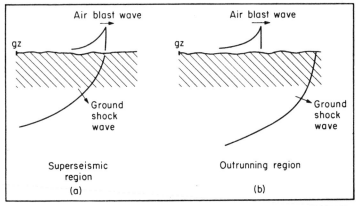

FIGURE D.8. Airblast-induced ground shock wave in the superseismic (a) and outrunning (b) region.

as the inverse second power of distance from the point of burst. Thus, the intensity of the airblast-induced ground shock could be much greater at large distances from ground zero than the directly induced shock. However, for those geologies in which seismic velocity layers underlie lower velocity layers, the ground motion at large distances is dominated by the directly induced effects.*

Formulae that predict approximate peak values for acceleration, velocity, and displacement of the ground near the surface due to *airblast-induced* ground motion in the superseismic and outrunning regions are given below [10].

For the superseismic region:

Vertical acceleration

$$\ddot{S}_{vs} \simeq 340 \frac{P_o}{C_s} \pm 30\% \tag{13}$$

Vertical velocity

$$\dot{S}_{vs} \simeq 75 \frac{P_o}{C_s \cdot \rho} \pm 20\% \tag{14}$$

Vertical displacement

$$S_{vs} \simeq 20 \cdot I \cdot \frac{P_o^{.25}}{C_s \cdot \rho} \pm 30\% \tag{15}$$

* Seismic velocity is the velocity at which the ground stress wave travels.

For the outrunning region:

Vertical acceleration $\qquad \ddot{S}_{VO} \simeq \dfrac{2 \cdot 10^5}{C_S r^2} \left\{ {+ \text{ factor of } 4 \atop - \text{ factor of } 2} \right.$ (16)

Vertical velocity $\qquad \dot{S}_{VO} \simeq \dfrac{4 \cdot 10^5}{C_S \cdot \rho \cdot r^2} \pm 50\%$ (17)

Vertical displacement $\qquad S_{VO} \simeq \dfrac{6 \cdot 10^4 \cdot Y^{1/3} \cdot \rho}{C_S \cdot r^2}$ (18)

where P_O = the peak overpressure at the point of interest in psi
C_S = the wave velocity in the medium in ft/sec
ρ = the specific gravity of the earth
I = the overpressure impulse in psi-sec
r = $R/Y^{1/3}$ kilofeet/(Mtons)$^{1/3}$ the scaled distance
Y = the yield of the weapon in Mtons, and
R = the distance from the point of detonation in kilofeet

In the above formulae $\ddot{S}$ is in g's, $\dot{S}$ is feet/sec, and displacement S in feet [10].

Values of C_S for various soils are listed in Table D.1. By using this table and Figure D.4, one can determine the distance from the point of detonation that the outrunning mode starts. For example, since $C_S \simeq 6000$ ft/sec for wet soils, the outrunning region will start at a point where the peak overpressure is 500 psi. Knowing the yield of the weapon and using this value of peak overpressure in equation (6), it is possible to calculate the desired range. For example, in a 1-Mton surface burst, the distance is

$$500 = \frac{16.4 \cdot 1}{R^3}$$
$$R = .32 \text{ nautical miles}$$

A good theoretical approximation, applicable to homogeneous media, is to calculate the corresponding horizontal components from the vertical components of motion given above by using the relation

(horizontal component of $S, \dot{S}, \ddot{S}$) =
= (vertical component of $S, \dot{S}, \ddot{S}$) × tan (arc sin C_S/U)   (19)

where for values of tan (arc sin C_S/U) equal or larger to 1, the peak horizontal component is taken equal to the corresponding peak vertical component [6]. As a practical matter, however, in most real soils the transmission through underlying higher seismic velocity layers cause a series of transseismic and then outrunning signals, so that at the distance from the explosion where one would expect to find the silo, the motion is often upward and outward due to an airblast-induced wave without a directly induced motion component.

The values for maximum acceleration attenuate rapidly with depth because the hysteresis of the soil dissipates the energy of the pulse by the preferential removal of the high-frequency components of the pulse and therefore lengthens its rise-time as a function of depth. The vertical displacement experiences an exponential decrease with depth:

$$S = S_O \cdot \exp(-.017 \cdot Z)$$

where S_O is the displacement near the surface and Z is the depth in feet. This relationship was derived to fit small-yield airburst detonations over a dry bed in Nevada and may not be generally applicable to all geologies [1].

The airblast-induced stress and strain values in the ground as a function of overpressure P_O and depth Z are given by [5].

Vertical peak stress
$$\sigma_V = \alpha_Z \cdot P_O$$
where α_Z = the geometric attenuation factor

$$\alpha_Z = \cfrac{1}{1 + \cfrac{Z \cdot P_O^{1/2}}{2.3 \cdot 10^3 \cdot Y^{1/3}}}$$ (20)

Z = depth in feet
P_O = peak overpressure in psi
Y = yield in Mton

TABLE D.1
Typical seismic velocities for soils and rocks

MATERIAL	SEISMIC VELOCITY ft/sec	SEISMIC VELOCITY m/sec
Loose and dry soils	600– 3,300	180–1,000
Clay and wet soils	2,500– 6,300	760–1,900
Coarse and compact soils	3,000– 8,500	910–2,600
Sandstone and cemented soils	3,000–14,000	910–4,300
Shale and marl	6,000–17,500	1,800–5,300
Limestone—chalk	7,000–21,000	2,100–6,400
Metamorphic rocks	10,000–21,000	3,000–6,400
Volcanic rocks	10,000–22,000	3,000–6,700
Sound plutonic rocks	13,000–25,000	4,000–7,600
Jointed granite	8,000–15,000	2,400–4,600
Weathered rocks	2,000–10,000	600–3,100

Source: Ref. 9.

Vertical peak strain

$$\epsilon_V \simeq 1.1 \cdot 10^5 \cdot P_O / \rho \cdot C_S^2 \pm 30\% \quad \text{(parts per thousand)} \quad (21)$$

$$\text{where } \rho = \text{soil density}$$
$$C_S = \text{soil seismic velocity}$$

The corresponding horizontal quantities σ_H and ϵ_H are given by

$$\sigma_H = \xi \cdot \sigma_V$$

and

$$\epsilon_H = \xi \cdot \epsilon_V$$

where ξ is between 1/3 and 1/2 depending on soil conditions. For very soft saturated soils ξ can reach 1 [11].

When the soil in the vicinity of the explosion is layered, reflections from the layer interfaces complicate the prediction of ground motion even further. In general, however, layering tends to dampen the vertical and enhance the horizontal components of motion. Therefore, these values of horizontal stress and strain can be taken as lower limits.

Ground shock and cratering effects of nuclear weapons cannot be simulated with conventional explosives. As a result, there is very little information available for quantitative predictions of directly induced ground motion resulting from nuclear explosions on the surface of the earth.

The following formulae that relate kinetic variables to weapon yield and distance from detonation are extrapolations from the results of deeply buried nuclear tests. In such tests, all the energy released in the explosion is directly coupled to the ground. Thus with proper instrumentation, accurate relationships between the weapon yield and the magnitude of ground motion can be derived. For a surface burst, however, the initial coupling of energy from the exploding weapon to the ground is rather uncertain. Since the extrapolation from a completely buried explosion to a surface one depends delicately on this coupling, the predictions made based on this approach are very uncertain.

When a nuclear weapon explodes on the ground, the very high temperatures and pressures present in the vapors of the weapon material transmit kinetic energy to the ground material and cause it to fly away, generating a crater immediately below and around the point of detonation. The airblast caused by the explosion spreads quickly over a large area and, therefore, has pressures which are thousands of times smaller than the concentrated impact of the vaporized weapon debris. Thus, airblast does not contribute substantially to crater formation, although it does play a role, for example, in its final shape and size by inhibiting excavation. If the weapon detonates aboveground, the energy of its vaporized debris is quickly expended in driving the shock front through the surrounding air. The resulting crater will, therefore, be much smaller, and for scaled heights of burst of $100 \cdot Y^{1/3}$ ft (where Y is in kilotons) or above there is no significant cratering at all [9].

The dimensions of the crater caused by a surface detonation should satisfy the same scaling relations:

$$r_{C_1} = r_{C_2}(Y_1/Y_2)^{1/3} \tag{22}$$

$$d_{C_1} = d_{C_2}(Y_1/Y_2)^{1/3} \tag{23}$$

where r_C is the crater radius and d_C the crater depth. But r_C and d_C depend on the geology and the type of soil in the vicinity of the explosion, and on the height of burst of the weapon, so that the scaling relations can be used only for purposes of comparison between two explosions at the same type of geology. Experimental data and recent more detailed calculations show that the radius r_C, in meters, of a crater caused by a surface burst of a weapon of yield Y in megatons is given by:

$$r_C = \Lambda Y^{.3} \qquad (24)$$

where Λ is a constant dependent on the type of soil on which the explosion occurs.

The respective expression for the crater depth is:

$$d_C = \beta Y^{.3} \qquad (25)$$

Reference [4] lists, for surface nuclear explosions above 1 kton, $\Lambda = 190$ m/Mton for dry soil and $\Lambda = 150$ m/Mton for sandstone with $\beta = 55$ m/Mton and 70 m/Mton for dry soil and sandstone respectively. But reference [5], based on data from Pacific atoll explosions, gives $\Lambda = 260$ m/Mton and 230 m/Mton for dry soil and sandstone, and $\beta = 28$ m/Mton and 24 m/Mton for dry soil and sandstone. It is possible that these latter results may reflect the presence of underlying higher-density geological strata that enhance the horizontal and limit the vertical extent of the crater.

As Table D.2 shows, the cratering efficiency varies with the yield of the weapons and becomes *smaller* with increasing yield (that is, deviates from the scaling law, since yield becomes *less* important for cratering as its value increases). On the other hand, as was indicated above, if the soil on which the weapon explodes is layered with relatively soft surface rock sitting on a layer of harder rock, the radius of the crater formed in such soil will tend to be larger and the depth smaller than predicted by the formula. The former effect is due to the fact that for high-yield weapons the energy density at the point of detonation is higher and, therefore, both the coupling efficiency to the soil is smaller and the proportion of energy released as radiation is larger. The latter is due to reflections from the higher-density subsurface layer.

Figure D.9, a freehand drawing, indicates that although r_C can be taken as the limit of survivability for any silo, a more realistic limit would be $2r_C$ since it is almost certain that a missile protected in a silo located in the rupture zone or covered by the explosion ejecta could not remain operational.

TABLE D.2

Surface-burst cratering efficiencies in idealized geologies*

GEOLOGY	CRATERING EFFICIENCY		
	TNT	HIGH-YIELD NUCLEAR $Y \geq 1$ KT	LOW-YIELD NUCLEAR $Y < 1$ KT
Dry soil (e.g., alluvium, clay, sand)	1,400 ft³/ton	70 ft³/ton	210 ft³/ton
Wet soil (e.g., surface water table)	4,000 ft³/ton	200 ft³/ton	600 ft³/ton
Dry soft rock (e.g., shale, sandstone)	1,000 ft³/ton	50 ft³/ton	150 ft³/ton
Wet soft rock (e.g., surface water table)	2,000 ft³/ton	100 ft³/ton	300 ft³/ton
Hard rock (e.g., basalt, granite)	600 ft³/ton	30 ft³/ton	90 ft³/ton

Source: Ref. 5.

As Figure D.9 roughly illustrates, $r_\ell \simeq 1.5\ r_C$ and $r_t = 2r_C$. In the rupture zone the soil is transversed by many radial cracks and in the plastic zone the soil has been compressed to a state of permanent deformation that causes part of the sloping around the crater.

* The expected uncertainty in the table values is plus or minus a factor of 1.6. The TNT cratering efficiency is 20 times the high-yield nuclear cratering efficiency and 20/3 times the low-yield nuclear cratering efficiency.

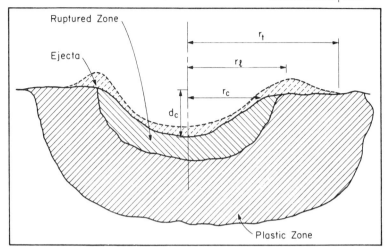

FIGURE D.9. Schematic definition of parameters of a crater formed by nuclear surface burst.

The formulae for the variation of various nuclear explosion effects given weapon yield and distance from the point of detonation permit the calculation of the free-field values of these effects for different attack levels. Given the yield of a warhead, one can calculate the severity of ground motions or the peak overpressure at a given distance. Knowing the CEP of the reentry vehicle that carries the warhead permits one to estimate the probability that given values of overpressure, or stress, or nuclear radiation, will be felt at the silo site as a result of the nuclear explosion.

REFERENCES TO APPENDIX D

1. S. Glasstone and P. Dolan, "The Effects of Nuclear Weapons," 1977, pp. 7–8.
2. H. L. Brode, "Review of Nuclear Weapon Effects," *Annual Review of Nuclear Sciences*, 1968, pp. 153–202.
3. *Effects of Radiation on Materials and Components*, Reinholt Publishing Company, 1964.
4. Glasstone, op. cit., p. 24.

5. *Air Force Manual for Design and Analysis of Hardened Structures*, Kirtland Air Force Base, New Mexico, 1974, p. 35.
6. Brode, op. cit.
7. *Mathematical Background and Programming Aids for Physical Vulnerability System for Nuclear Weapons*, DI-550-27-1, Defense Intelligence Agency, Washington, D.C., 1974.
8. H. L. Brode and J. G. Lewis, *Implications of Recent Airblast Studies to Damage of Hardened Structures*, R&D Associates, Marina del Ray, California, 1975.
9. H. L. Brode, *Height of Burst Effects at High Overpressures*, RM-6301 DASA Rand Corporation, Santa Monica, California, 1970.
10. H. L. Brode, *A Review of Nuclear Radiation Phenomena Pertinent to Protective Construction*, Rand Report R-425 PR, Rand Corporation, Santa Monica, California, 1964.
11. N. Newmark et al., *Principles and Practices for Design of Hardened Structures*, Air Force Design Manual, Kirtland Air Force Base, New Mexico, 1962.

APPENDIX E
INERTIAL NAVIGATION
OF BALLISTIC MISSILES

THE ACCURATE DELIVERY of a warhead to its target by a ballistic missile requires the ability to steer the rocket thrust of the missile so that at the moment the thrust is terminated, the missile's speed, direction of motion, and position are such that the warhead, when released, will be on one of the many possible trajectories that lead to its target. This ability in turn requires the measurement of all the forces that act on the missile during its flight and cause its motion. Once these forces are measured, the motion of the missile—that is, its position, velocity, and acceleration—can be computed with the aid of the simple formulae of Newtonian mechanics.

A technique known as inertial sensing is used to guide the ballistic missiles of the United States and the Soviet Union to their targets. This technique utilizes sensitive gauges to measure the forces acting on a small test mass m inside an instrument known as accelerometer.

Two forces act on the missile during its boost phase: the force of gravity F_g and the force of the booster rocket F_a. The force of gravity F_g is equal to

$$F_g = m \cdot \bar{g} \tag{1}$$

where m is the test mass that can be carefully weighed before it is put into the accelerometer, and $\bar{g}$ is the acceleration of gravity.

$$\bar{g} = \frac{G \cdot M_e \cdot \bar{r}}{r^3} \tag{2}$$

291

where $G \cdot M_e$ is the earth's gravitational constant and r is the distance of the missile from the center of the earth. Notice that r is a vector (that is, it has both magnitude and direction). The accelerometer is constructed and attached to the missile so that the acceleration ā experienced by the entire missile is the same as the acceleration experienced by the test mass inside the accelerometer. So

$$\bar{a} \cdot m = F_a + F_g \tag{3}$$

where ā is the total acceleration sensed by the accelerometer, which is also the total acceleration of the missile. So using equation (1):

$$\bar{a} \cdot m = F_a + m \cdot \bar{g} \tag{4}$$

$$\text{or} \qquad \bar{a} = \bar{F}_a/m + \bar{g} \tag{5}$$

Thus, in order to know ā the acceleration of the missile, one must know F_a, m, and $\bar{g}$. The test mass m is known. The acceleration of gravity $\bar{g}$ cannot be measured by the accelerometer and therefore its value must be fed into the equation. Equation (2) says that $\bar{g}$ varies with $\bar{r}$, the position of the missile. So the values of $\bar{g}$ must be stored in the memory of the missile computer as a function of $\bar{r}$ and fed continuously into equation (5). The quantity the accelerometer measures is F_a, the force the test mass (and the entire missile) senses as a result of the rocket booster. Since ā in equation (5) is a vector quantity, provisions must be made to determine both its magnitude and direction, and therefore to measure the magnitude and direction of $\bar{F}_a$. Traditionally, this is done by analyzing the force vector F_a into three mutually perpendicular components F_{a_x}, F_{a_y}, F_{a_z} which cause the respective accelerations $\bar{a}_x$, $\bar{a}_y$, $\bar{a}_z$.

The measurement of the acceleration is implemented by mounting three accelerometers with their sensitive axes perpendicular to each other, and aligned with the coordinate system of axes in which the missile is guided: Once the acceleration of the missile along each of the three axes of this coordinate system is known it is possible to compute its velocity and position. Knowing these quantities the computer on board the missile can command the booster rocket to shut off the instant the missile has the requisite velocity and position to release its warhead.

In order to maintain the alignment of the accelerometers with the initial coordinate system they are mounted on a gyroscopically stabilized platform (see Figure E.1). Gyroscopes are devices that contain a rapidly rotating wheel. Conservation of the angular momentum of the wheel causes resistance to any motion the gyroscope is subjected to. The magnitude of the resistance is proportional to the motion, so when the gyroscopes and accelerometers are all mounted on a three-axis gimbaled platform the resistance each gyroscope exhibits to motion is used to activate torque motors that keep the gimbaled platform in its initial alignment even though the missile is moving and rotating. The entire system of accelerometers, gyroscopes, and the gimbaled platform that is kept in an invariant position by torque motors is called an inertial measurement unit (IMU). Using such an IMU, a missile can navigate inertially —that is, it can determine at any point during its boosting trajectory its position, velocity, and acceleration. (See Figure E.2.)

This information is in turn used as input by the steering and thrust termination computers of the missile, first to steer the missile through the high aerodynamic loading of the early endoatmospheric portion of its flight and then, after the missile leaves the atmosphere, to reach the precomputed required position and velocity toward its target after thrust has terminated. This is achieved by opening a large port at the front end of the solid-fuel rocket, which reverses the rocket thrust. If at the same instant the reentry vehicle (or MIRV bus) containing the warheads is detached from the rocket, the two separate, leaving only the force of gravity to act upon the warhead.

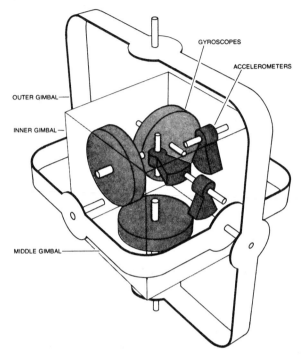

FIGURE E.1. Inertial-guidance system suitable for monitoring the exact position and velocity of a long-range ballistic missile continuously during the period between launch and thrust termination relies on data from three mutually perpendicular accelerometers; each of these extraordinarily sensitive devices measures the forces acting in a given direction on an enclosed test mass. In this design the accelerometers are mounted on a gimbaled platform that is gyroscopically stabilized to maintain the original direction of each accelerometer.
From *Scientific American*, vol. 233, No. 1, p. 13.

FIGURE E.2. (*opposite*) Block diagram of a closed-loop guidance system. In the navigation diagram note how the value of the acceleration due to gravity can be obtained either from the gravity model stored in the memory of the guidance computer, or by actually measuring the gravitational field variations with a gradiometer.

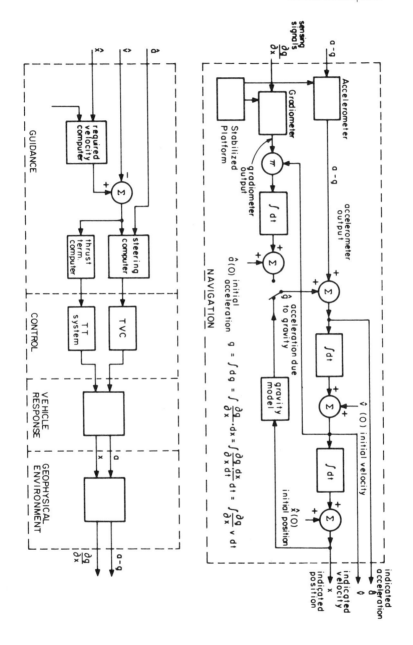

APPENDIX F
SOURCES AND SIZE
OF TARGET MISS
OF BALLISTIC MISSILES

THERE ARE many known sources of errors in the guidance of a ballistic missile that cause the reentry vehicle to miss the target. Experience with testing of ballistic missiles indicates that there may be sources of errors that are still not quite understood, since a reentry vehicle often misses its target by a distance that cannot be accounted for by the known error sources. There are seven categories of known errors:

1. Errors in specifying initial conditions
2. Errors in inertial sensing (malfunctions of the accelerometers and gyroscopes)
3. Errors in guidance formulation and computations by the missile's on-board computer
4. Errors in thrust termination
5. Errors in accounting for in-flight gravity anomalies
6. Errors in specifying the position of the target with respect to the launch point
7. Reentry anomalies and unexpected atmospheric effects

The first four types of errors contribute to an overall error in position and velocity of the missile at the instant of boost termination. In examining the target miss that results from this overall error, it must be remembered that the miss is proportional to the size of the error. The exact proportionality constants that relate the target miss to the errors at warhead release are a function of the exact trajectory of the missile. Table F.1 lists the proportionality constants for a 10,000-km minimum-energy trajectory.*

TABLE F.1

Constants relating horizontal miss at the target to errors at warhead release

Errors at Warhead Release		Horizontal Miss at Target	
		Range (in trajectory plane)	Lateral or Track (out of plane)
Velocity Errors at Warhead Release	Vertical	$2000 \dfrac{\text{meters}}{\text{meter/sec}}$	—
	Horizontal in Plane	$6000 \dfrac{\text{meters}}{\text{meter/sec}}$	—
	Horizontal out of Plane	—	$1000 \dfrac{\text{meters}}{\text{meter/sec}}$
Position Errors at Warhead Release	Vertical	$3.5 \dfrac{\text{meters}}{\text{meter}}$	—
	Horizontal in Plane	$1 \dfrac{\text{meter}}{\text{meter}}$	—
	Horizontal out of Plane	—	(zero)

In considering each class of errors separately, it is necessary to assign values to the specific errors and then list the resulting target miss caused by each one in order to illustrate the relative sizes of the errors and the misses they cause. The values of error presented here are not characteristic of any specific guidance system.

The initial conditions that must be given to the inertial

* From D. Hoag, "Ballistic Missile Guidance," in Feld et al., *Impact of New Technologies on the Arms Race* (M.I.T. Press, 1970).

guidance system are the position, velocity, and alignment of the platform with respect to the local vertical and the Z-axis (azimuth). The errors result in the following misses in meters:

		RANGE	TRACK
Position error		20	20
Velocity error		20	0
Vertical alignment		60	6
Azimuth error		0	60
	Root mean square	66 m	63 m

Next we consider the miss caused by inertial sensing errors during the powered portion of the flight. These can come from six possible malfunctions:

a. *Accelerometer bias* caused by inaccurate measurement of the force on the test mass. An error of a tenth of a dyne on a 10-gram force will give an acceleration error of $10^{-5} \cdot g$. Assuming that the boost phase of the missile is 3 minutes, i.e. 180 seconds, that error will result at boost termination in a velocity error of $10^{-5} \cdot g \cdot 180 = 1.7$ cm/sec and a distance error of $1/2 \cdot 10^{-5} \cdot g \cdot (180)^2 = 147$ cm.

b. *Accelerometor scale factor* caused by inappropriate calibration of the accelerometer. Such an error is proportional to the magnitude of the quantity measured. For a minimum-energy trajectory the accelerometer will have been recording velocity change of 9000 m/sec, and so if the bias were only one part per million the thrust termination velocity error almost would be 1 cm/sec.

c. *Accelerometer nonorthogonality* can occur if the actual direction of the accelerometer measuring axis is not the one assumed by the computer. Such misalignment can be caused by the nonperpendicularity of the axes of the three accelerometers or by platform distortions because of the boosting force. If the accelerometers are not orthogonal by one microradian the resulting velocity error at thrust will be about 1 cm/sec.

d. *Platform misalignment* may contribute little to the error budget. Assuming good design the platform distortion should be about an additional microradian in each axis.

e. *Gyroscope bias drift* can be caused by a fixed extraneous torque on the gyroscope wheel. A .1 dyne-cm torque on a 10^6 dyne-cm per rad/sec wheel will cause a drift rate of 10^{-7} rad/sec. If each of the three gyroscopes in an IMU has such a drift, the velocity errors at thrust termination will be 11 cm/sec in the vertical direction, 1 cm/sec in the horizontal (range) direction, and 13 cm/sec in the horizontal (track) direction.

f. *Gyroscope drift* can be caused by the acceleration of the missile. If the gyroscopes have a drift rate of 10^{-8} rad/ sec per g of acceleration, the resulting velocity errors at thrust termination will be 1.9 cm/sec vertical, 1.2 cm/sec horizontal (range), and 2.4 cm/sec horizontal (track).

g. *Gyroscope compliance drift* can be caused by the vibration of the missile during the boost phase. According to Hoag the resulting velocity errors at thrust termination will be about half those caused by the acceleration-induced gyroscope bias (see f. above).

Using Table F.1 it is possible to calculate the target miss distance in range and track each of these errors will cause. The results are listed in Table F.2.

TABLE F.2
Target miss caused by inertial sensing errors

	RANGE	TRACK
Accelerometer bias	45	7
Accelerometer scale factor	40	0
Accelerometer nonorthogonality	70	30
Platform misalignment	10	10
Gyroscope bias drift	45	13
Gyroscope drift	70	20
Gyroscope compliance drift	35	10
Root mean square	130 m	40 m

Target miss distances are also due to guidance formulation and computation. These errors must now be considered small with respect to the rest of the error sources, since powerful computers can be used both to store a more detailed polynomial that describes the value of the gravitational field as a function of position and to perform the calculations with greater precision. It is possible to assign —more or less arbitrarily—target miss of 15 meters in range and 5 meters in track to this source of error.

Thrust-termination errors, the fourth cause of target miss, can be quite large. At thrust termination the missile is accelerating by about 100 m/sec^2 (10 g's); therefore an error of a millisecond in the precise termination time can cause a velocity error of 10 cm/sec. But the use of small vernier jets can give the missile the last few cm/sec^2 acceleration. Thus the velocity error will be about one-tenth or less, that is, about 1 cm/sec, resulting in a combined range error of 40 meters and a negligible track error.

It is very difficult to estimate the miss error due to unaccounted gravitational anomalies, the fifth cause of target miss. Perhaps the miss they cause can be as large as 100 meters at the target or as little as 10 meters. Over familiar trajectories the miss will be toward the lower end of this range; for untested trajectories it may be toward the upper end, especially if the missile is launched from a mobile platform, in which case the gravitational anomalies near the launch point could not have been determined in advance. I assume error of 50 meters in range and 15 meters in track caused by uncorrected-for gravity anomalies.

It is reasonable to expect that modern methods of geodesy and mapmaking that use satellite-gathered data have reduced the contribution of the sixth source of target miss —inaccurate mapping of the target location with respect to the launch point—to a few tens of meters. Target miss is probably no more than 30 meters due to mapping errors.

Finally let us examine the target miss size caused by the unguided reentry and passage of the warhead through the atmosphere. A number of factors can contribute to errors during reentry. The atmospheric conditions, such as barometric pressure over the target, can affect the reentry of the warhead in a manner not predicted by the guidance computer of the missile. The density of the atmosphere can affect the range of the warhead. Local winds can blow it off target both in range and track. Rain or snow can also affect its range. The slightest asymmetry in the ablation of the reentry vehicle's heat shield can create lift forces that will unpredictably change the direction of motion of the warhead. Small changes in the location of the center of gravity of the reentering body as its heat shield wears out can add significant deflection away from its intended trajectory toward the target. The actual miss caused by all these effects is quite unpredictable, but it would not be surprising if it were as big as 100 meters in range and 60 meters in track.

By adding all these contributions to the total distance by which the reentry vehicle misses the target, we can relate its expected performance to the characteristics of its guidance system, the amount of information available to the guidance computer, and the size of the uncertainty inherent in its voyage through the atmosphere. The net miss is the vector sum of all the individual contributions, so the size of the total error is the square root of the sum of the squares of the individual contributions as shown in Table F.3. The table also shows that with a total range miss of 190 meters and track miss of 99 meters, the hypothetical missile will have a CEP of 170 meters.

TABLE F.3

Contributions to the final target miss from various sources of guidance error

	RANGE	TRACK
Initial condition	66	63
Inertial sensing	130	40
Guidance and computation	15	5
Thrust termination	40	0
Gravity anomalies	50	15
Targeting	20	20
Reentry	100	60
Root mean square	190 m	99 m

$CEP = .59(190 + 99) = 170$ m

APPENDIX G
WORKING PRINCIPLES OF
GLOBAL POSITIONING SYSTEM

THE NAVSTAR Global Positioning System (GPS) is a constellation of twenty-four satellites in 12-hour orbits at an altitude of 20,183 km. The satellites are positioned in such a fashion that any point on earth will be visible from at least six and as many as eleven of the satellites at 5° or more above the horizon. Each satellite transmits signals exactly synchronized with those of all the other satellites in the constellation. It also continuously transmits information that gives its position in space with respect to the center of the earth. (See Figure G.1.)

Signals that leave all satellites simultaneously arrive at different times at the receiver of a user such as a missile, ship, or plane. By measuring the time each signal takes to come from each satellite the receiver can determine the distance of its position, $D_1 \ldots D_4$, from each satellite. So

$$D_1 = ct_1$$
$$D_2 = ct_2$$
$$D_3 = ct_3$$
$$D_4 = ct_4$$

(see Figure G.1). In addition to transmitting the timing signal each satellite broadcasts its position in space. So the user also knows the quantities R_1, R_2, R_3, R_4 or equivalently, the coordinates $X_1, Y_1, Z_1; X_2, Y_2, Z_2; X_3, Y_3, Z_3;$ and X_4, Y_4, Z_4 of the four satellites. By solving the system of four simultaneous equations the receiver can determine its position in a geocentric reference frame.

302

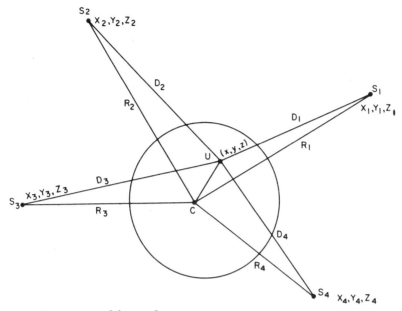

C = center of the earth
U_X, U_Y, U_Z = receiver position of coordinates
D_1, D_2, D_3, D_4 = the distances of 4 satellites from receiver
R_1, R_2, R_3, R_4 = the positions of 4 satellites in space
         with respect to the center of the earth

FIGURE G.1. Illustration of the relevant quantities of the Global Positioning System.

$$(X_1 - U_X)^2 + (Y_1 - U_Y)^2 + (Z_1 - U_Z)^2 = D_1^2\epsilon$$
$$(X_2 - U_X)^2 + (Y_2 - U_Y)^2 + (Z_2 - U_Z)^2 = D_2^2\epsilon$$
$$(X_3 - U_X)^2 + (Y_3 - U_Y)^2 + (Z_3 - U_Z)^2 = D_3^2\epsilon$$
$$(X_4 - U_X)^2 + (Y_4 - U_Y)^2 + (Z_4 - U_Z)^2 = D_4^2\epsilon$$

The four unknowns are U_X, U_Y, U_Z, the coordinates of the receiver's position in that reference frame, and ϵ, a correction factor that takes into account possible inaccuracies in the clock of the receiver and the fact that the signals from the satellites may be distorted or delayed in passing through the ionosphere. Since four equations are needed to determine U_X, U_Y, U_Z, and ϵ, the user must receive signals from at least four satellites. Determination of U_X, U_Y, U_Z is possible with an accuracy of 10 meters 90% of the time and 7 meters 50% of the time, depending on the ionospheric conditions. When a user such as a missile is moving its velocity can be determined by measuring the Doppler shift of the carrier-wave frequency from the satellites. The velocity can be determined to 2 cm/sec within a dynamic range of 0–25 m/sec while the missile is accelerating up to 100 m/sec² (10 g's). It is possible then to use NAVSTAR to supplement and make final corrections to the guidance of a ballistic missile shortly before the warheads are released toward their targets. Such corrections in sensed position and velocity of the missile could rectify the errors accumulated during the missile's boost phase.

APPENDIX H
DERIVATION OF
KILL PROBABILITY EQUATION

A REENTRY VEHICLE from a ballistic missile which upon repeated firings against an aim point would land in a normal distribution with a standard deviation σ about that aim point will have a single-shot kill probability against a target

$$P_K = 1 - P_S = 1 - \exp(-r_K^2/2\sigma^2) \qquad (1)$$

where r_K is the distance from the point of detonation beyond which the target would survive.

It is necessary to be able to rewrite (1) in terms of the characteristics of the target, say a silo, and the attacking warhead. A silo is characterized by its *hardness*, which is the amount of blast overpressure it can withstand. An attacking warhead is characterized by the energy yield of its explosive charge, its accuracy, its bias, and its reliability. We will assume in this calculation that the bias is zero.

The overpressure P_O (in psi) caused by the explosion of a warhead of yield Y (in megatons of TNT) at a point r (in nautical miles*) from the point of detonation is given by:

$$P_O = 14.7\left[\frac{Y}{r^3}\right] + 12.8\left[\frac{Y}{r^3}\right]^{1/2} \qquad (2)$$

This is an empirical formula derived from early atmospheric tests.

Solving for $\left[\dfrac{Y}{r^3}\right]^{1/2}$

* A nautical mile is 1.85 kilometers.

305

$$\left[\frac{Y}{r^3}\right]^{1/2} = \frac{-1 \pm (1 + .36P_O)^{1/2}}{2.3}$$

Now for $P_O \gg 300$ psi (which is the case with silos)

$$.36P_O \gg 1$$

therefore we can omit the 1 in the parenthesis. So

$$\left[\frac{Y}{r^3}\right]^{1/2} = -.432 \pm .026P_O^{1/2}$$

or

$$r^3 = \frac{Y}{P_O \cdot f(P_O)}$$

where $f(P_O)$ is a slowly varying function of P_O.

$$f(P_O) = .19P_O^{-1} - .23P_O^{-1/2} + .068$$
$$\approx .061 \text{ for } P_O \text{ around } 1000 \text{ psi}$$

Now if one substitutes the hardness H of the silo for P_O, r is equal to r_K, the distance at which the silo would survive a blast overpressure P_O. Therefore

$$r_K = \frac{Y^{1/3}}{H^{1/3}f(H)^{1/3}} \quad \text{where } f(1000) = .061 \tag{2}$$

Substituting (2) into (1) we have

$$P_K = 1 - P_S = 1 - \exp(-Y^{2/3}/.3\sigma^2 \cdot H^{2/3})$$

This assumes somewhat arbitrarily that all silos for which r $< r_K$ will be destroyed and all those for which r $> r_K$ will survive. This assumption, known as the "cookie-cutter" approximation, is satisfactory for all purposes other than detailed targeting.

It is important now to describe σ in terms of the precision of the warhead expressed by its CEP or "circular error probable," a measure of accuracy used in characterizing missiles. By definition CEP is the radius of the circle centered at the aim point and containing 50% of the projectiles launched against the aim point. Assuming a normal distribution in r and θ we write

$$P(r) = C \cdot \exp(-r^2/2\sigma^2)$$

so

$$1 = C \cdot \int_0^{2\pi} d\theta \cdot \int_0^{\infty} r \cdot \exp(-r^2/2\sigma^2) dr$$

$$1 = 2\pi C\sigma^2 \qquad \text{so } C = \frac{1}{2\pi\sigma^2}$$

Then by definition of the CEP

$$.5 = \frac{1}{2\pi\sigma^2} \int_0^{2\pi} d\theta \int_0^{(CEP)} r \cdot \exp(-r^2/2\sigma^2) dr$$

$$.5 = 1 - \exp[-(CEP)^2/2\sigma^2]$$

$$ln\ .5 = -(CEP)^2/2\sigma^2$$

$$\text{so} \quad CEP = 1.17\sigma \quad \text{Therefore } \sigma = .85\ CEP \qquad (3)$$

Now we substitute:

$$P_K = 1 - \exp(-Y^{2/3}/.22H^{2/3} \cdot CEP^2) \qquad (4)$$
$$\text{for perfect reliability}$$

Now define

$$K = \frac{Y^{2/3}}{(CEP)^2} \qquad (5)$$

a quality that describes the lethality of a missile warhead against a silo. The target has to be a silo or something harder than 300 psi to use this formalism.)

So we can rewrite P_K

$$P_K = 1 - \exp(-K/.22 \cdot H^{2/3}) \qquad (6)$$

where the numerator describes the missile and the denominator describes the silo.

Note that K can become ridiculously large as $CEP \to 0$. In reality K has a maximum numerical value beyond which its magnitude has no physical meaning. This limiting value comes about because when $CEP \leq r_C$ where r_C is the radius of the crater that the explosion excavates, $P_K \simeq 1$—that is, the kill probability for the silo is unity.* Making the missile more accurate, or the K larger, loses physical significance and operational importance because a missile inside the silo cannot survive if the silo is inside the crater.

So one defines:

$$K_{max} = \frac{Y^{2/3}}{r_C^2} \qquad \text{for CEP} = r_C$$

but

$$r_C = \alpha Y^{1/3}$$

where α is an excavation constant depending on the soil. Therefore

$$K_{max} = \frac{2/3}{\alpha^2 Y^{2/3}} = \frac{1}{\alpha^2} \approx 100$$

So it is not meaningful to speak of lethality values where K is between 100 and 125.

These calculations have been based upon a missile reliability of 1, or 100% reliability. But if the missile reliability ρ smaller than 1 then

$$P_K(\rho < 1) = \rho \cdot P_K(\rho = 1)$$

And what about using n warheads against one silo? If all n come from the same launcher

$$P_K(\rho, n) = \rho \cdot \{1 - [P_S(\rho = 1)]^n\} \qquad \text{for } \rho < 1$$

but if they come from different launchers

$$P_K(\rho, n) = 1 - [1 - \rho \cdot P_K(\rho = 1)]^n$$

* This is a "defense-conservative" calculation. An "offense-conservative" assumption would be that $K = K_{max}$ when CEP $< R_C$, say CEP $= .3 \cdot R_C$. The rest of the calculation would be the same.

APPENDIX I
PRINCIPLES OF
RADAR OPERATION

USING RADAR is the best method to detect an aircraft and determine its direction of travel and distance from a given point. Radar (which is an acronym for *r*adio *d*etection *a*nd *r*anging) consists of an antenna that transmits and receives electromagnetic waves, a generator of these waves, and a detector and receiver of such waves. The transmitted radiation travels with the speed of light. When it hits an object, such as a plane, part of the radiation is absorbed by the object and part is reradiated back. The receiving antenna intercepts part of this reradiated energy and the radar receiver processes it into a signal that contains information not only about the presence of the object but also about its distance (or range) from the radar antenna and its velocity. The velocity of the target object is determined by the Doppler shift in the frequency of the received radar wave; its distance is calculated by measuring the time it took the radar signal to reach the target and return. If the time is T, the range to the target is $R = cT/2$, where c is the velocity of light. If R is in kilometers and T is in microseconds, we have the simple relationship

$$R(km) = .15T(\mu sec) \qquad (1)$$

In order to be able to predict the performance of a radar we need a relationship between the amount of radiation it emits per unit time, the size of its antenna, and the maximum distance at which it can detect a given object. If the radar emitted radiation energy isotropically and its power (energy per unit time) were W, then at a distance R away the power density of the electromagnetic waves from the radar would be $W/4\pi R^2$. This isotropic arrangement, however, is wasteful because the radiation of the radar can be focused into a narrow beam. So using an antenna of area A and radiation of wave length λ, the power density at a distance R away will be

$$[W/4\pi R^2] \cdot [4\pi A/\lambda^2]$$

The second factor is called G, the *gain* of the radar.

An object at a distance R that is illuminated by the radar beam will reradiate a portion of the radar's electromagnetic energy isotropically into space. So the power density of the reradiated wave that will reach the radar will be

$$\frac{W\cdot G}{4\pi R^2} \cdot \frac{\sigma}{4\pi R^2} = \frac{W\cdot A}{\lambda^2 R^2} \cdot \frac{\sigma}{4\pi R^2}$$

where σ is a measure of the size and reflectivity of the target and has the units of area. (This is called the "cross section" of the target.)

The portion of this reflected power density received by the radar is proportional to the area of the antenna, so the received power W_R is

$$W_R = \frac{W\cdot A}{\lambda^2 R^2} \cdot \frac{\sigma}{4\pi R^2} \cdot A$$

$$= \frac{WA^2\sigma}{\lambda^2 4\pi R^4} \tag{2}$$

The maximum range of the radar can now be determined by equating W_R with the minimum power the receiver can detect W_{min}. So

$$W_{min} = \frac{WA^2\sigma}{\lambda^2 4\pi R_{max}^4} \quad \text{or} \quad R_{max} = \left[\frac{WA^2\sigma}{4\pi\lambda^2 W_{min}}\right]^{1/4} \tag{3}$$

APPENDIX J
THE PRINCIPLE
OF PHASED ARRAYS

CONSIDER A LINEAR ARRAY of n hydrophones at a distance l from each other (see Figure J.1) and a sound wave arriving at the array at an angle θ with respect to it. Let us assume that the wave arrives at hydrophone 1 at time t and at hydrophone 2 at time t + τ. The instant the wave is at hydrophone 1 it is at a distance d away from hydrophone 2. So we have d/l = tan θ. But d = $V_s \cdot \tau$ where V_s is the speed of sound in water, so

$$\tan \theta = \frac{V_s \cdot \tau}{l}$$

and

$$\theta = \text{arc tan} \left[\frac{V_s}{l} \cdot \tau \right]$$

Upon its arrival at hydrophone 1 the acoustical wave will generate a sound pulse which the electronics that accompany the hydrophone transform into an electrical pulse, an electrical signal. The same thing will happen at hydrophone 2 at time τ later, at hydrophone 3 at time 2τ later, and at hydrophone n at time $(n-1)\tau$ later. Plotted against time, these output signals will look something like sum B in Figure J.2. Now if the output of hydrophone 1 is delayed by a time $(n-1)\tau$ and the output from hydrophone 2 by a delay $(n-2)\tau$ and so on, and then the delayed outputs from all the hydrophones are added together, the result will be the large pulse shown in sum A in Figure J.2.

Acoustical signals that arrive at the array from angles other than θ will not add up coherently after the delays have been added because τ is a function of θ. By rapidly

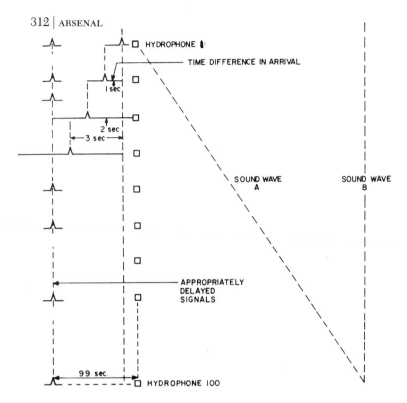

FIGURE J.1. Geometry of an acoustical wave arriving at a 100-hydrophone array.

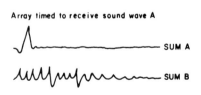

Array timed to receive sound wave A

SUM A

SUM B

FIGURE J.2. Added outputs of n hydrophones.

changing the delays at the output of each hydrophone, it is possible to listen for sounds arriving at the array from different directions. For example, to listen for a wave that is coming from a direction perpendicular to the array all the delays are equal to zero, since the wave would arrive at all the hydrophones simultaneously.

By utilizing a fast computer that inserts different delays into the hydrophones of the array sequentially, the array can be made to sweep the ocean in front of it for weak sounds.

APPENDIX K
THE CELL CONCEPT
IN SIGNAL PROCESSING

THE CONCEPT of the resolution cell lies at the center of any description of a sonar signal-processing system and its performance characteristics. To analyze this performance it is assumed that all space surrounding the detection system (be it passive or active) is divided into elements of volume. The size of each element is defined to be such that the system cannot resolve the presence of more than one sound source within it. That is, for the system to distinguish two sources as separate, they must be in separate cells or elements of volume. As a simple example of such volumes, consider a line of hydrophones deployed horizontally in the ocean. If variable delays are introduced at the output of each hydrophone this array can be made to "scan" on a horizontal plane and therefore distinguish two sound sources as distinct from each other provided they are separated in bearing by an amount greater than some angle θ. Each resolution cell in this case is an angular sector of width θ. The number of such cells for this system is $C = 360°/θ°$.

Theta can be as small as 5°, and in that case C = 72. If the system consisted of a planar array of hydrophones, and again by appropriate delays this array could scan the ocean in two orthogonal directions but could distinguish two sound sources only if they were at least a solid angle ω apart, then the number of cells would be $C_A = 4\pi/\omega$. So if ω were 10 millisteradians, $C_A \simeq 1.2 \cdot 10^3$.

It is not only physical space that can be divided into resolution cells. Consider for example a two-dimensional passive array of hydrophones that is equipped with a set of contiguous band-pass filters, of bandwidth f. If F is the entire bandwidth of the system, the number of spectral resolution cells is F/f, and since each space resolution cell has F/f such spectral cells the total number of resolution cells of the system is now

$$C_S = \frac{4\pi}{\omega} \cdot F/f$$

For F = 3 kilohertz and f = 30 hertz the total number of cells is

$$C_S = 1{,}200 \cdot 100 = 1.2 \cdot 10^5$$

The advantage of this approach can be displayed readily. Consider an array of omnidirectional hydrophones without angular or spectral resolution. Suppose that such a system receives a signal power of S, and noise power of N. The presence of a sound source in this case is detected by recognizing the difference between power level S + N (yes, there is a source) and N (no, there is no source). The ratio is $(S + N)/N = S/N + 1$. Consider now the same array but capable of resolving one source 10 millisteradians of solid angle away from another. The total number of resolution cells is now 1,200, of which only one contains the source. As the system scans these cells, the output will be N/1200 for all the empty cells and S + N/1200 for the cell that contains the target. The ratio of the input power in the presence of the signal to that in the absence of such signal is

$$\frac{S + N/1200}{N/1200} = 1200 \cdot S/N + 1$$

It is clear that this system will resolve the presence of a source in an isotropic ambient noise field with a signal 10 log (1/1200), roughly 30 db lower than the previous nondirectional system. If in addition the system is equipped with spectral resolution and its F/f is 100, the ratio of power to "signal present" to "no signal" is now

$$\frac{S + N/1.2 \cdot 10^5}{N/1.2 \cdot 10^5} = 1.2 \cdot 10^5 \cdot S/N + 1$$

Therefore, for the same listening time (same search rate) as in the other two cases, this system will resolve a signal 50 db smaller than the first, and 20 db smaller than the second system. Although spectacular, there are two reasons why this is a somewhat misleading example of the improvement of the signal-to-noise ratio. First, it is not always true that the same amount of listening time is possible in the different examples. Second, it must always be kept in mind that the final output of any processor is scanned by a human being whose ability to decide whether a given signal is a "target" or a "false alarm" decreases with the increasing number of resolution cells he has to monitor. It must also be remembered that the "false alarm" rate increases with the number of resolution cells and as a result may force a reduction in the sensitivity of the system.

APPENDIX L
DERIVATION OF THE FORMULA
FOR RESOLVING POWER
IN TERMS OF f, A, AND R

THE RESOLUTION δ of an optical system of focal length f (that is, the size of the smallest object it can detect on the ground) from an altitude A above the surface of the earth with a focal plane resolution d is:

$$\delta = \frac{A \cdot d}{f} \qquad \text{meters}$$

where all distances are in meters. The combined optical resolution at the focal plane and the resolving characteristics of the recording device, be it film or an array of electro-optical devices, can be expressed in terms of the number of lines R drawn with 2:1 contrast within 1 millimeter. R is then 1/d and the overall resolution of the sensor is

$$\delta = \frac{A}{10^3 \cdot R \cdot f} \qquad \text{meters}$$

since there are 10^3 millimeters in 1 meter. As a rule of thumb, two lines across an object are required to resolve it from the background, that is, to detect it; three to five lines to orient it and determine its aspect ratio, eight to recognize it (e.g., truck or tank), and thirteen to identify it (e.g., Cadillac or Oldsmobile). If an object is 10 meters long, the combined ground resolution of the sensor δ must be 5 meters in order to detect it, 2–3 meters to determine its geometric shape, 1–2 meters to recognize its function, and about 70 cm to positively identify it. One now can determine, given the altitude A of the platform that carries the sensor, the combined f·R value required for each of these tasks. For example, detection of an object 10 meters long by a satellite on a 200-km orbit would require

$$10^3 \cdot f \cdot R = \frac{2 \cdot 10^5}{10/2} = 4 \cdot 10^4$$

since two lines across it are sufficient for detection. If the R value of the system is 100/mm

$$f = \frac{4 \cdot 10^4}{10^5} = 40 \text{ cm}$$

while for identification

$$f = \frac{2 \cdot 10^5}{(10/13) \cdot 10^5} = 2.85 \text{ m}$$

Photographic film commonly used in surveillance applications has an R larger than 180 lines/mm. There are films with R = 300 ℓ/mm and some commercially available film has R = 400 ℓ/mm. Industry is experimenting with an optical storage computer memory using film with R = 500 ℓ/mm.

Such high focal-plane resolutions, however, are not easily attainable because of the limit imposed by diffraction effects. This limiting value of R is given by the relationship

$$R_{limit} = \frac{L}{\lambda \cdot f}$$

where L is the diameter of the lens, λ the wavelength of light to which the system is sensitive, and f the focal length of the lens. For visible light λ = .55·10⁻⁶ meters and for a lens 30 cm in diameter with a 2.8-meter focal length

$$R_{lim} = \frac{.3}{.55 \cdot 10^{-6} \cdot 2.8} = .214 \cdot 10^6$$

or 214 lines/mm. Conversely, a system having a lens with f = 25 meters and R = 500 lines, would result in a ground resolution of less than 2 cm; the lens diameter at which the system becomes diffraction-limited is 6.87 meters. Since actual systems usually use much larger diameters than the limiting value, the technical difficulty of employing very high-resolution recording devices becomes apparent. The diffraction limit becomes more severe at longer wavelengths, for example in infrared-sensitive sensors. The overall limit in resolution then is practically set by the physical size of the lens of the sensor.

These rather simple calculations would indicate that lenses with 3-meter focal length and less than 1 meter in diameter can yield diffraction-free ground resolution of about 25–30 cm on the ground from altitudes of 250 km. Such resolutions allow the detection of objects half a meter in one dimension and the complete identification of objects like passenger cars. Even larger systems with better resolutions seem quite feasible. For example, the 3-meter solar telescope orbited by the United States, if inverted and made to observe the ground, would have a ground resolution of $\delta = 16$ meters from a geosynchronous altitude of 40,000 km, an indication that from a monitoring satellite the system would achieve, in principle at least, a resolution of 8–10 cm on the ground. At this level of resolution atmospheric turbulence starts being an important factor.

Atmospheric turbulence that distorts telescopic images of astronomical telescopes is a well-known phenomenon. A new technique, made possible by very fast electronics and new piezoelectric materials, permits the detection and subsequent correction of the phase distortion that the turbulence introduces to different parts of a plane light wave arriving at a detector. The technique involves a detector of the phase error (usually a shearing interferometer), an active optical element that compensates for the error in real time, and a processor that calculates the response of the optical element based on the output signal from the detector. In a successful model of this system the phase error detector generates a wavefront map by measuring the phase error in about 1 msec in regions each about 10 cm on a side that cover the entire aperture of the optical system. The active optical element is a one-piece piezoelectric mirror divided into regions, each driven by a separate electrical actuator. The processor receives the map from the detector and distorts the mirror in order to compensate for phase errors in adjacent regions. Although this approach was shown to be theoretically possible in 1953, it is only very recently that the technology has been available to attempt its practical application.

With the removal of atmospheric turbulence as a limiting factor in visible-light-sensor resolution, it is possible to expect optical resolutions restricted only by the diffraction limit. This fact permits the application of new microelectronic techniques for the real-time transmission of images from spaceborne sensors.

APPENDIX M
PRINCIPLES OF
SIDE-LOOKING RADAR
OPERATION

SIDE-LOOKING synthetic-aperture radar is an image-forming airborne radar of high resolution. Its main advantage over other systems capable of surveillance beyond national borders is that it is largely unaffected by weather conditions, such as cloud cover or rain. The high resolutions it can achieve result from the motion of the radar-carrying aircraft, which effectively creates a very large antenna. In an ordinary radar with an antenna of length L, the angular resolution β is equal to the ratio of the radar wavelength λ and the size of the antenna L:

$$\beta = \lambda/L$$

Thus for reflecting objects at ranges $r \gg L$, the linear resolution would be

$$\delta = r\lambda/L = r\beta$$

So for a given λ and r, the resolution δ improves with the size of the antenna. Consider now an aircraft flying along the line AA' with velocity v, at a vertical distance r_0 from a radar-reflecting object and an actual distance r (see Figure M.1), forming an angle θ with respect to the flight direction. Assuming that the aircraft has a radar that transmits signals along r_0 and receives reflections from the target at each point along its flight path, the Doppler shift of the reflected signal will be

$$f_D = (2v \cos \theta)/\lambda$$

and the difference in Doppler shifts from two adjacent reflecting targets subtending an angle $\Delta\theta$ at the radar will be

$$\Delta f_D = (2v \sin \theta)\Delta\theta/\lambda$$

If the observation of the two signals lasts for time Δt, then $\Delta f_D = 1/\Delta t$ and therefore

$$1/\Delta t \simeq (2v \sin \theta)\Delta\theta/\lambda$$

Using the known quantities f_D, λ, v, and θ, the angular distance $\Delta\theta$ between points 1 and 2 can be computed. At a direction exactly normal to the aircraft path, $\sin \theta$ is unity and the Doppler shift is zero, but $\Delta f_D/\Delta\theta$ is a maximum, giving the best possible resolution.

If the radar on the plane has several receiving dipoles each of which receives the return of the signal it has beamed out, and if the received signals can be stored in each dipole while retaining both amplitude and phase, then signals from all the dipoles can be summed together with appropriate added phase shifts so that the antenna is a focusing one. At this point the antenna of physical length L will "look" (or behave electromagnetically) as if it had a "synthetic" length L_S

$$L_S = r_0\lambda/L$$

and the resulting linear resolution δ will be in the theoretical limit $L_S/2$.

Although this suggests that infinitely small resolutions could be achieved, practical considerations dictate the minimum size of L. For example, the radar must be pulsed at least twice per effective antenna length L_S traveled by the aircraft. Thus either the pulse rate must be very high or the aircraft very slow, or L_S must have a reasonable value. But in order to avoid overlapping returning pulses from two points a distance δr apart, the time between pulses cannot be smaller than $2\delta r/c$. These conditions imply that

$$L \geq 4v\delta r/c$$

Under these conditions the synthetic antenna has an equivalent length $L_S \simeq v\Delta t$.

The intrinsic reason for achieving better resolution with

a synthetic antenna of length L_S is that each dipole sends out signals in sequence (one per radar pulse), receives them again in sequence while preserving phase and amplitude, and stores and processes them separately. After a number of return signals from a given reflector are stored (in each dipole, so to speak) they are read back simultaneously, giving the maximum possible sum. It is this ability to process the received information optimally that gives such good resolution parallel to the flight path of the plane. In the "cross-track" plane the resolution is very poor (the physical antenna is only 30 cm in that dimension) and therefore SLAR (side-looking airborne radar) pictures are difficult to interpret because of the poor relief patterns they generate. Side-looking radar detects vehicles quite easily because of their large radar cross sections, even if they are smaller than the nominal resolution of the radar at a given range. They appear as bright spots, but 3-meter resolution is needed in order to classify the vehicle. Individual vehicle signatures are often unreliable, but in a SLAR picture concentrations of bright spots with changing patterns would be features calling for further monitoring.

To avoid errors caused by unexpected departures of the antenna from straight-line travel along AA', caused by angular rotations of the aircraft or sudden changes in its altitude, an inertial measuring unit containing gyroscopes and accelerometers is made an integral part of the side-looking radar antenna. The gyroscopes provide signals to servomotors that keep the antenna pointing in the proper direction when the plane rotates. Gyroscope drifts can be corrected by electronically sampling Doppler shifts around the zero shift and detecting its drift. The accelerometers provide information that permits the insertion of the proper phase-shift corrections to compensate for unexpected displacement changes.

The amplitudes of the electronic signals produced by adding the stored returns in each dipole of the antenna are transformed to light intensities on a cathode ray tube face and recorded, generating a picturelike record of the landscape on either side of the aircraft's path. This process involves recording the signals on magnetic tape, elaborate computer processing of the data upon return of the aircraft

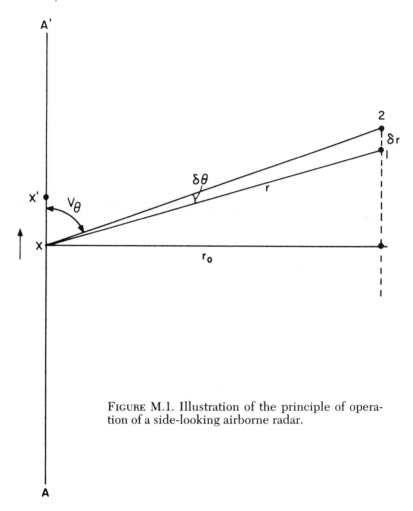

FIGURE M.1. Illustration of the principle of operation of a side-looking airborne radar.

to its base, and finally the development of the optical image. Thus, several hours may pass between the actual surveillance and the decoding of the data. Recently the United States has initiated development of a dedicated array processor computer that can process side-looking radar data almost on-line and identify changes from the image of the landscape generated at an earlier pass. In addition, efforts are made to use digital rather than analog processing of the return pulses to enhance the resolution of the final image. More recently, with the applictions of powerful on-board microprocessors, the United States has achieved real-time image-forming SLARs capable of being flown by fighter aircraft. This is a valuable ability in environments with long periods of inclement weather.

Existing military SLARs deployed, for example, with NATO forces have a long track resolution of 2 m to 3 m at ranges of 100 km. This performance is achieved with a radar weighing about 200 kg and having a physical antenna 30 cm by 120 cm, which generates a synthetic aperture L_s over 500 m long. These resolution values are in a direction parallel to the flight line of the plane.

INDEX

accelerometers, 109–10, 112, 116–18, 291–94, 298, 323
see also inertial guidance systems
acoustical waves, 68–69, 215–217, 311–12
aircraft, 147–53, 158–59
in antisubmarine warfare, 223–24, 229–32, 234, 236–237
jet propulsion in, 148–50
navigation in, 152–53
wing design in, 150–51
see also bombers
Alamogordo (N. Mex.), atomic testing at, 25–27
alpha particles, 14–15, 56, 267
animals, effect of nuclear detonations on, 50–51, 85, 95, 99–100
antiballistic missile (ABM) systems, 167–82, 235
antimissile missiles in, 168, 173–78
blinding of, 176–79, 181
cities defended by, 168–70, 178
computer systems in, 168, 171–75, 178, 180–82
decoy reentry vehicles and, 168, 173–75, 178, 180–81
early warning system in, 168, 180

infrared detection in, 180–181
missile silos defended by, 169–70, 178–79
nonnuclear adaptations of, 179–81
placement of, 171, 178
radar in, 168, 173–82
reliability of, 169–70, 177–178, 181
testing of, 168, 181
vulnerability of, 177–78
see also intercontinental ballistic missiles; lasers; particle-beam weapons
antisubmarine warfare, 124–125, 212–39
active detection (sonars) in, 213–14, 224–25, 230–31, 233
aircraft in, 223–24, 229–32, 234, 236–37
computers in, 226–28, 232
continuous trailing in, 235–236
detection threshold in, 231–232
discrimination in, 226–27, 231–32, 237–38
effectiveness of, 234–35, 237–39
electromagnetic radiation and, 214–15, 222

.